Ayu
Watanabe

L♥DK

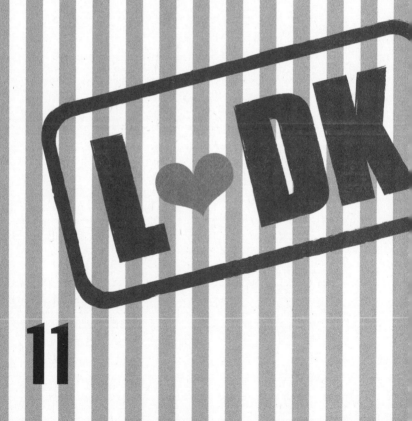

11

L♥DK

Ayu Watanabe

11

c o n t e n t s

L♥DK

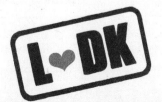

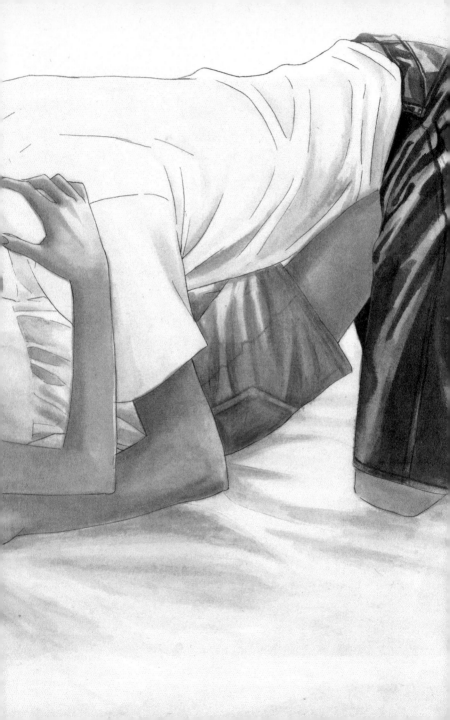

#41 Forbidden Confession

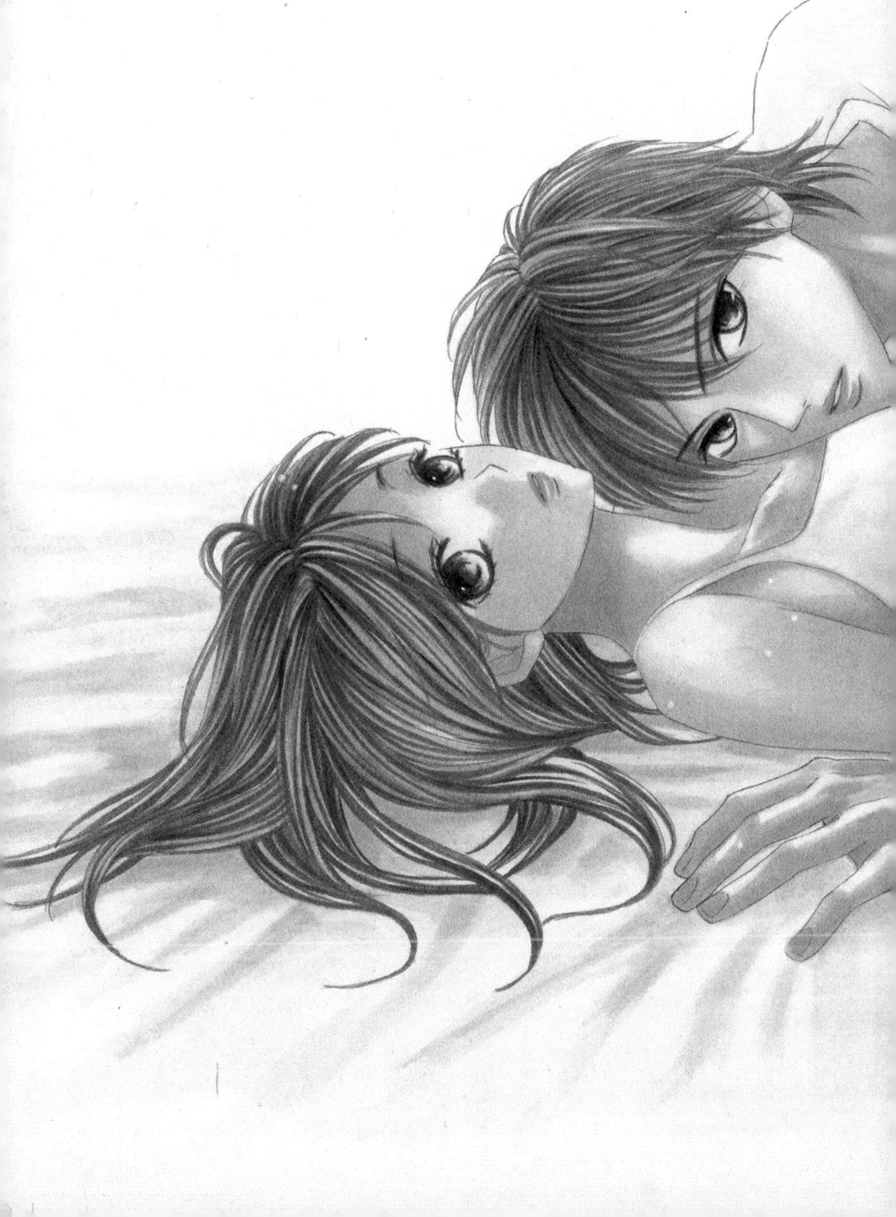

Story So Far

L♥DK

Story

High schooler Aoi is living in the secret arrangement of sharing an apartment with the love of her life and the school's hottest student, Shusei. Now that they're third-years, they're in the same class together, and Aoi's thrilled to become friends with Haru and Kaede! Or so she thought. She's shocked when Haru reveals having feelings for Shusei. And now, Aoi's relationship with Shusei has been outed to Kaede?!

Cast

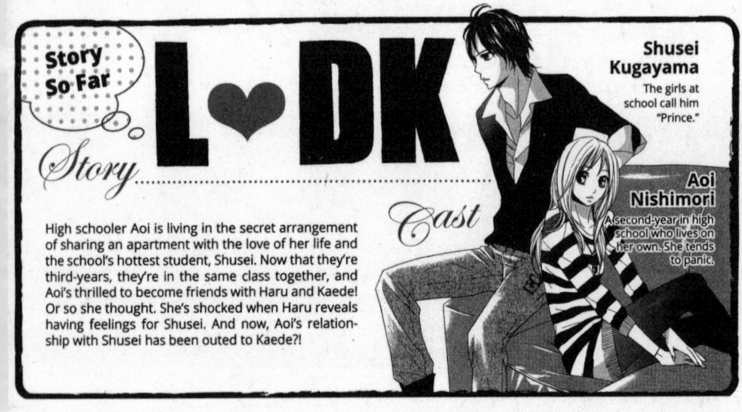

Shusei Kugayama
The girls at school call him "Prince."

Aoi Nishimori
A second-year in high school who lives on her own. She tends to panic.

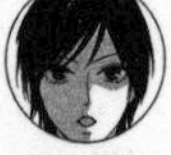

Haru Ono
Aoi's classmate. She was in the same basketball club with Shusei.

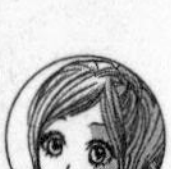

Kaede Igarashi
Also a classmate of Aoi. She and Haru are good friends.

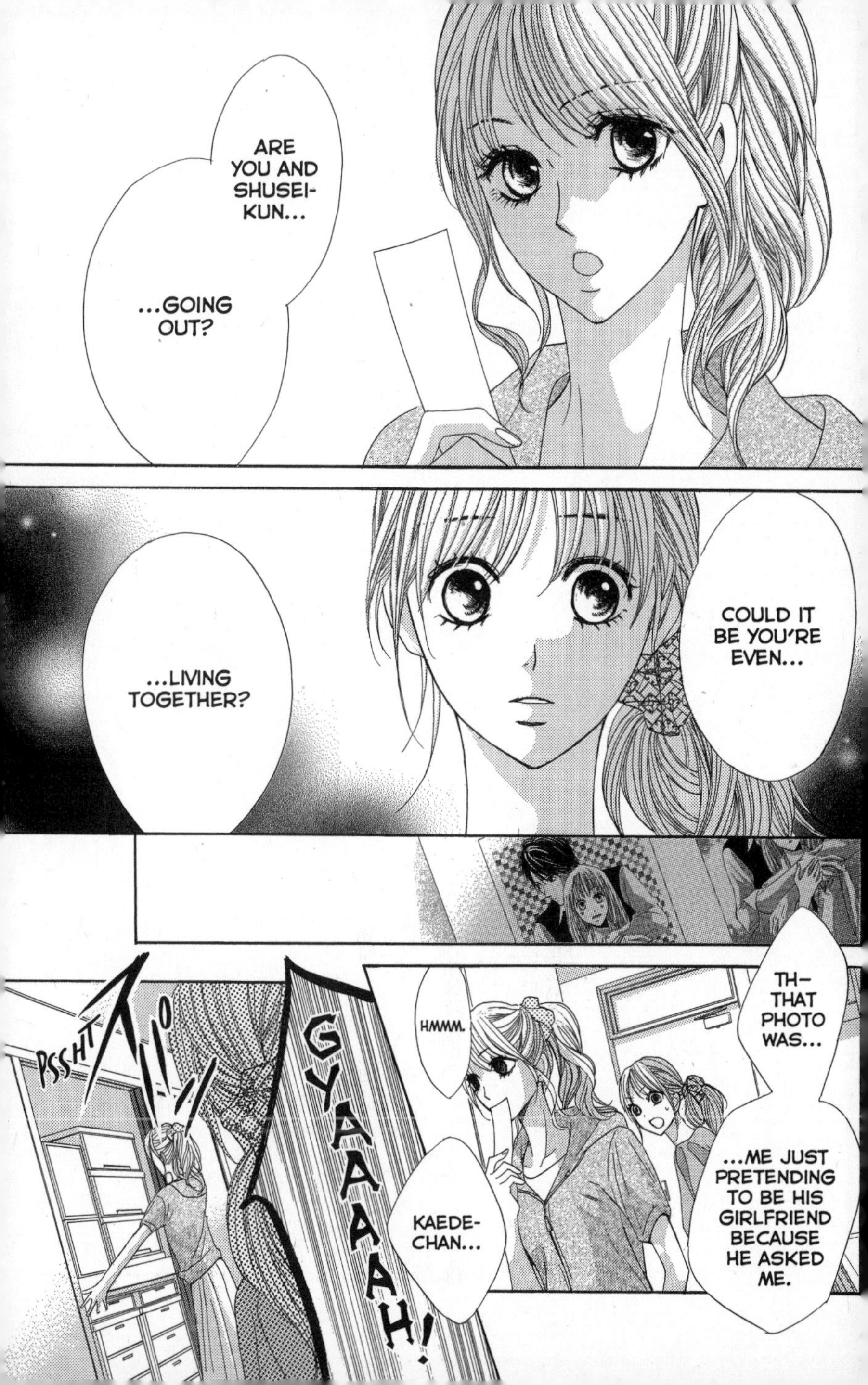
ARE YOU AND SHUSEI-KUN...
...GOING OUT?
COULD IT BE YOU'RE EVEN...
...LIVING TOGETHER?
TH— THAT PHOTO WAS...
...ME JUST PRETENDING TO BE HIS GIRLFRIEND BECAUSE HE ASKED ME.
HMMM.
KAEDE-CHAN...
GYAAAAH!
PSSHT

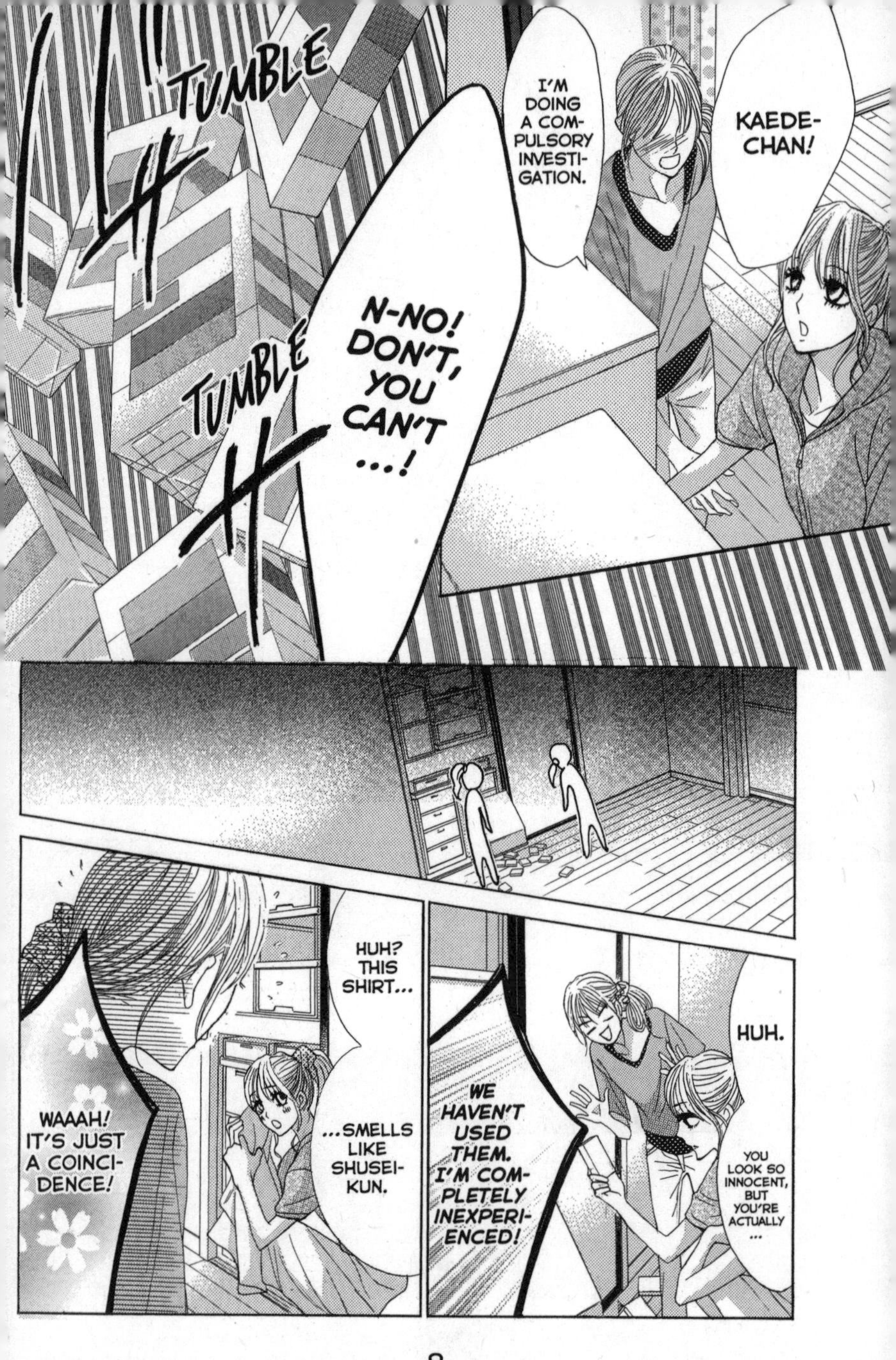
KAEDE-CHAN!
I'M DOING A COMPULSORY INVESTIGATION.
N-NO! DON'T, YOU CAN'T ...!
TUMBLE
TUMBLE
HUH.
YOU LOOK SO INNOCENT, BUT YOU'RE ACTUALLY ...
WE HAVEN'T USED THEM. I'M COMPLETELY INEXPERIENCED!
HUH? THIS SHIRT...
...SMELLS LIKE SHUSEI-KUN.
WAAAH! IT'S JUST A COINCIDENCE!

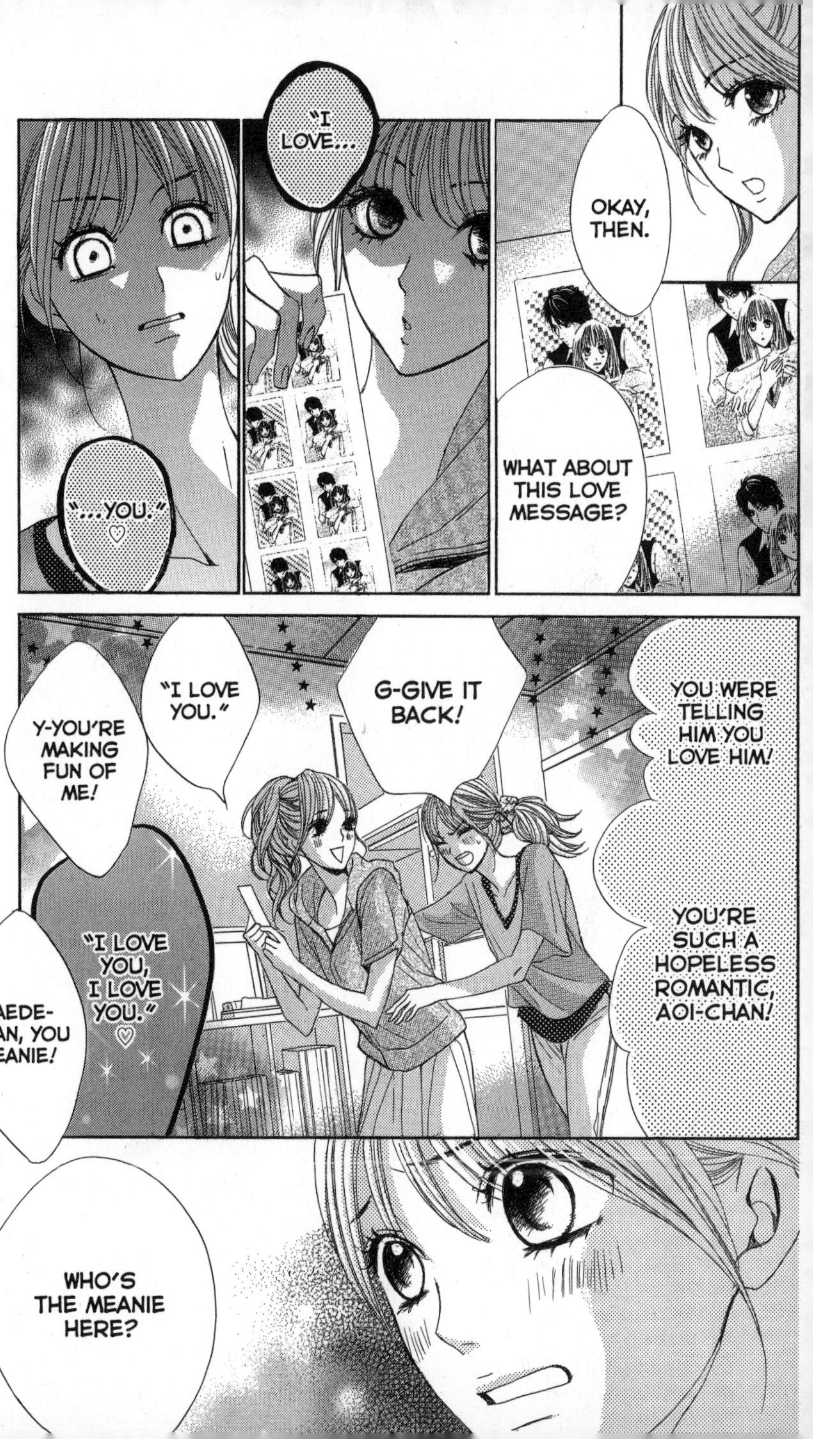
OKAY, THEN.
WHAT ABOUT THIS LOVE MESSAGE?
"I LOVE...
"...YOU." ♡
YOU WERE TELLING HIM YOU LOVE HIM!
YOU'RE SUCH A HOPELESS ROMANTIC, AOI-CHAN!
G-GIVE IT BACK!
"I LOVE YOU."
Y-YOU'RE MAKING FUN OF ME!
"I LOVE YOU, I LOVE YOU." ♡
KAEDE-CHAN, YOU MEANIE!
WHO'S THE MEANIE HERE?

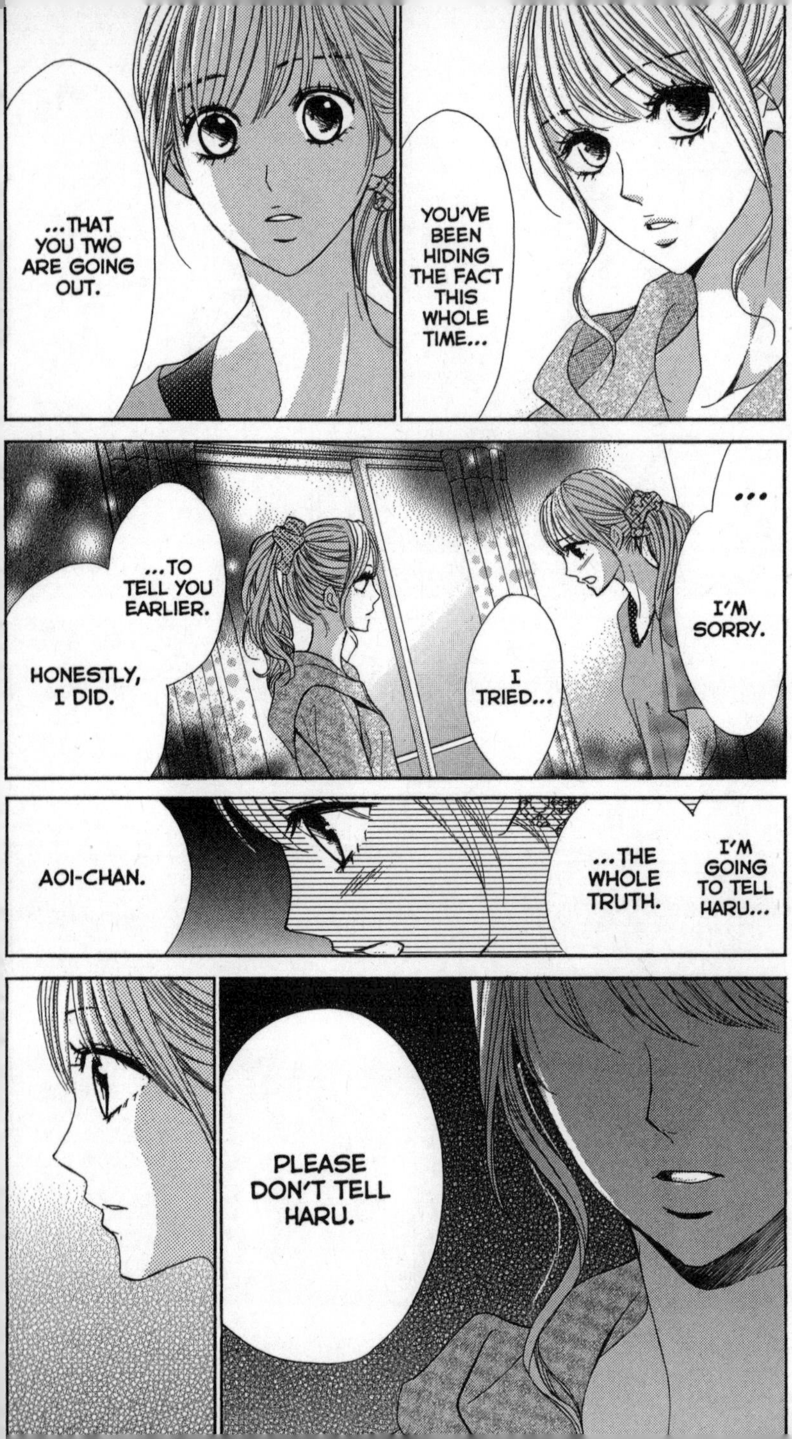
YOU'VE BEEN HIDING THE FACT THIS WHOLE TIME...
...THAT YOU TWO ARE GOING OUT.
...
I'M SORRY.
I TRIED...
...TO TELL YOU EARLIER.
HONESTLY, I DID.
I'M GOING TO TELL HARU...
...THE WHOLE TRUTH.
AOI-CHAN.
PLEASE DON'T TELL HARU.

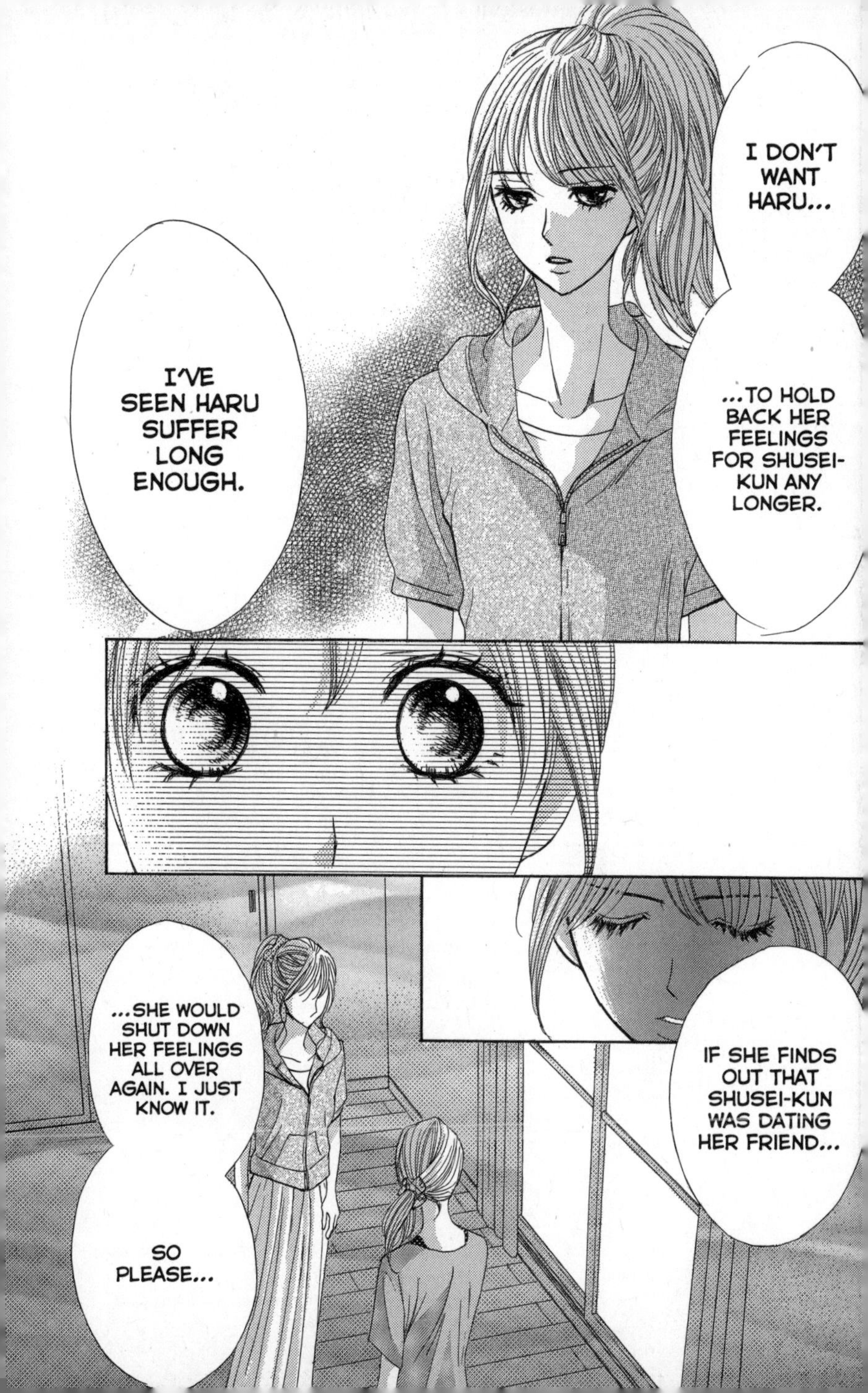
I DON'T WANT HARU...
...TO HOLD BACK HER FEELINGS FOR SHUSEI-KUN ANY LONGER.
I'VE SEEN HARU SUFFER LONG ENOUGH.
IF SHE FINDS OUT THAT SHUSEI-KUN WAS DATING HER FRIEND...
...SHE WOULD SHUT DOWN HER FEELINGS ALL OVER AGAIN. I JUST KNOW IT.
SO PLEASE...

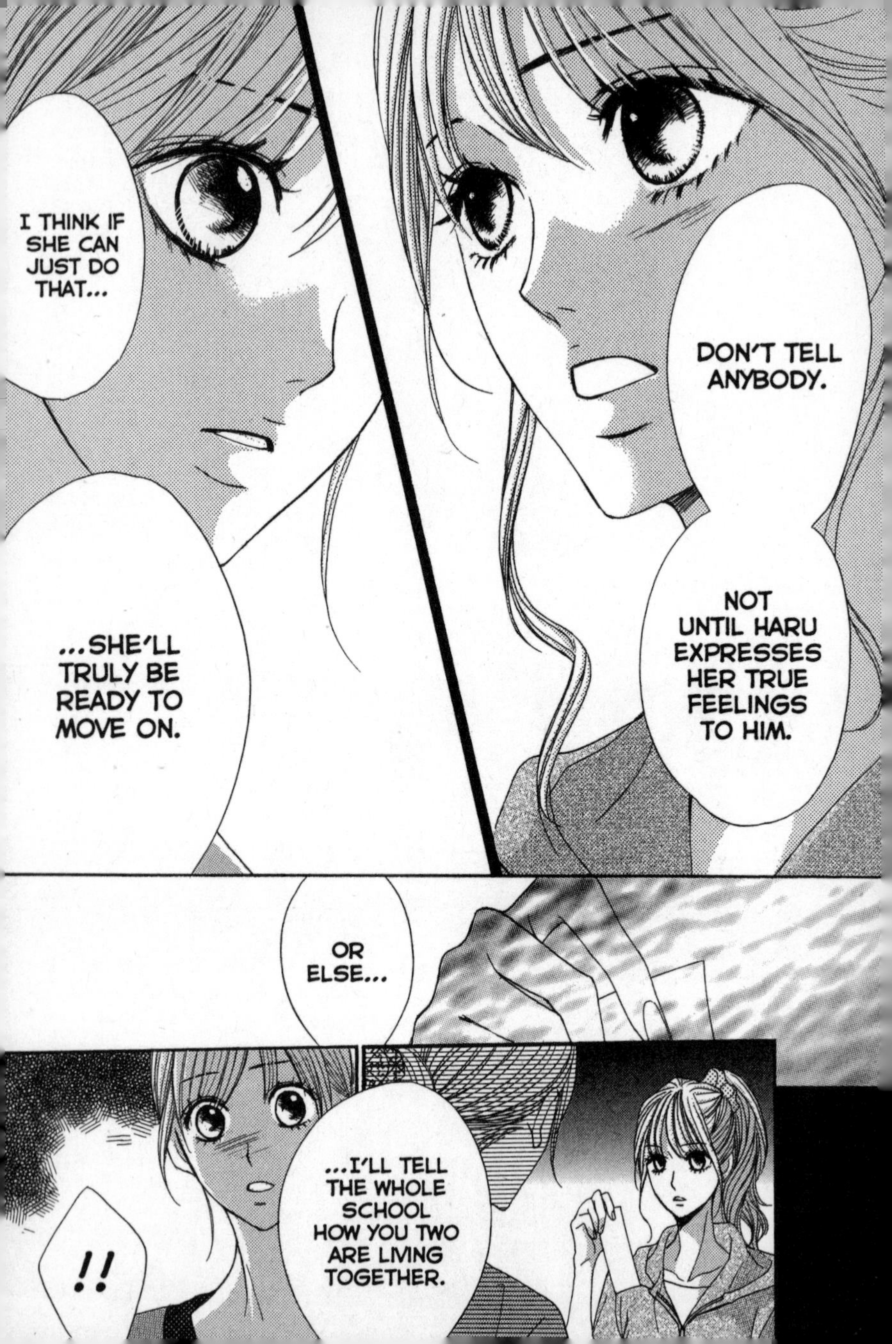

DON'T TELL ANYBODY.
NOT UNTIL HARU EXPRESSES HER TRUE FEELINGS TO HIM.
I THINK IF SHE CAN JUST DO THAT...
...SHE'LL TRULY BE READY TO MOVE ON.
OR ELSE...
...I'LL TELL THE WHOLE SCHOOL HOW YOU TWO ARE LIVING TOGETHER.
!!

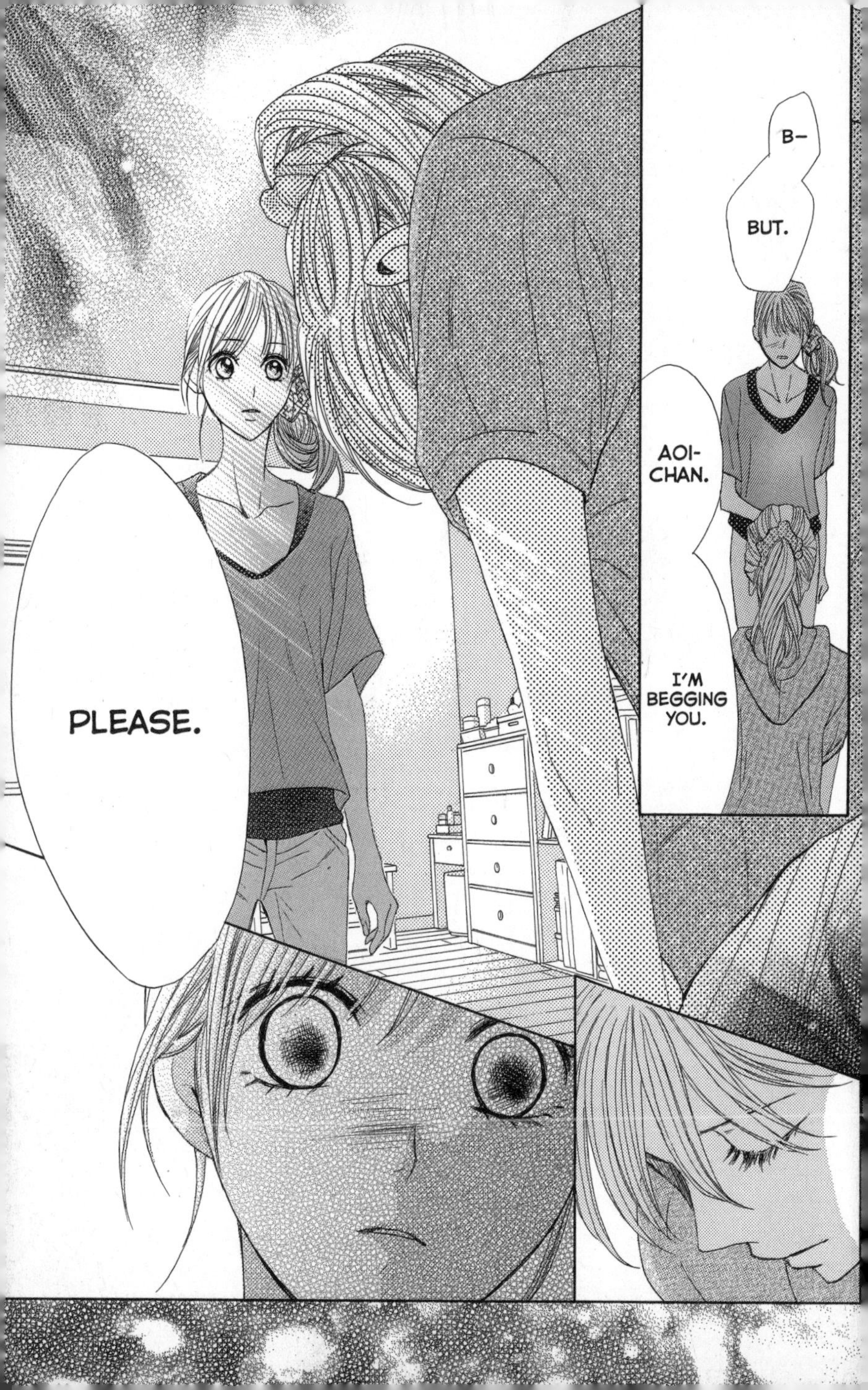
B—
BUT.
AOI-CHAN.
I'M BEGGING YOU.
PLEASE.

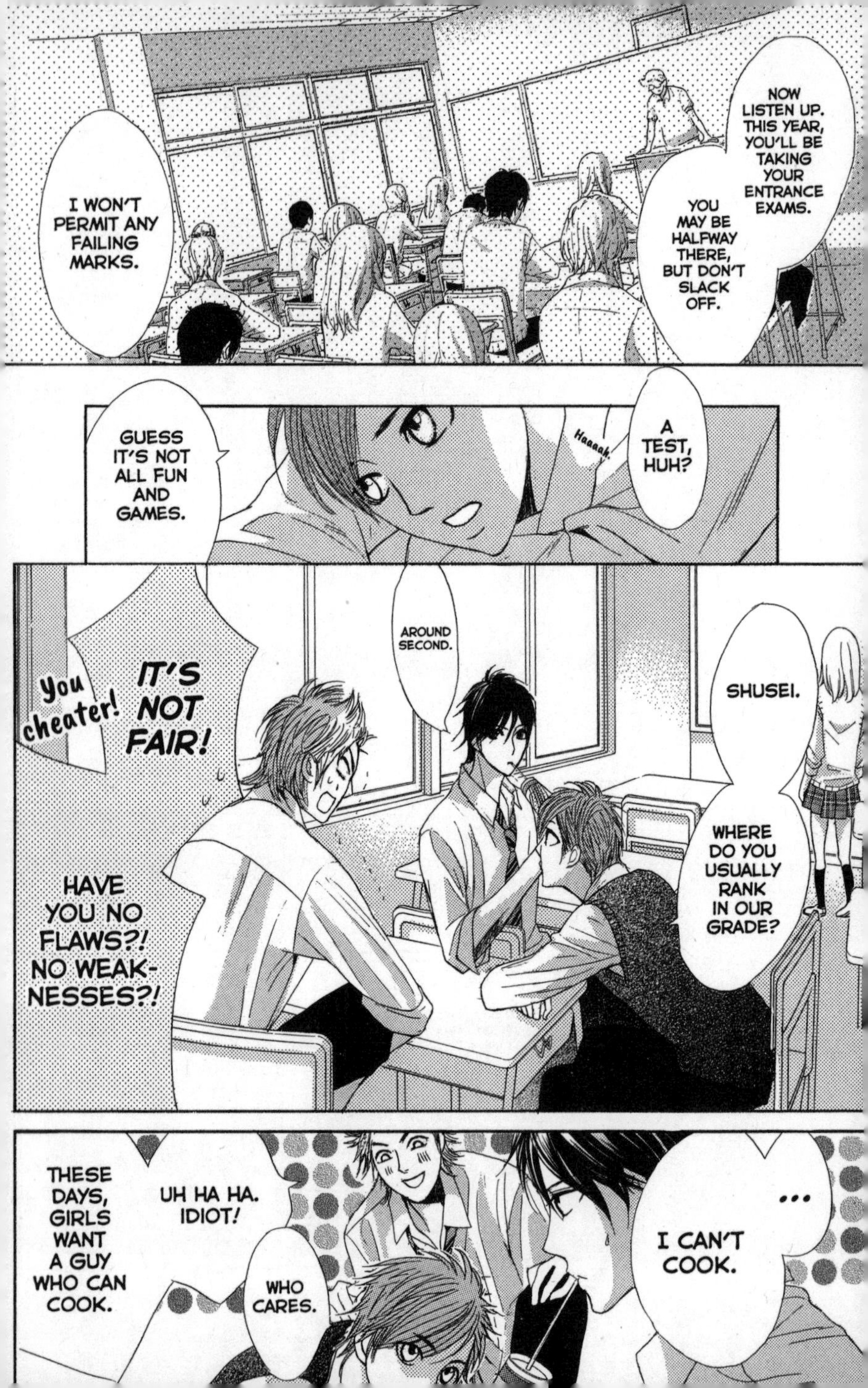
NOW LISTEN UP. THIS YEAR, YOU'LL BE TAKING YOUR ENTRANCE EXAMS.
YOU MAY BE HALFWAY THERE, BUT DON'T SLACK OFF.
I WON'T PERMIT ANY FAILING MARKS.
A TEST, HUH?
Haaaah.
GUESS IT'S NOT ALL FUN AND GAMES.
SHUSEI.
WHERE DO YOU USUALLY RANK IN OUR GRADE?
AROUND SECOND.
IT'S NOT FAIR!
You cheater!
HAVE YOU NO FLAWS?! NO WEAKNESSES?!
...
I CAN'T COOK.
WHO CARES.
UH HA HA. IDIOT!
THESE DAYS, GIRLS WANT A GUY WHO CAN COOK.

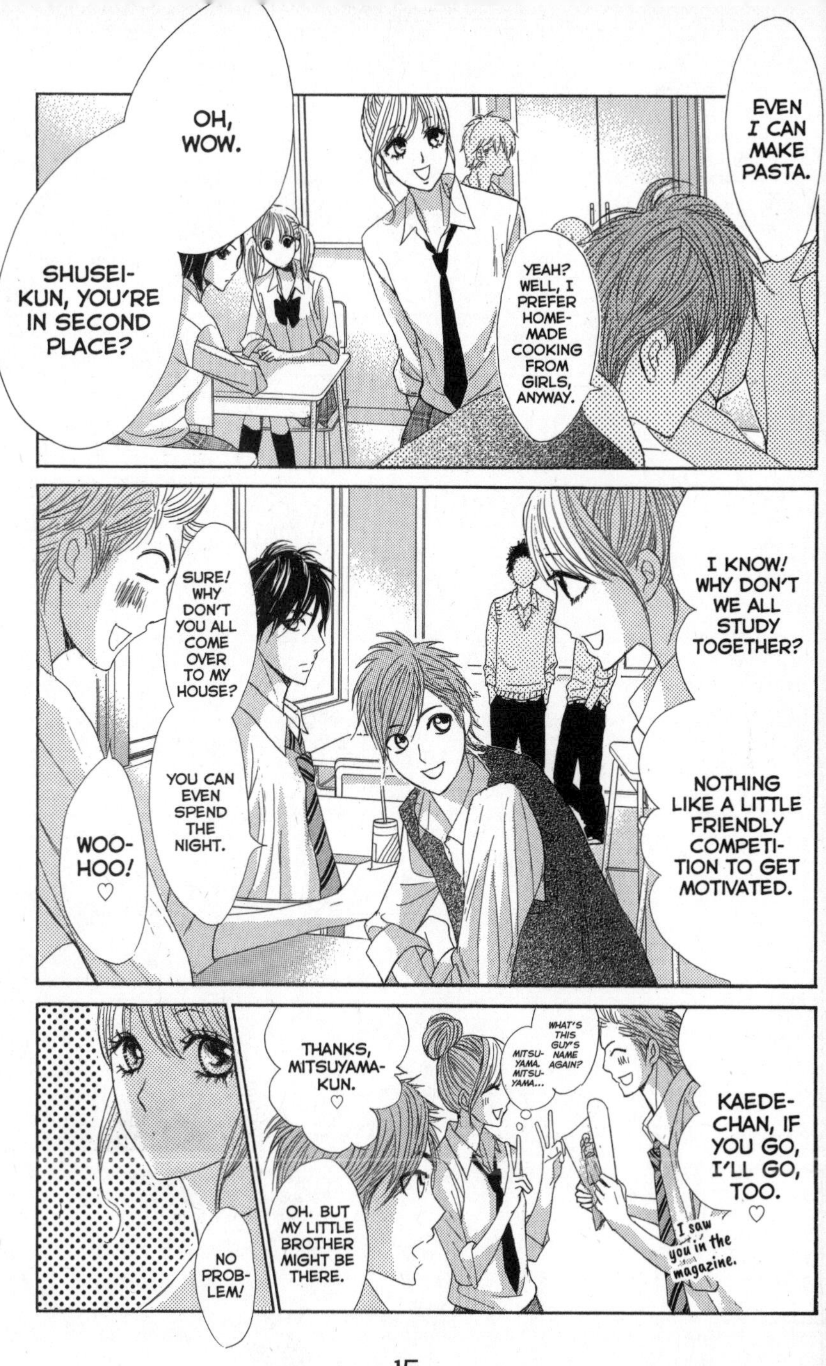
EVEN I CAN MAKE PASTA.
YEAH? WELL, I PREFER HOME-MADE COOKING FROM GIRLS, ANYWAY.
OH, WOW.
SHUSEI-KUN, YOU'RE IN SECOND PLACE?
I KNOW! WHY DON'T WE ALL STUDY TOGETHER?
NOTHING LIKE A LITTLE FRIENDLY COMPETI-TION TO GET MOTIVATED.
SURE! WHY DON'T YOU ALL COME OVER TO MY HOUSE?
YOU CAN EVEN SPEND THE NIGHT.
WOO-HOO! ♡
KAEDE-CHAN, IF YOU GO, I'LL GO, TOO. ♡
I saw you in the magazine.
WHAT'S THIS GUY'S NAME AGAIN?
MITSU-YAMA. MITSU-YAMA...
THANKS, MITSUYAMA-KUN. ♡
OH. BUT MY LITTLE BROTHER MIGHT BE THERE.
NO PROB-LEM!

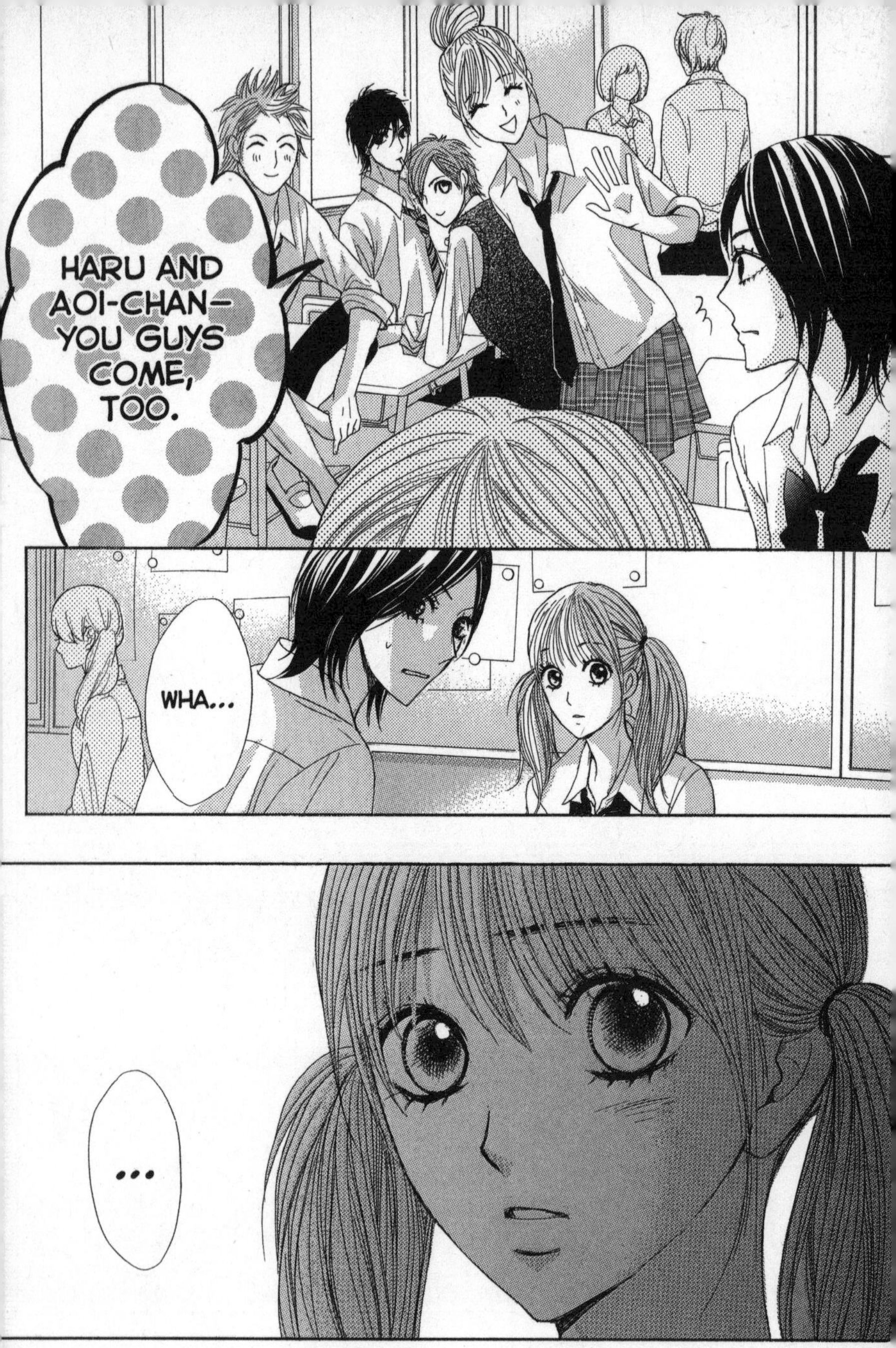
HARU AND AOI-CHAN– YOU GUYS COME, TOO.
WHA...
...

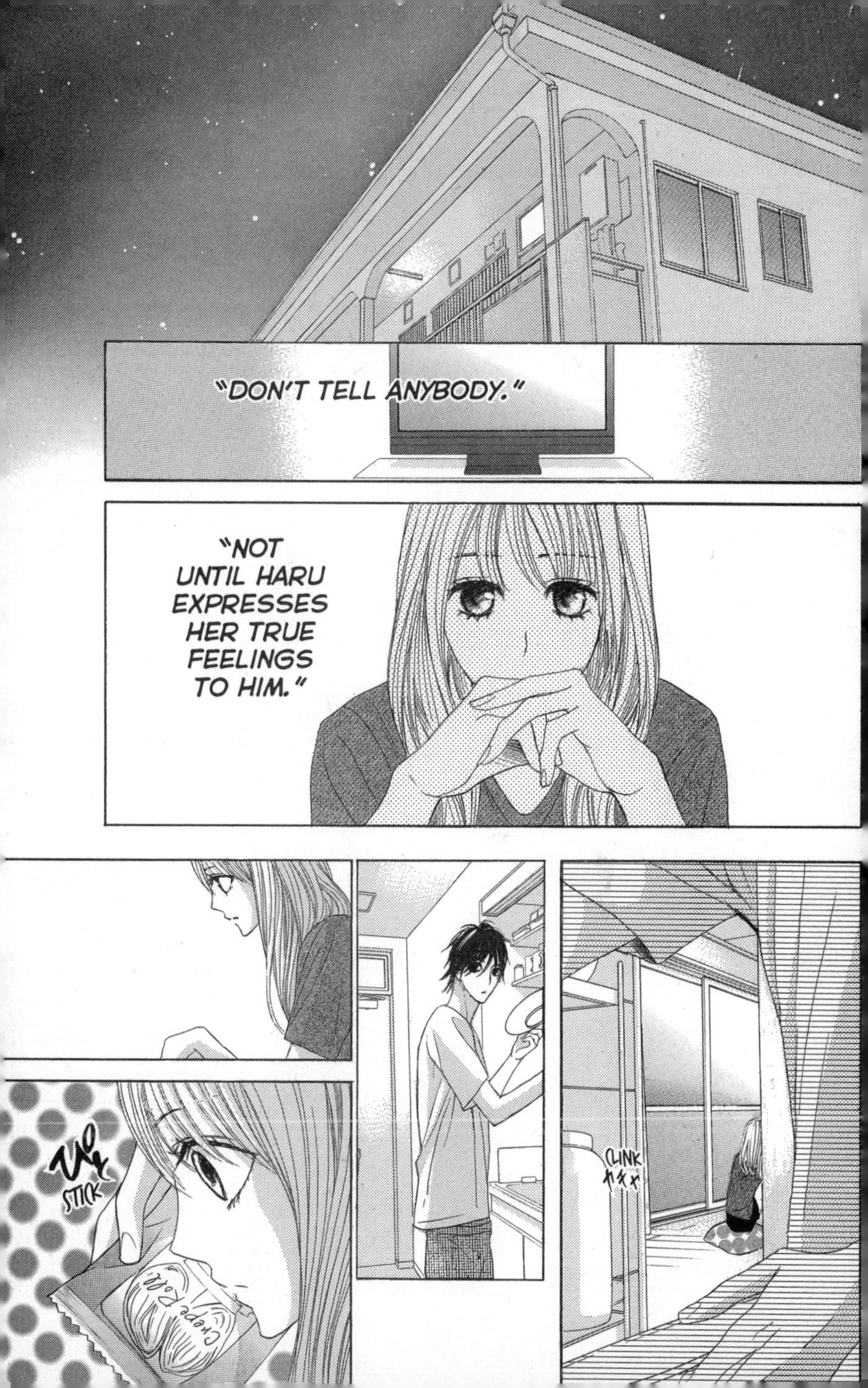
"DON'T TELL ANYBODY."
"NOT UNTIL HARU EXPRESSES HER TRUE FEELINGS TO HIM."
CLINK
STICK
Crepe Roll

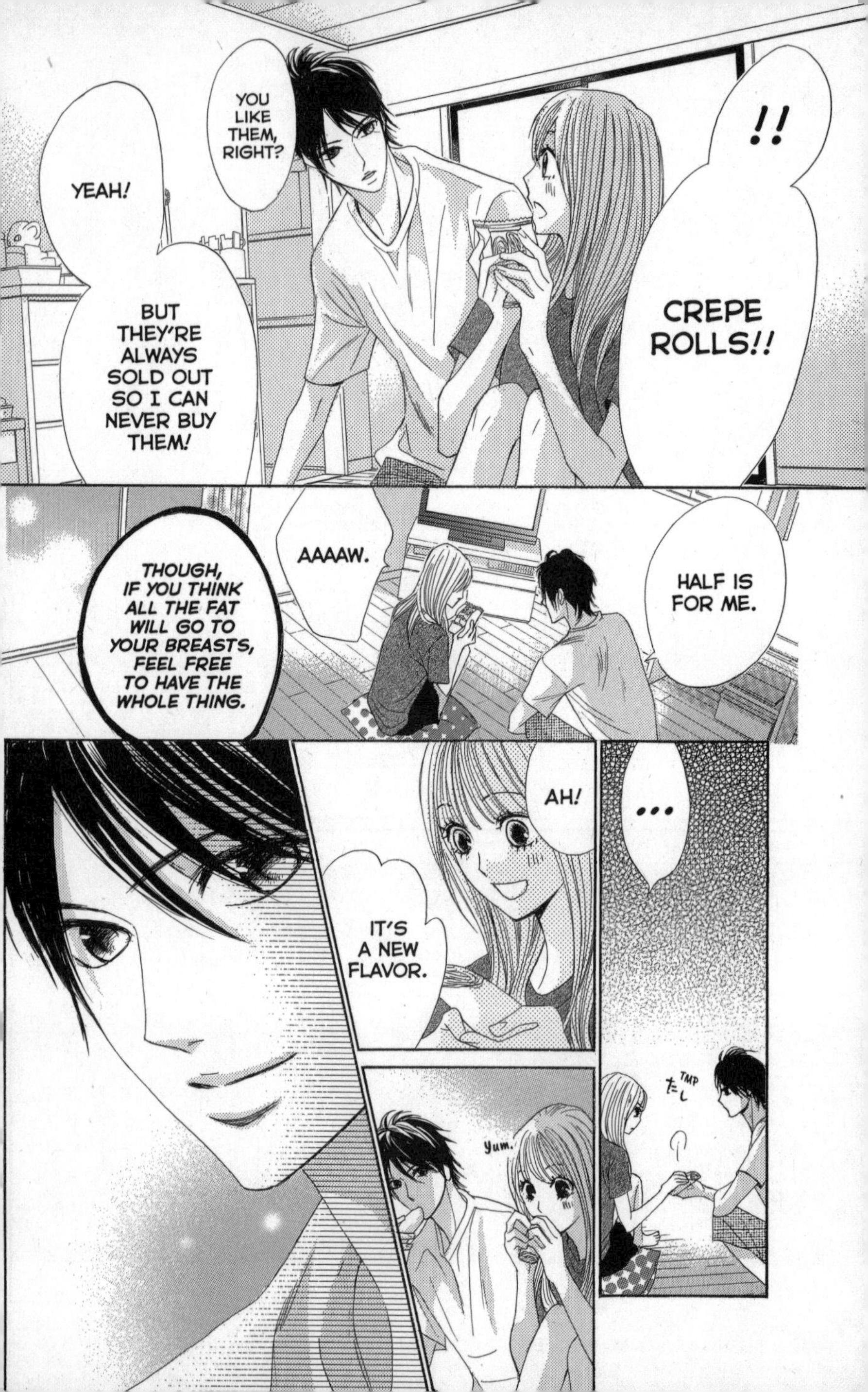
!!
CREPE ROLLS!!
YOU LIKE THEM, RIGHT?
YEAH!
BUT THEY'RE ALWAYS SOLD OUT SO I CAN NEVER BUY THEM!
HALF IS FOR ME.
AAAAW.
THOUGH, IF YOU THINK ALL THE FAT WILL GO TO YOUR BREASTS, FEEL FREE TO HAVE THE WHOLE THING.
...
TMP
AH!
IT'S A NEW FLAVOR.
yum.

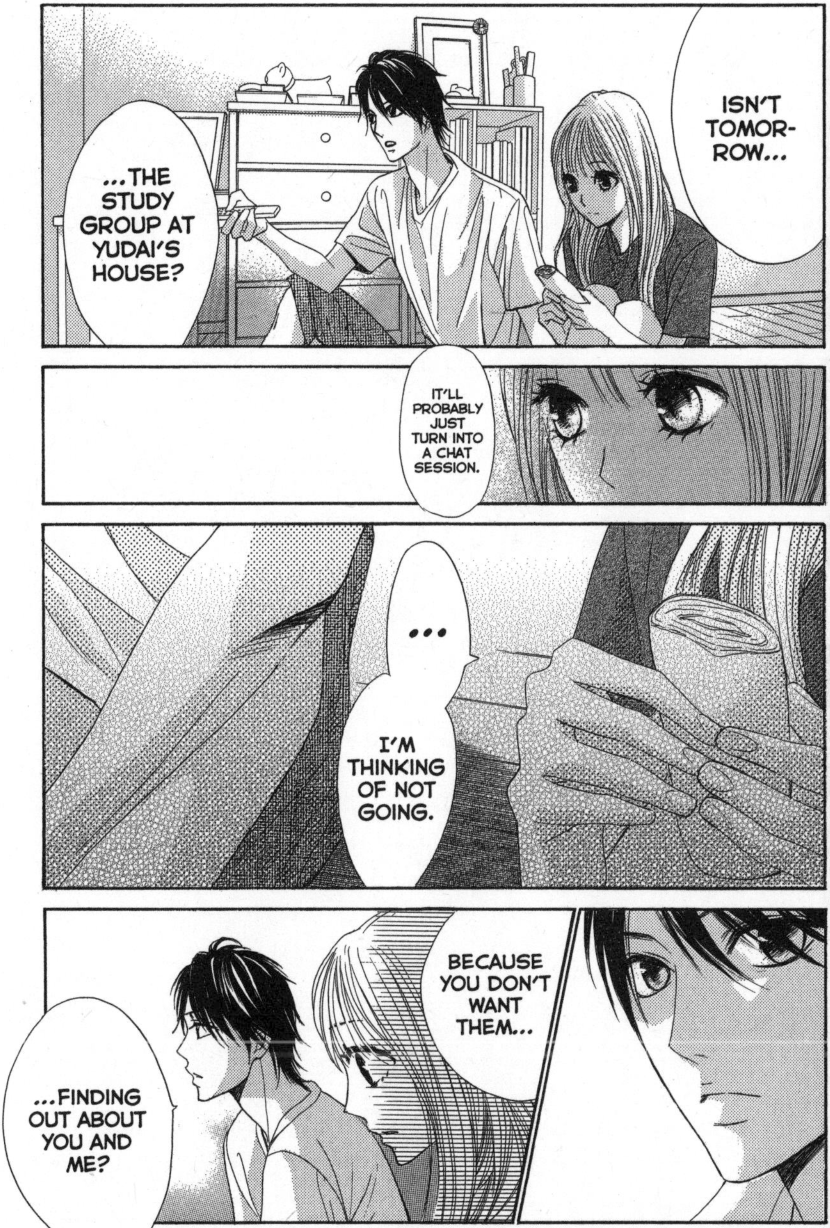
ISN'T TOMORROW...
...THE STUDY GROUP AT YUDAI'S HOUSE?
IT'LL PROBABLY JUST TURN INTO A CHAT SESSION.
...
I'M THINKING OF NOT GOING.
BECAUSE YOU DON'T WANT THEM...
...FINDING OUT ABOUT YOU AND ME?

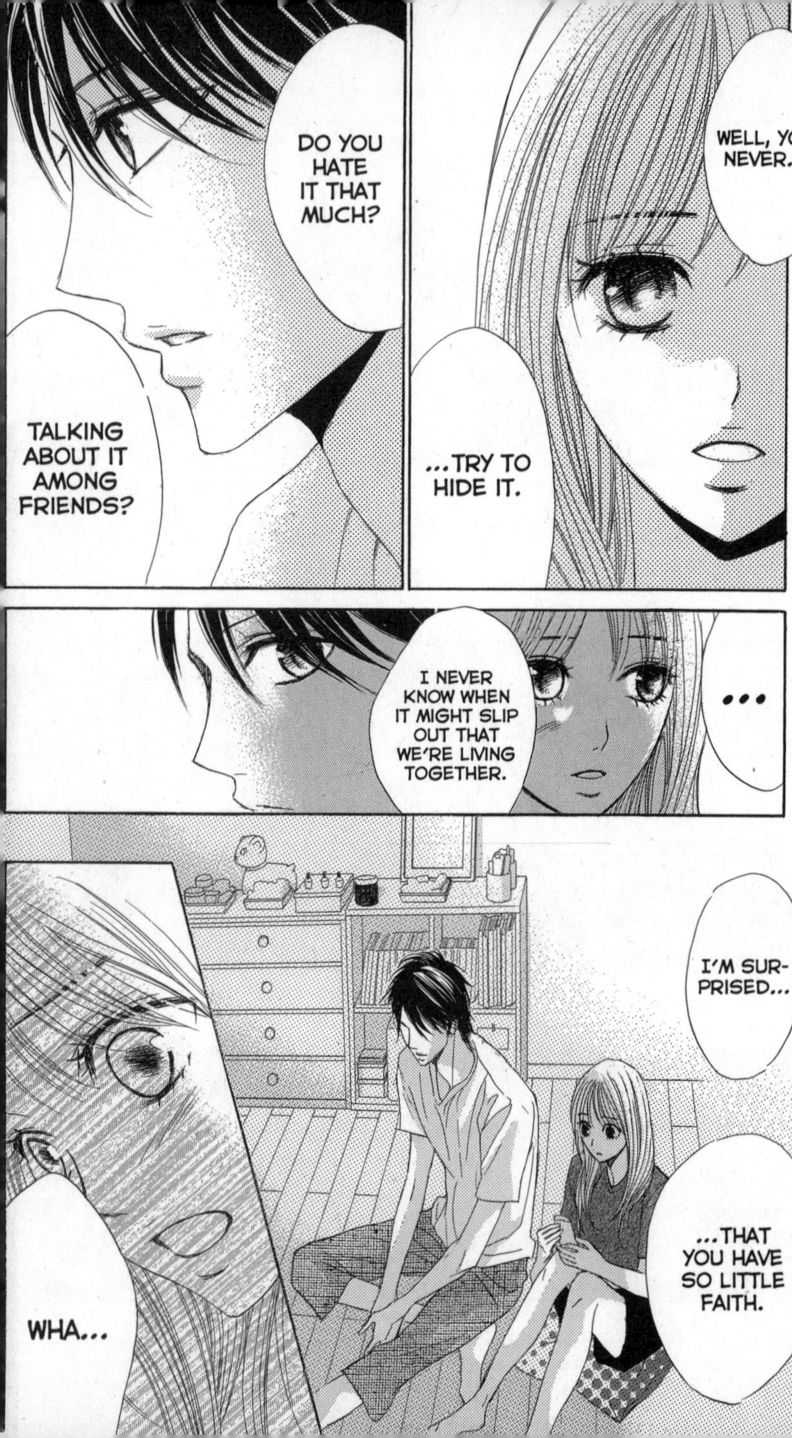
WELL, YOU NEVER...
...TRY TO HIDE IT.
DO YOU HATE IT THAT MUCH?
TALKING ABOUT IT AMONG FRIENDS?
...
I NEVER KNOW WHEN IT MIGHT SLIP OUT THAT WE'RE LIVING TOGETHER.
I'M SUR-PRISED...
...THAT YOU HAVE SO LITTLE FAITH.
WHA...

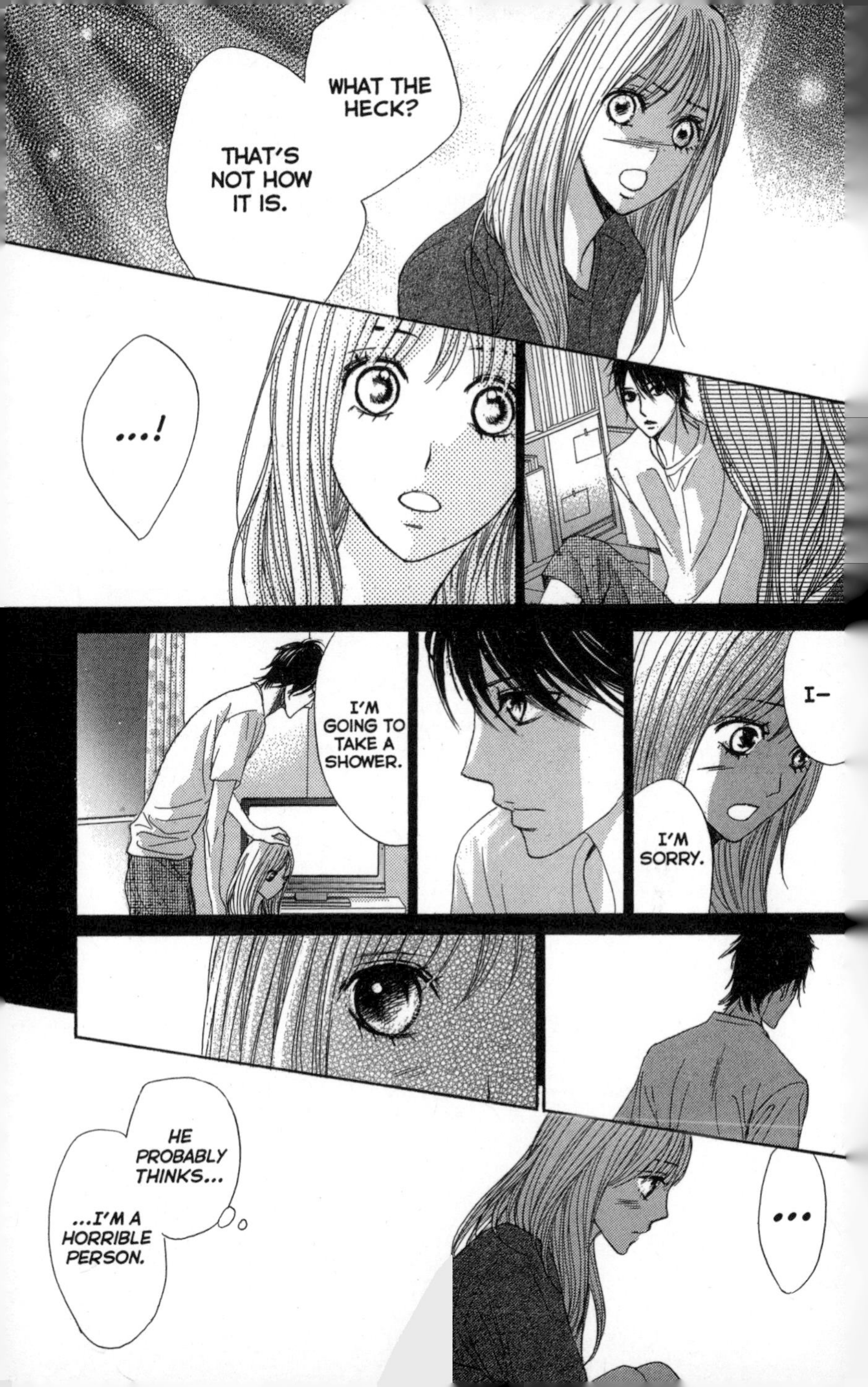
WHAT THE HECK?
THAT'S NOT HOW IT IS.
...!
I–
I'M SORRY.
I'M GOING TO TAKE A SHOWER.
...
HE PROBABLY THINKS...
...I'M A HORRIBLE PERSON.

MM.

HEY.

SLEEP ON THE FUTON.

MMM.

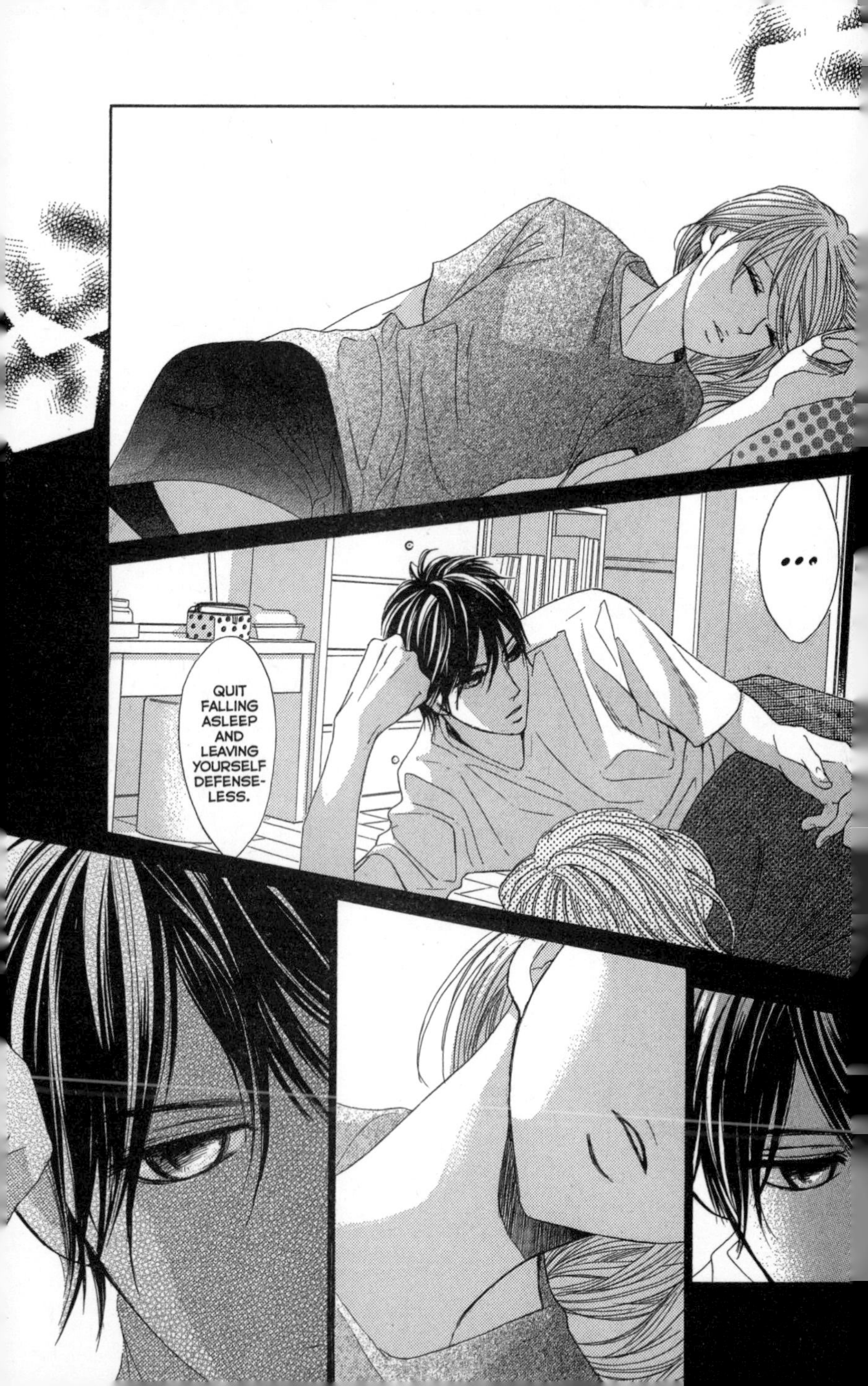
...
QUIT FALLING ASLEEP AND LEAVING YOURSELF DEFENSE-LESS.

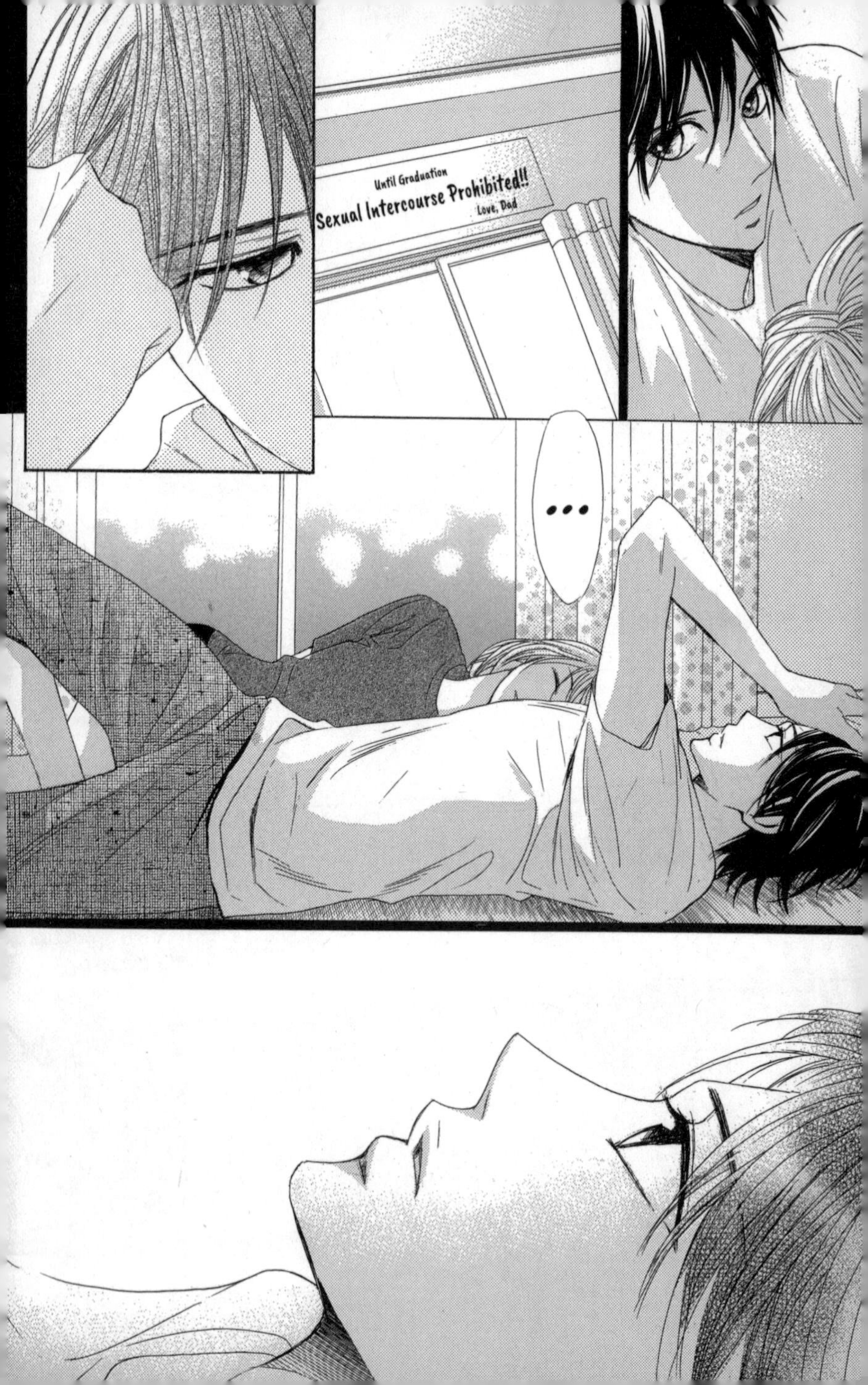
Until Graduation
Sexual Intercourse Prohibited!!
Love, Dad
...

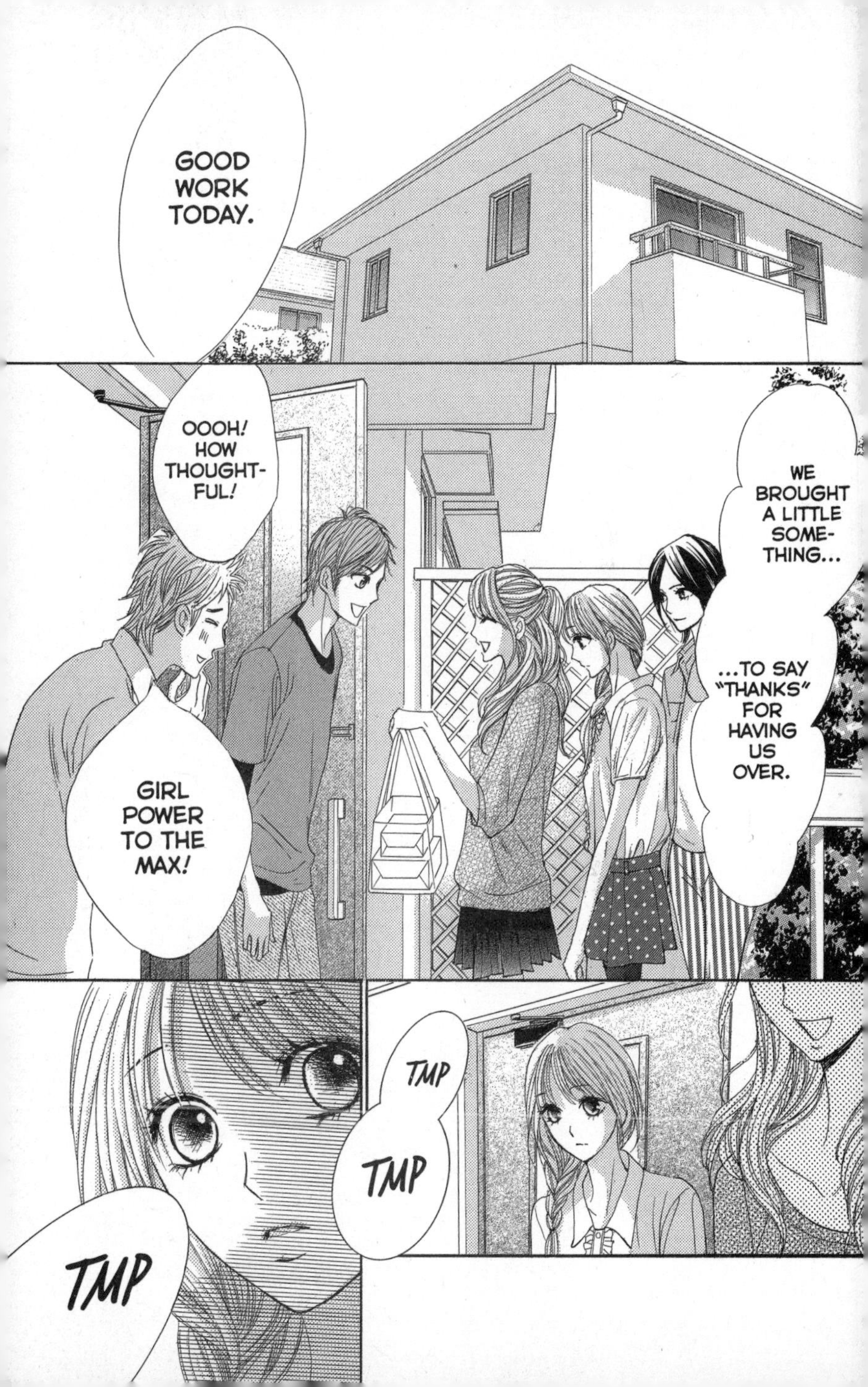
GOOD WORK TODAY.
WE BROUGHT A LITTLE SOME-THING...
...TO SAY "THANKS" FOR HAVING US OVER.
OOOH! HOW THOUGHT-FUL!
GIRL POWER TO THE MAX!
TMP
TMP
TMP

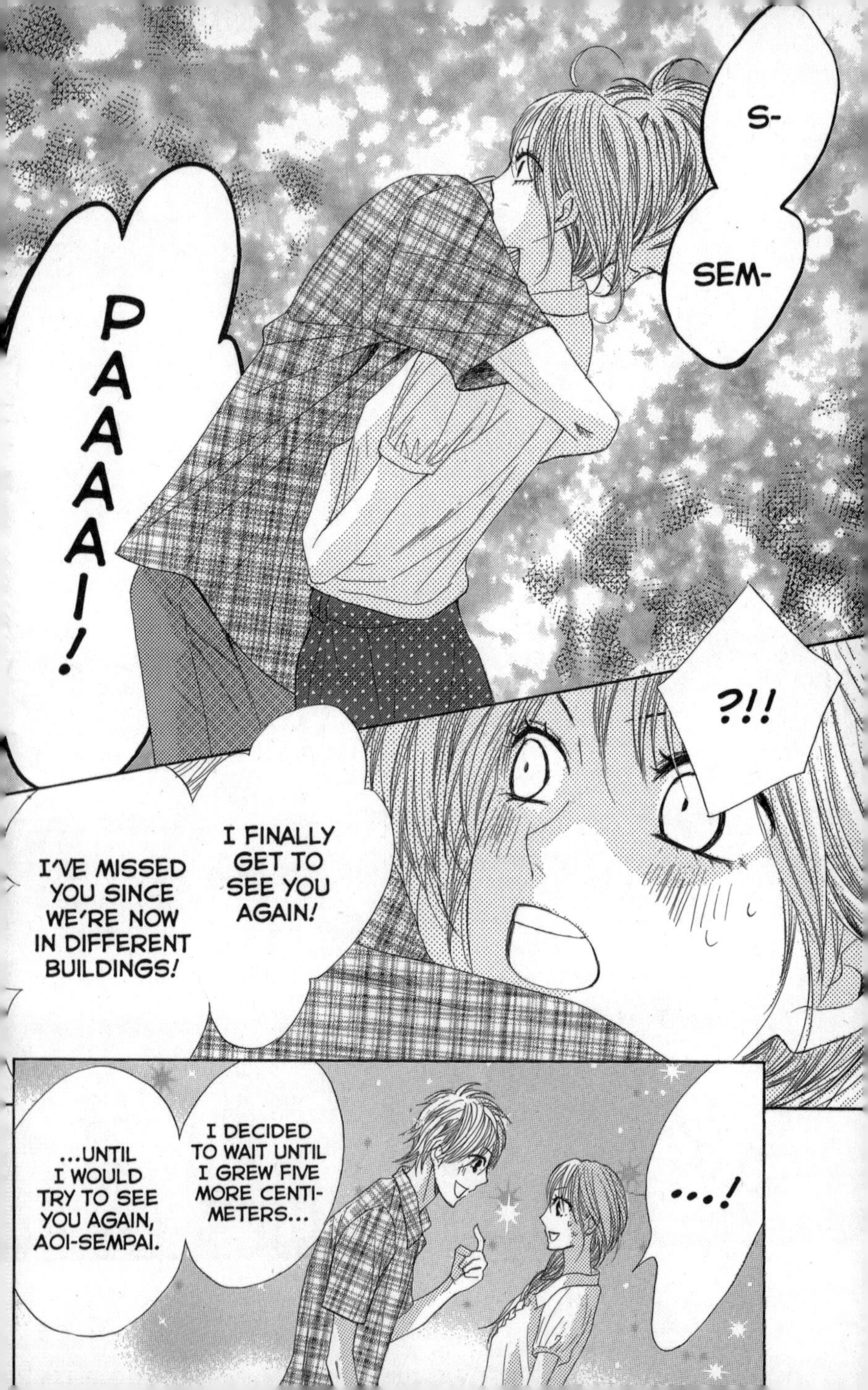
S-
SEM-
PAAAAI!!
?!!
I FINALLY GET TO SEE YOU AGAIN!
I'VE MISSED YOU SINCE WE'RE NOW IN DIFFERENT BUILDINGS!
...!
I DECIDED TO WAIT UNTIL I GREW FIVE MORE CENTIMETERS...
...UNTIL I WOULD TRY TO SEE YOU AGAIN, AOI-SEMPAI.

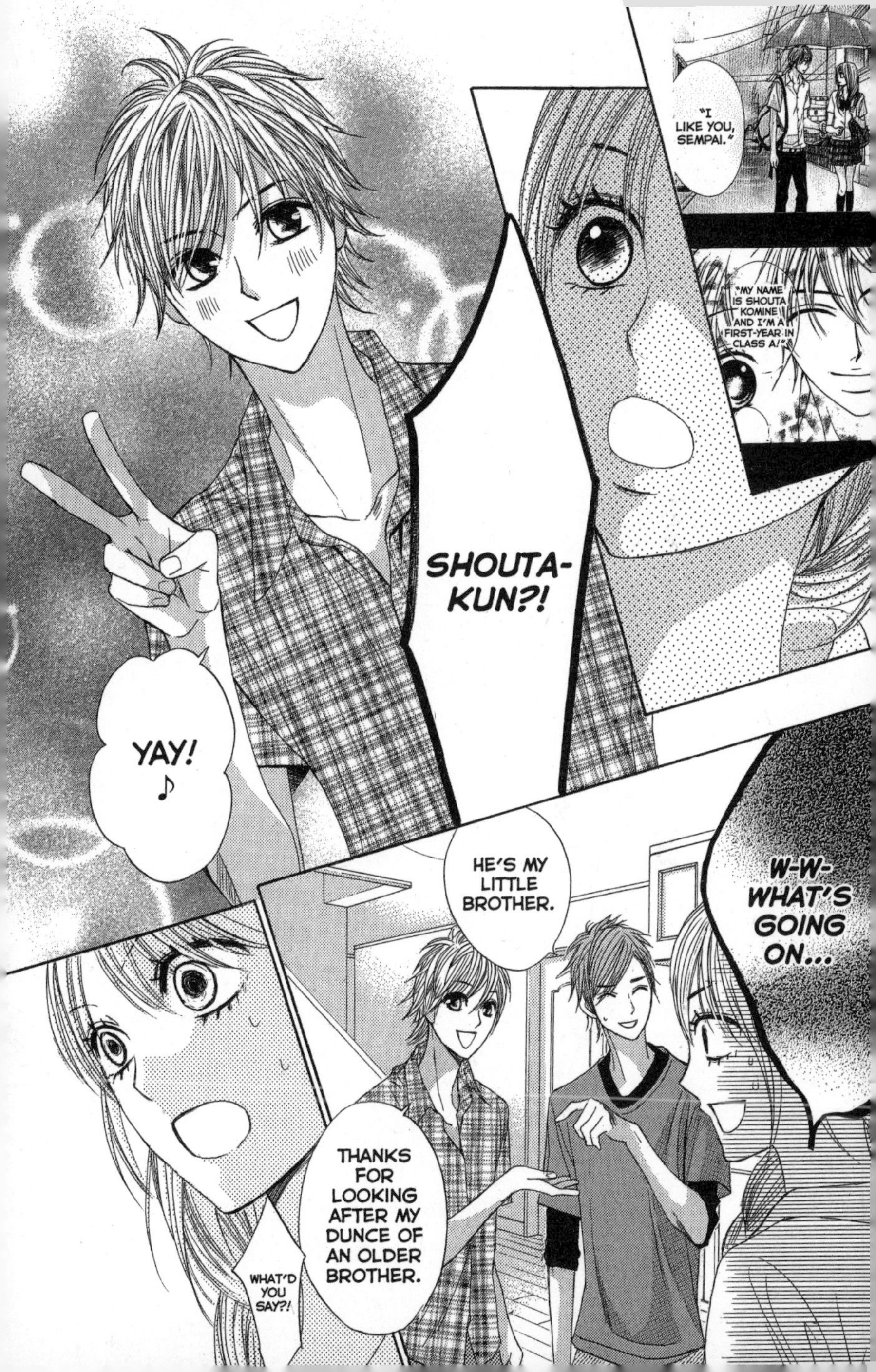
"I LIKE YOU, SEMPAI."
"MY NAME IS SHOUTA KOMINE AND I'M A FIRST-YEAR IN CLASS A!"
SHOUTA-KUN?!
YAY! ♪
W-W-WHAT'S GOING ON...
HE'S MY LITTLE BROTHER.
THANKS FOR LOOKING AFTER MY DUNCE OF AN OLDER BROTHER.
WHAT'D YOU SAY?!

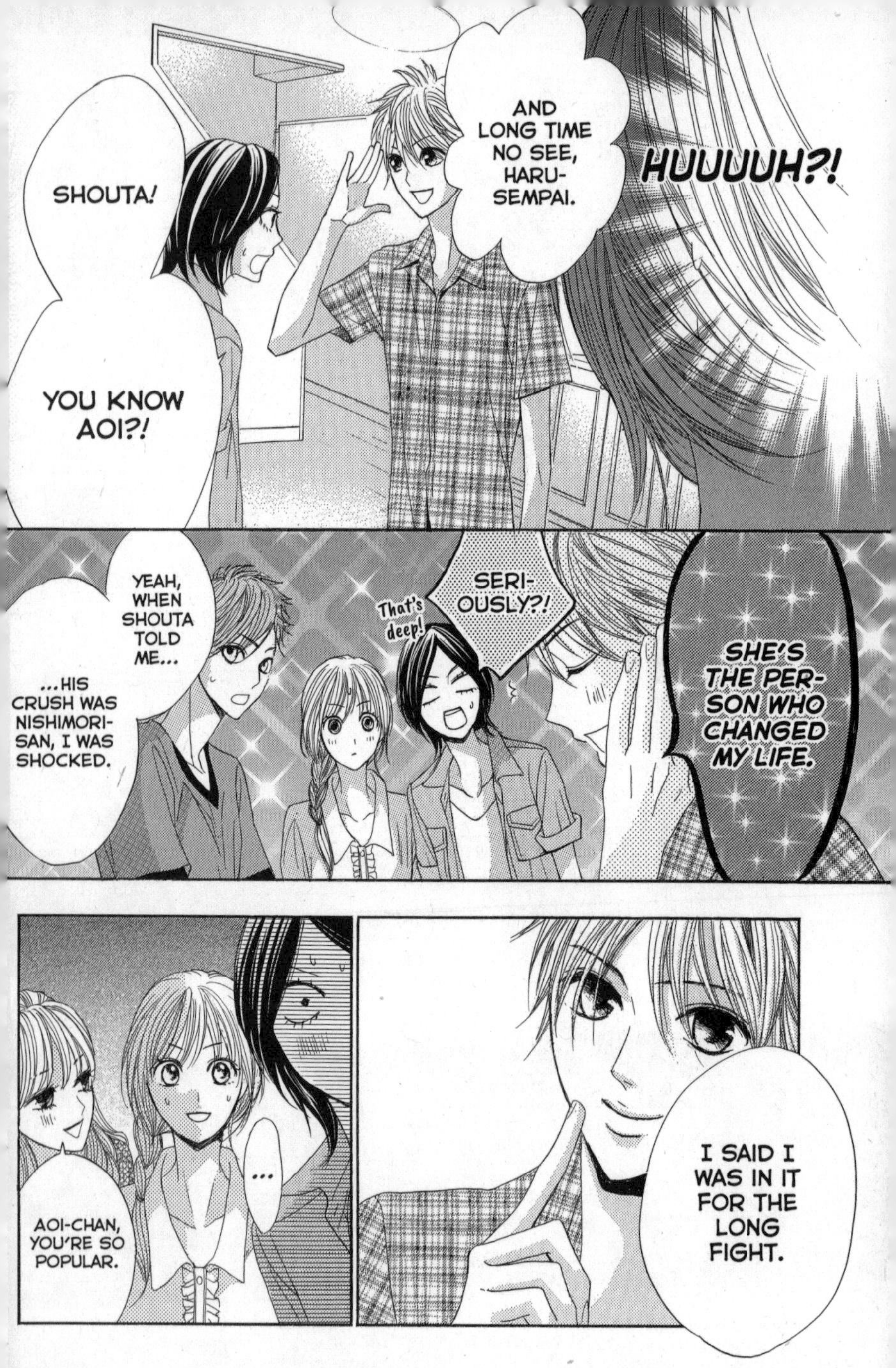

AND LONG TIME NO SEE, HARU-SEMPAI.
HUUUUH?!
SHOUTA!
YOU KNOW AOI?!
SHE'S THE PERSON WHO CHANGED MY LIFE.
SERI-OUSLY?!
That's deep!
YEAH, WHEN SHOUTA TOLD ME...
...HIS CRUSH WAS NISHIMORI-SAN, I WAS SHOCKED.
I SAID I WAS IN IT FOR THE LONG FIGHT.
...
AOI-CHAN, YOU'RE SO POPULAR.

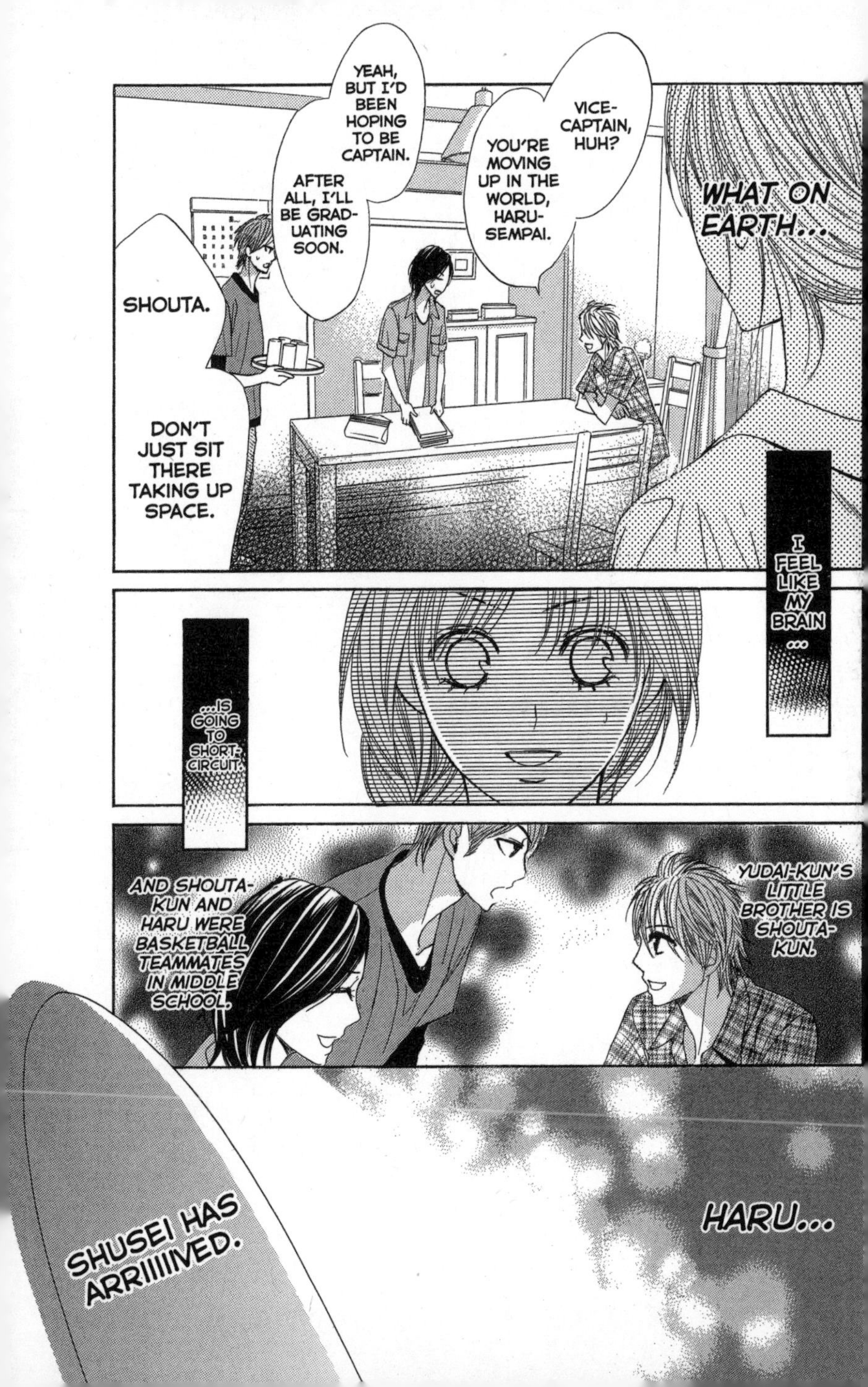
WHAT ON EARTH...
VICE-CAPTAIN, HUH?
YOU'RE MOVING UP IN THE WORLD, HARU-SEMPAI.
YEAH, BUT I'D BEEN HOPING TO BE CAPTAIN.
AFTER ALL, I'LL BE GRADUATING SOON.
SHOUTA.
DON'T JUST SIT THERE TAKING UP SPACE.
I FEEL LIKE MY BRAIN...
...IS GOING TO SHORT-CIRCUIT.
YUDAI-KUN'S LITTLE BROTHER IS SHOUTA-KUN.
AND SHOUTA-KUN AND HARU WERE BASKETBALL TEAMMATES IN MIDDLE SCHOOL.
HARU...
SHUSEI HAS ARRIIIIIVED.

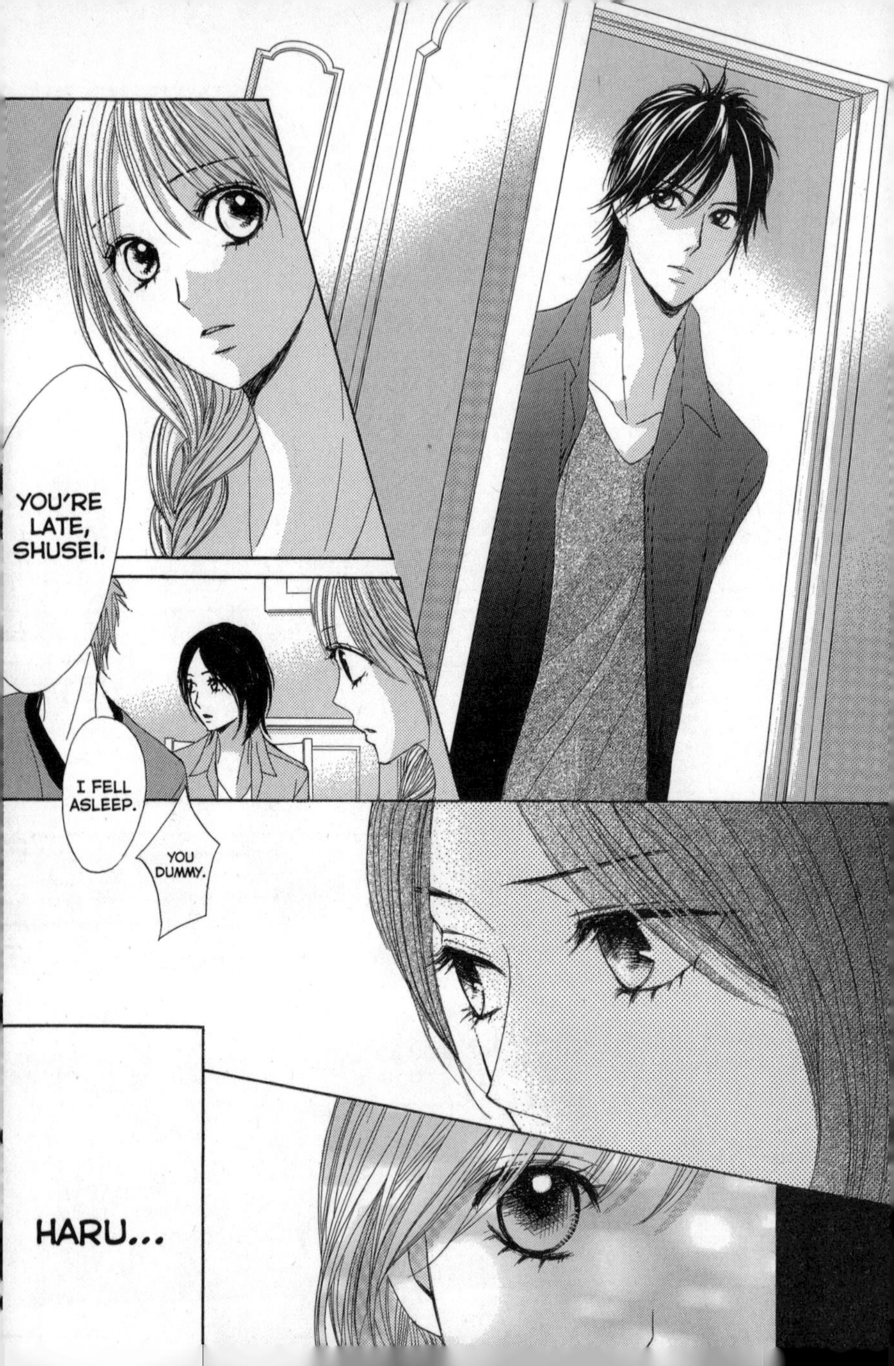
YOU'RE LATE, SHUSEI.
I FELL ASLEEP.
YOU DUMMY.
HARU...

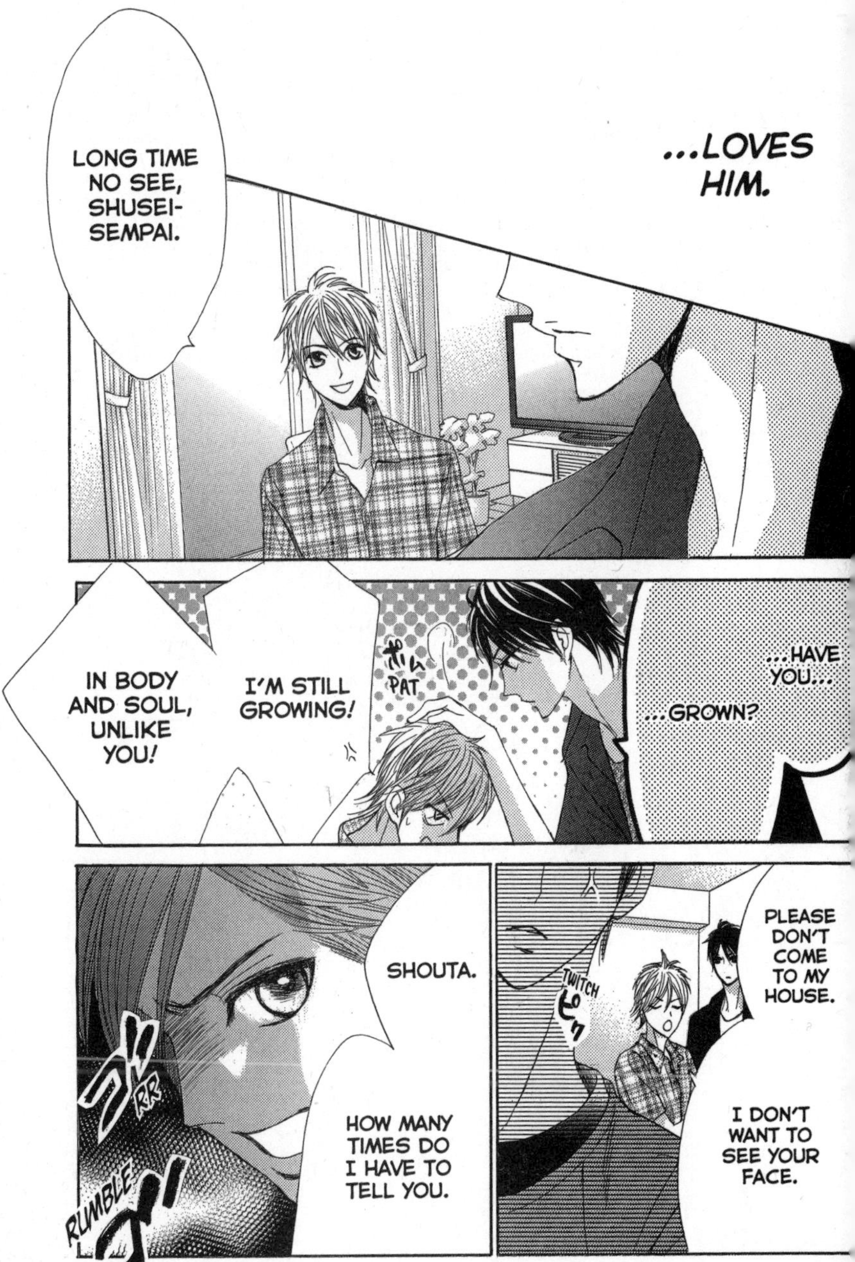
...LOVES HIM.
LONG TIME NO SEE, SHUSEI-SEMPAI.
...HAVE YOU...
...GROWN?
PAT
I'M STILL GROWING!
IN BODY AND SOUL, UNLIKE YOU!
PLEASE DON'T COME TO MY HOUSE.
TWITCH
I DON'T WANT TO SEE YOUR FACE.
SHOUTA.
HOW MANY TIMES DO I HAVE TO TELL YOU.
RR
RUMBLE

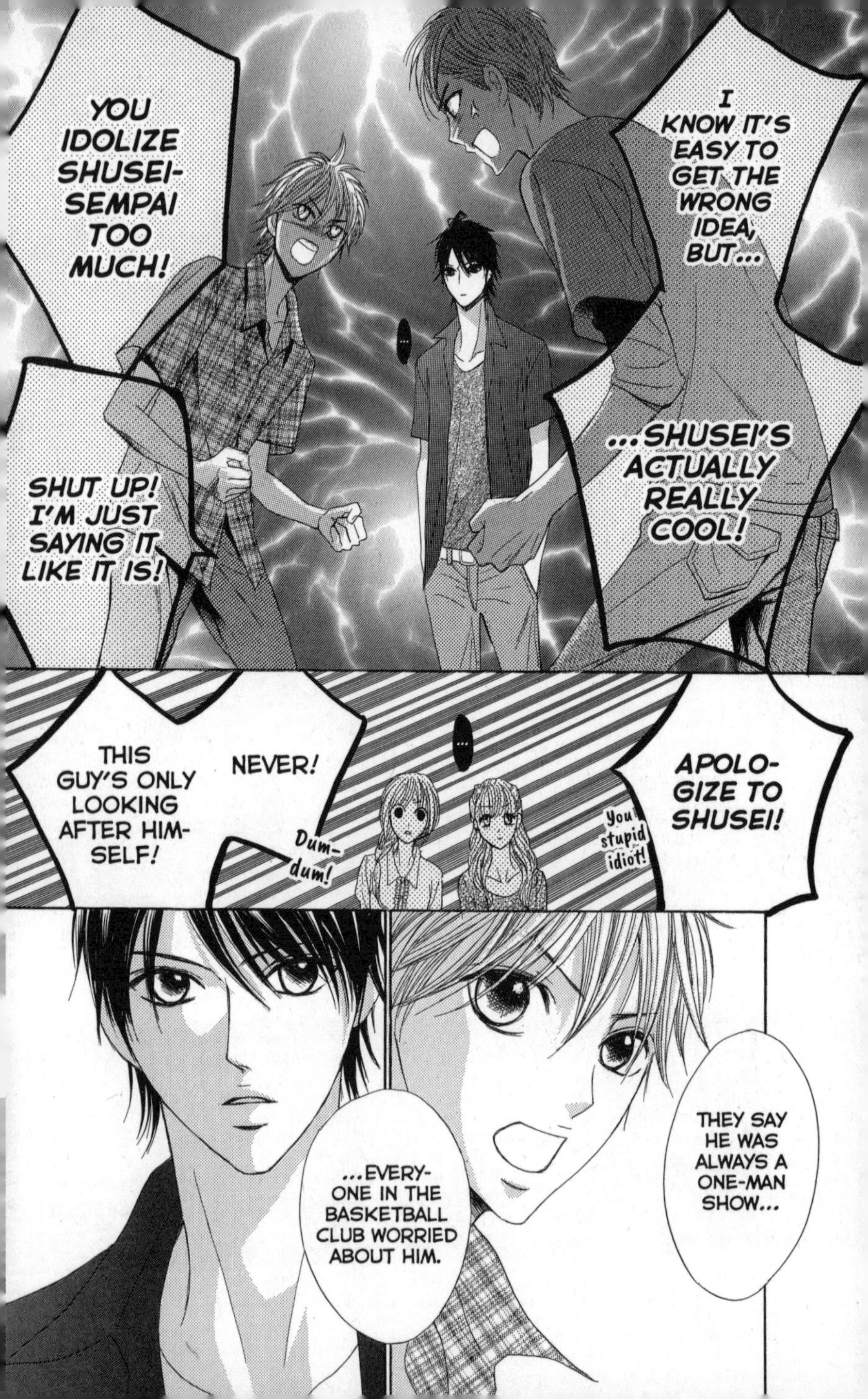

I KNOW IT'S EASY TO GET THE WRONG IDEA, BUT...
YOU IDOLIZE SHUSEI-SEMPAI TOO MUCH!
...
...SHUSEI'S ACTUALLY REALLY COOL!
SHUT UP! I'M JUST SAYING IT LIKE IT IS!
APOLO-GIZE TO SHUSEI!
...
You stupid idiot!
Dum-dum!
NEVER!
THIS GUY'S ONLY LOOKING AFTER HIM-SELF!
THEY SAY HE WAS ALWAYS A ONE-MAN SHOW...
...EVERY-ONE IN THE BASKETBALL CLUB WORRIED ABOUT HIM.

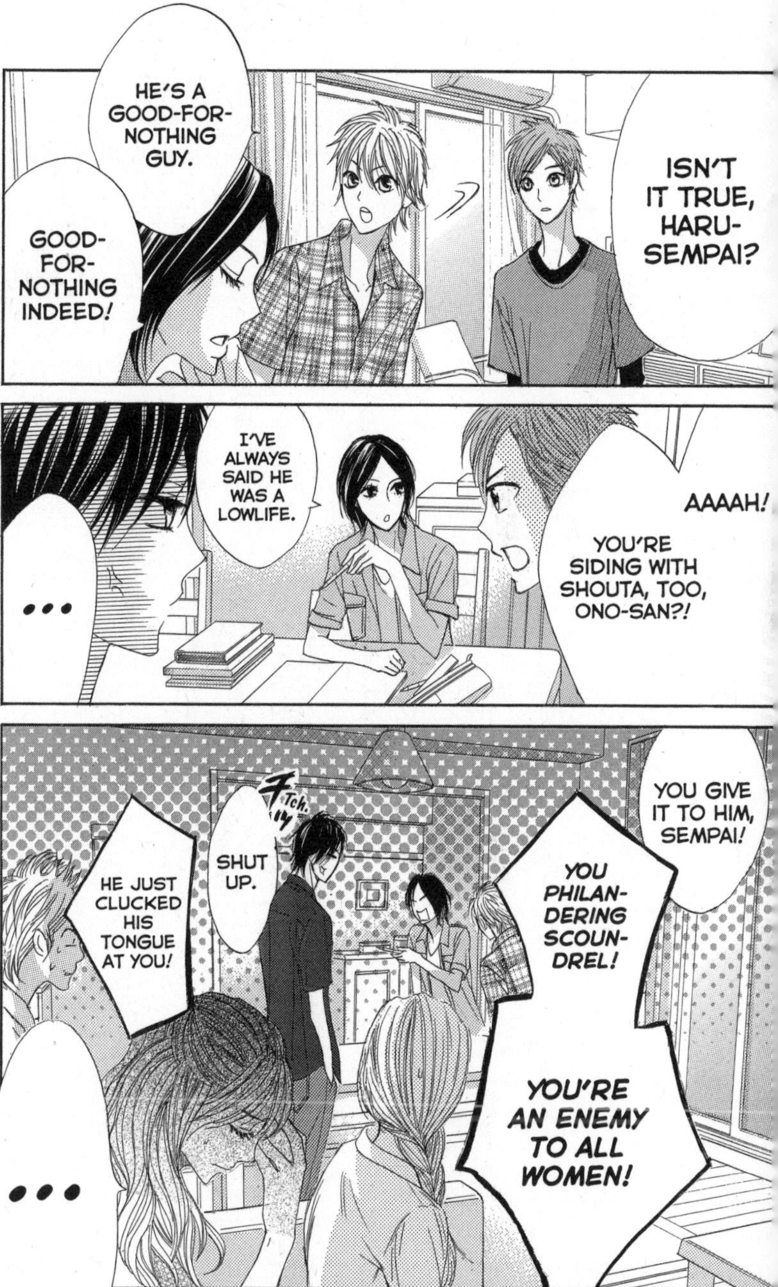
ISN'T IT TRUE, HARU-SEMPAI?
HE'S A GOOD-FOR-NOTHING GUY.
GOOD-FOR-NOTHING INDEED!
I'VE ALWAYS SAID HE WAS A LOWLIFE.
AAAAH!
YOU'RE SIDING WITH SHOUTA, TOO, ONO-SAN?!
...
YOU GIVE IT TO HIM, SEMPAI!
YOU PHILANDERING SCOUNDREL!
YOU'RE AN ENEMY TO ALL WOMEN!
チ Tch.
SHUT UP.
HE JUST CLUCKED HIS TONGUE AT YOU!
...

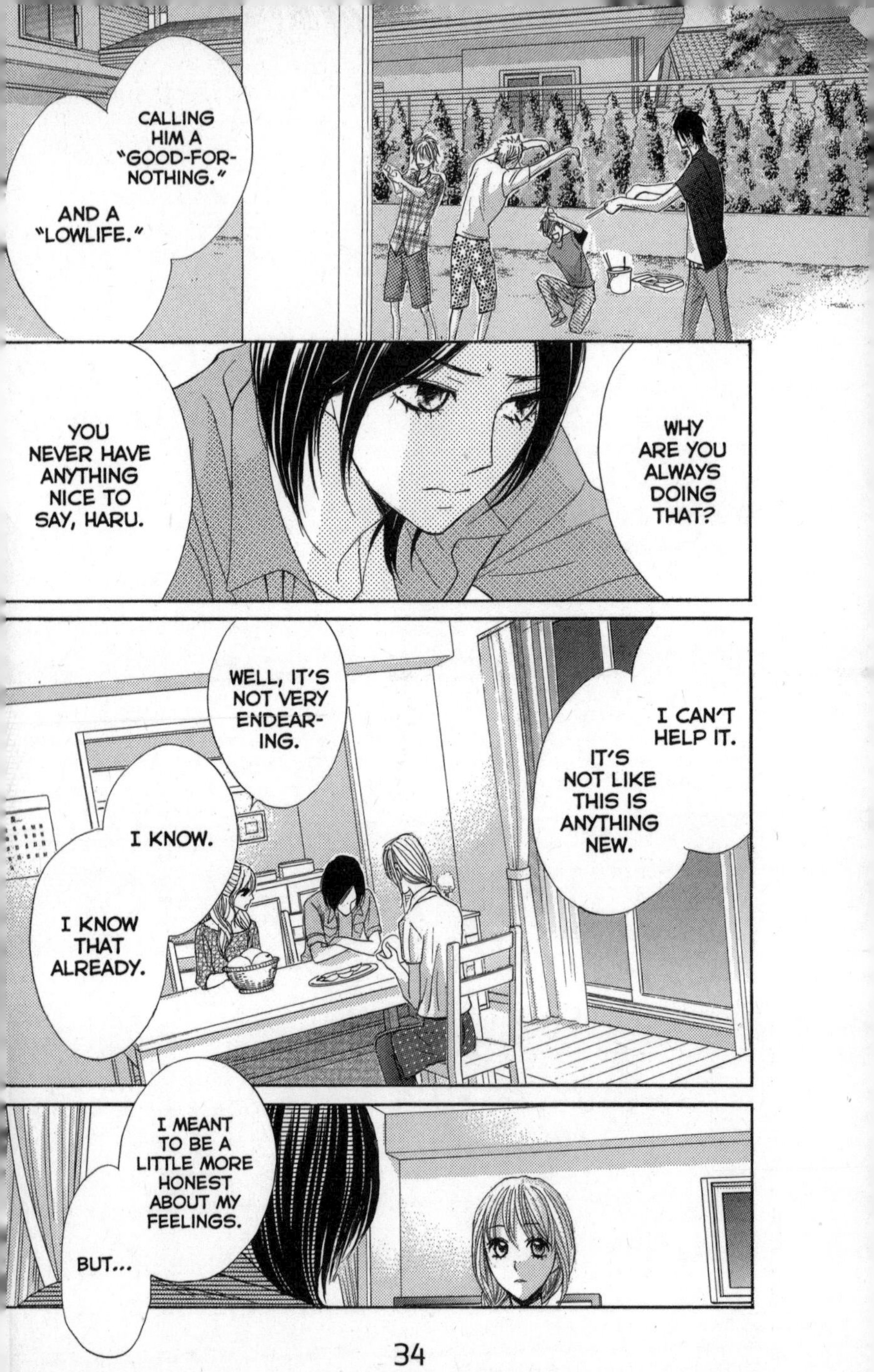
CALLING HIM A "GOOD-FOR-NOTHING."
AND A "LOWLIFE."
WHY ARE YOU ALWAYS DOING THAT?
YOU NEVER HAVE ANYTHING NICE TO SAY, HARU.
I CAN'T HELP IT.
IT'S NOT LIKE THIS IS ANYTHING NEW.
WELL, IT'S NOT VERY ENDEAR-ING.
I KNOW.
I KNOW THAT ALREADY.
I MEANT TO BE A LITTLE MORE HONEST ABOUT MY FEELINGS.
BUT...

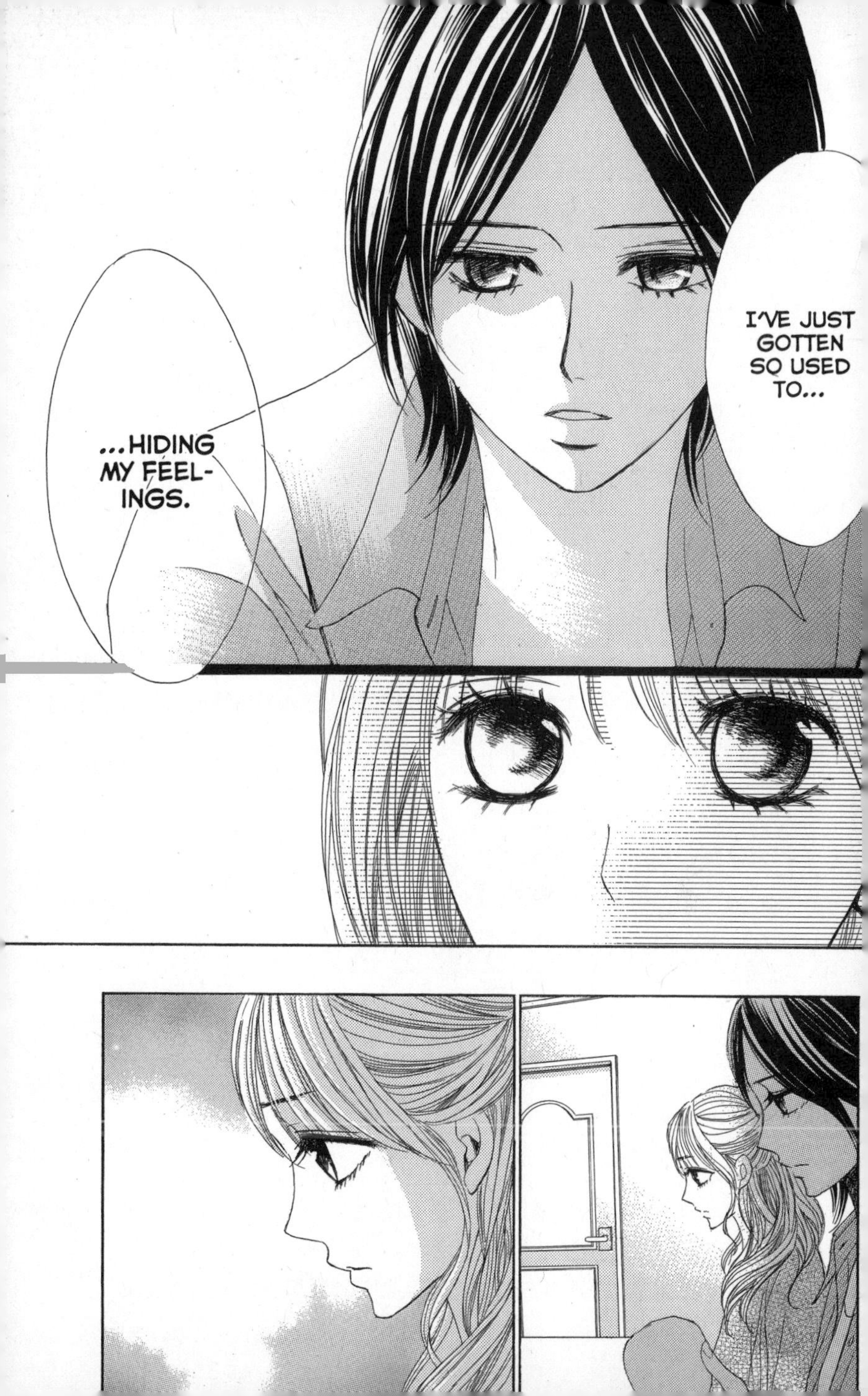
I'VE JUST GOTTEN SO USED TO...
...HIDING MY FEELINGS.

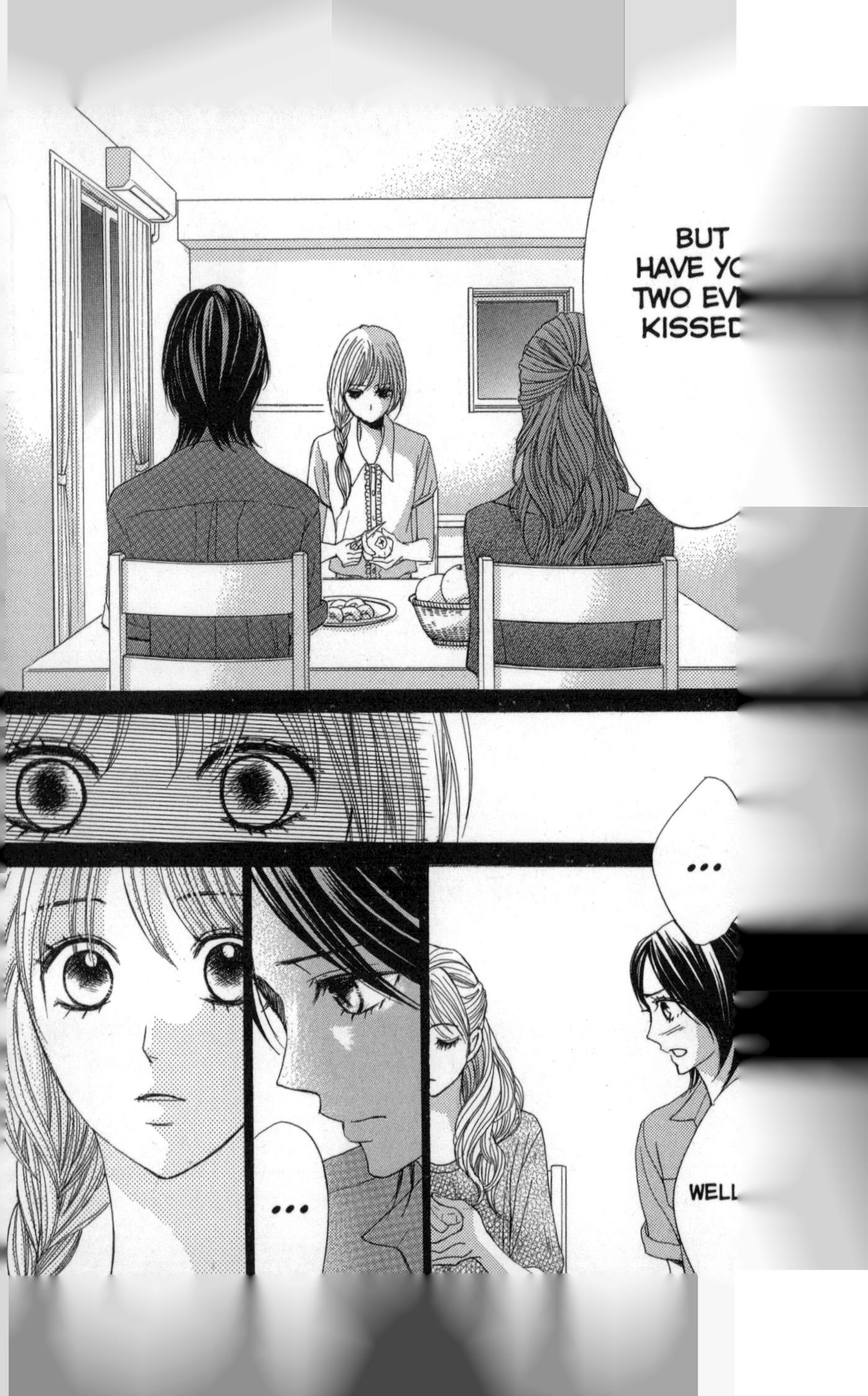
BUT HAVE YO TWO EV KISSED
...
...
WELL

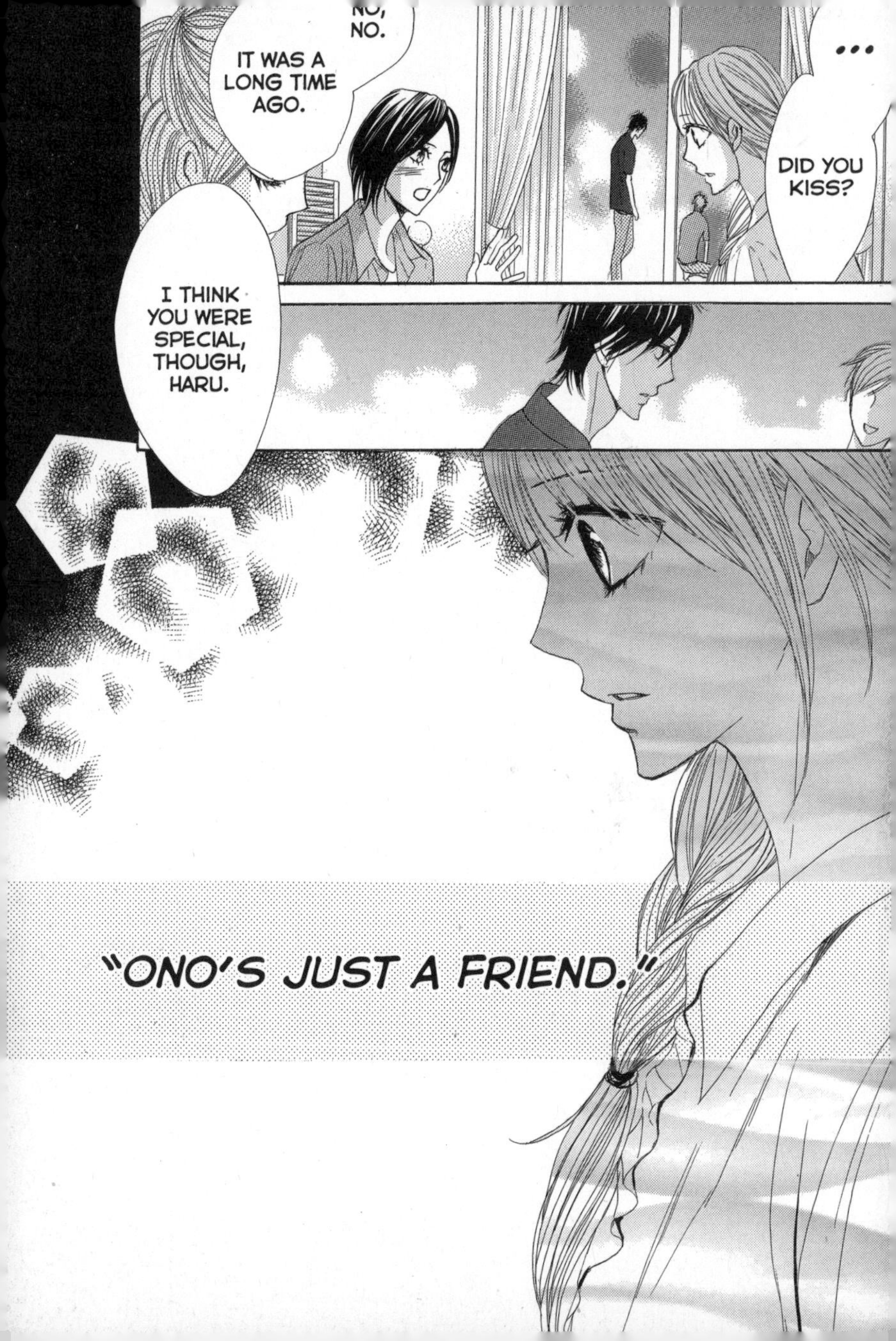
...
DID YOU KISS?
NO, NO.
IT WAS A LONG TIME AGO.
I THINK YOU WERE SPECIAL, THOUGH, HARU.
"ONO'S JUST A FRIEND."

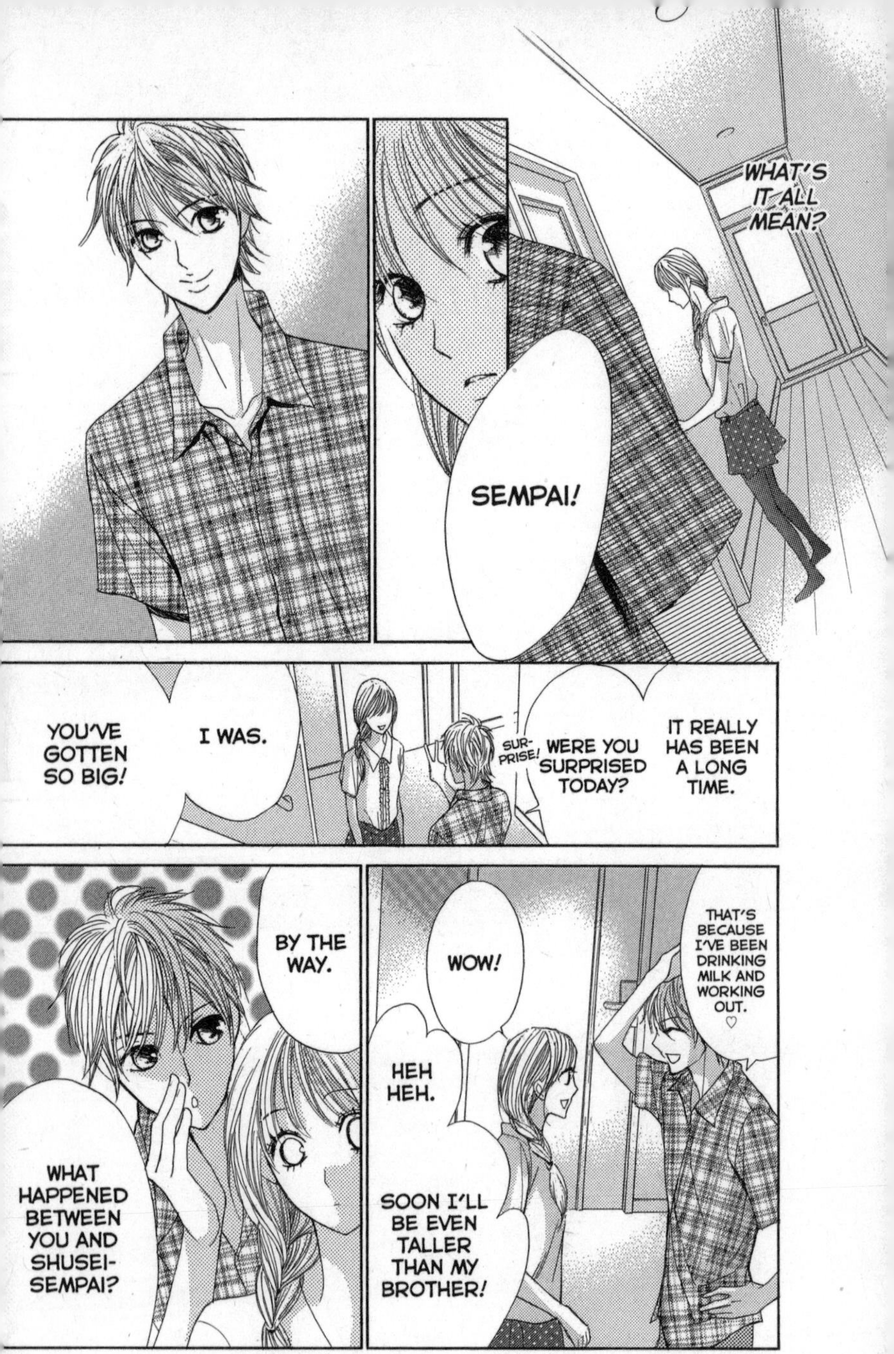
WHAT'S IT ALL MEAN?
SEMPAI!
IT REALLY HAS BEEN A LONG TIME.
WERE YOU SURPRISED TODAY?
SUR-PRISE!
I WAS.
YOU'VE GOTTEN SO BIG!
THAT'S BECAUSE I'VE BEEN DRINKING MILK AND WORKING OUT. ♡
WOW!
HEH HEH.
SOON I'LL BE EVEN TALLER THAN MY BROTHER!
BY THE WAY.
WHAT HAPPENED BETWEEN YOU AND SHUSEI-SEMPAI?

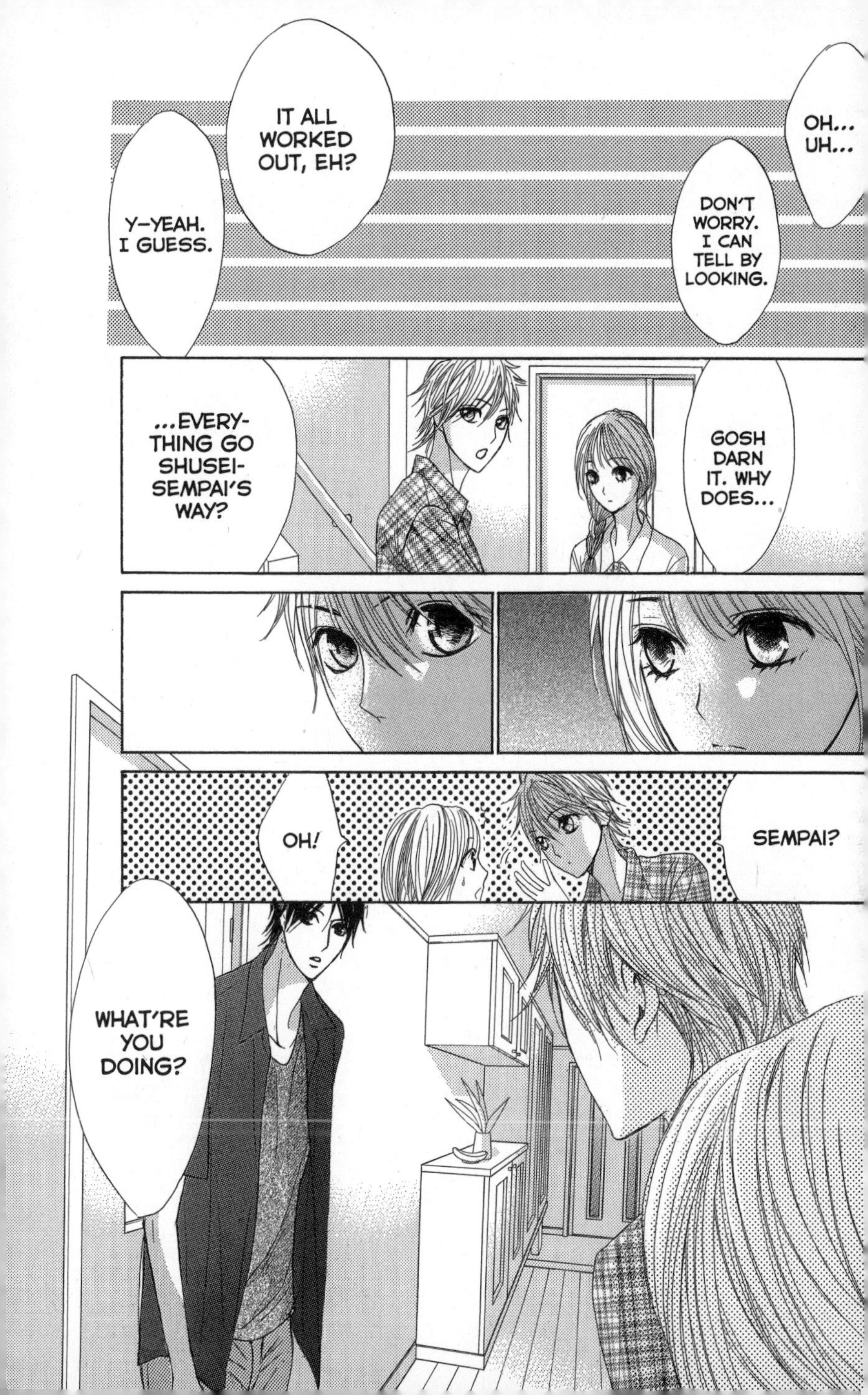
OH... UH...
DON'T WORRY. I CAN TELL BY LOOKING.
IT ALL WORKED OUT, EH?
Y-YEAH. I GUESS.
GOSH DARN IT. WHY DOES...
...EVERYTHING GO SHUSEI-SEMPAI'S WAY?
SEMPAI?
OH!
WHAT'RE YOU DOING?

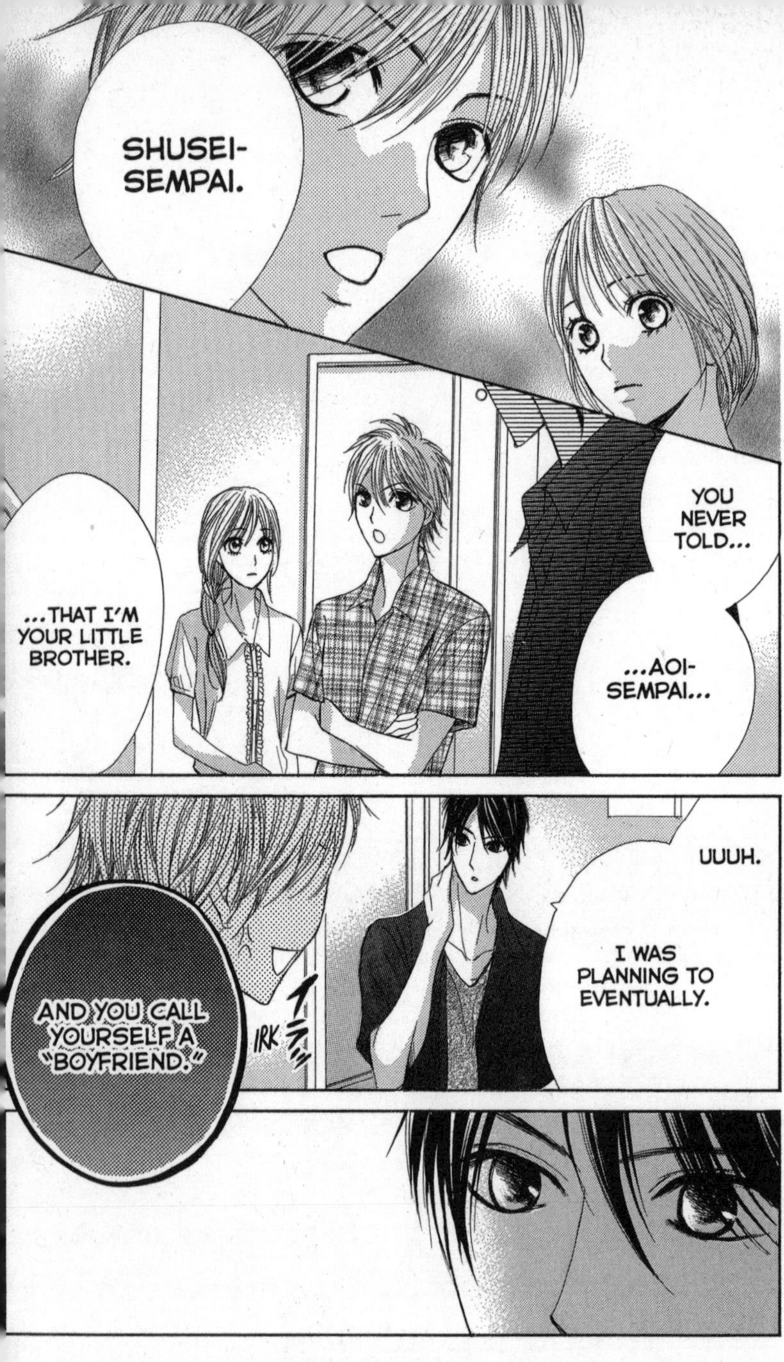
SHUSEI-SEMPAI.
YOU NEVER TOLD...
...AOI-SEMPAI...
...THAT I'M YOUR LITTLE BROTHER.
UUUH.
I WAS PLANNING TO EVENTUALLY.
IRK
AND YOU CALL YOURSELF A "BOYFRIEND."

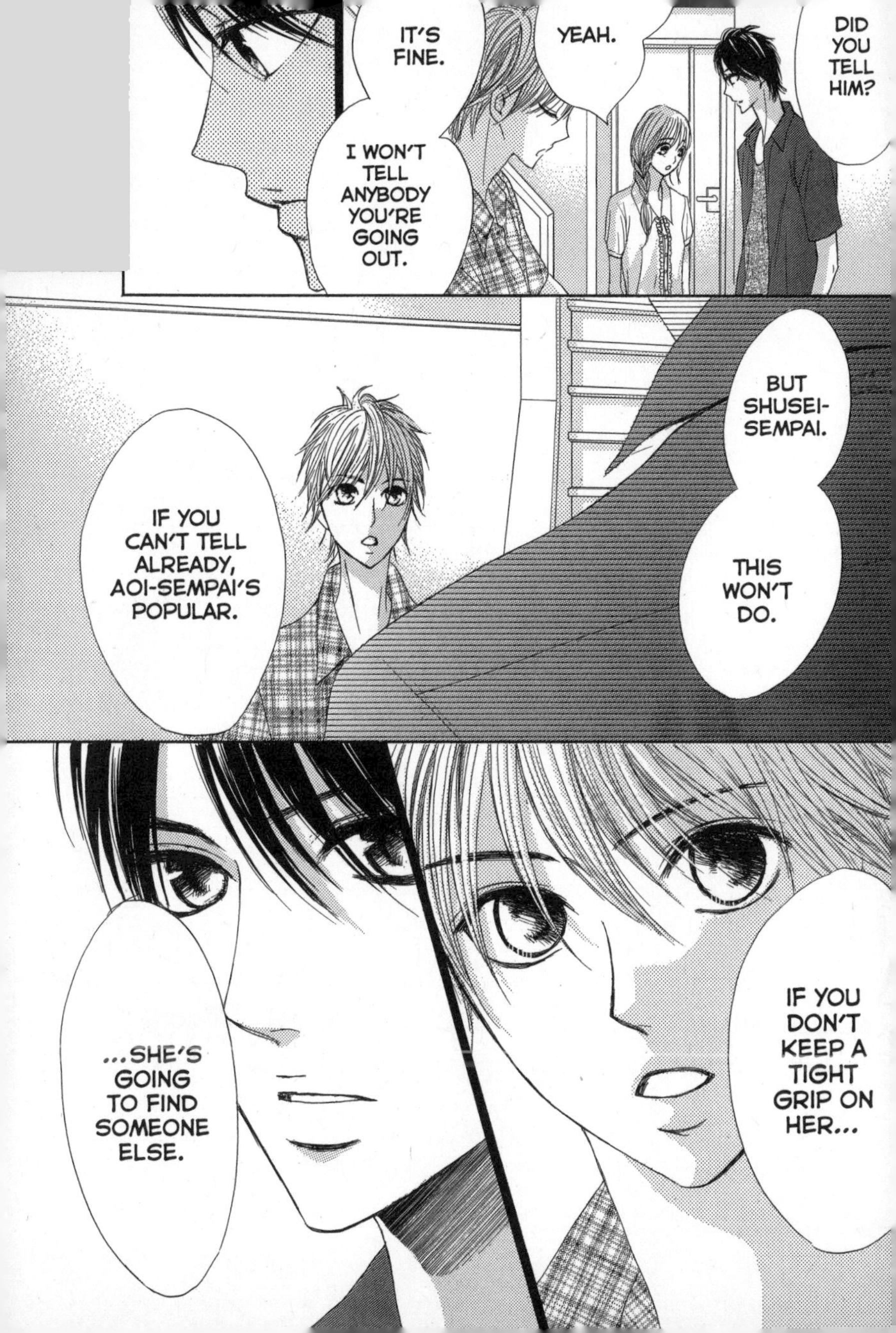
DID YOU TELL HIM?
YEAH.
IT'S FINE.
I WON'T TELL ANYBODY YOU'RE GOING OUT.
BUT SHUSEI-SEMPAI.
THIS WON'T DO.
IF YOU CAN'T TELL ALREADY, AOI-SEMPAI'S POPULAR.
IF YOU DON'T KEEP A TIGHT GRIP ON HER...
...SHE'S GOING TO FIND SOMEONE ELSE.

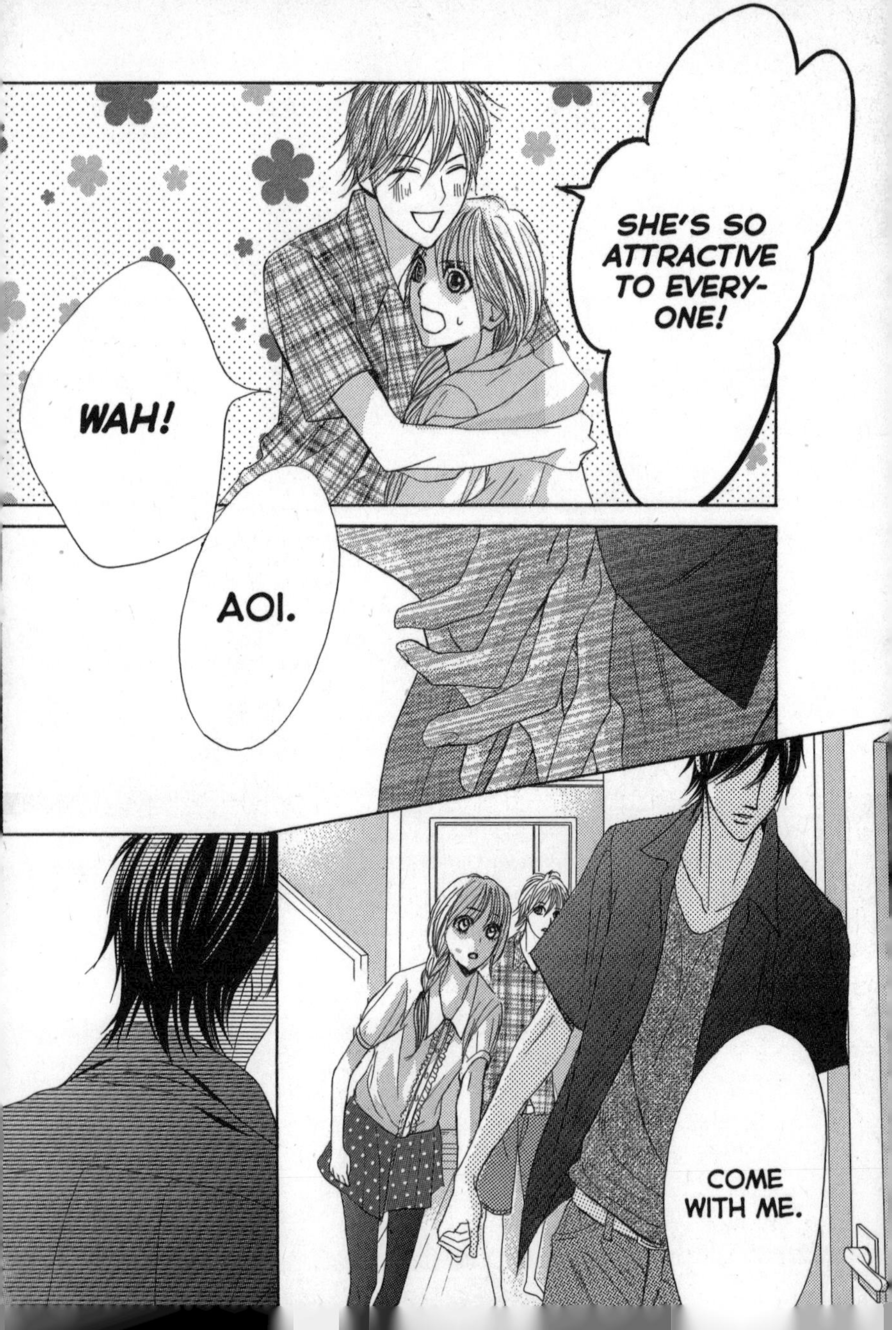
SHE'S SO ATTRACTIVE TO EVERY-ONE!
WAH!
AOI.
COME WITH ME.

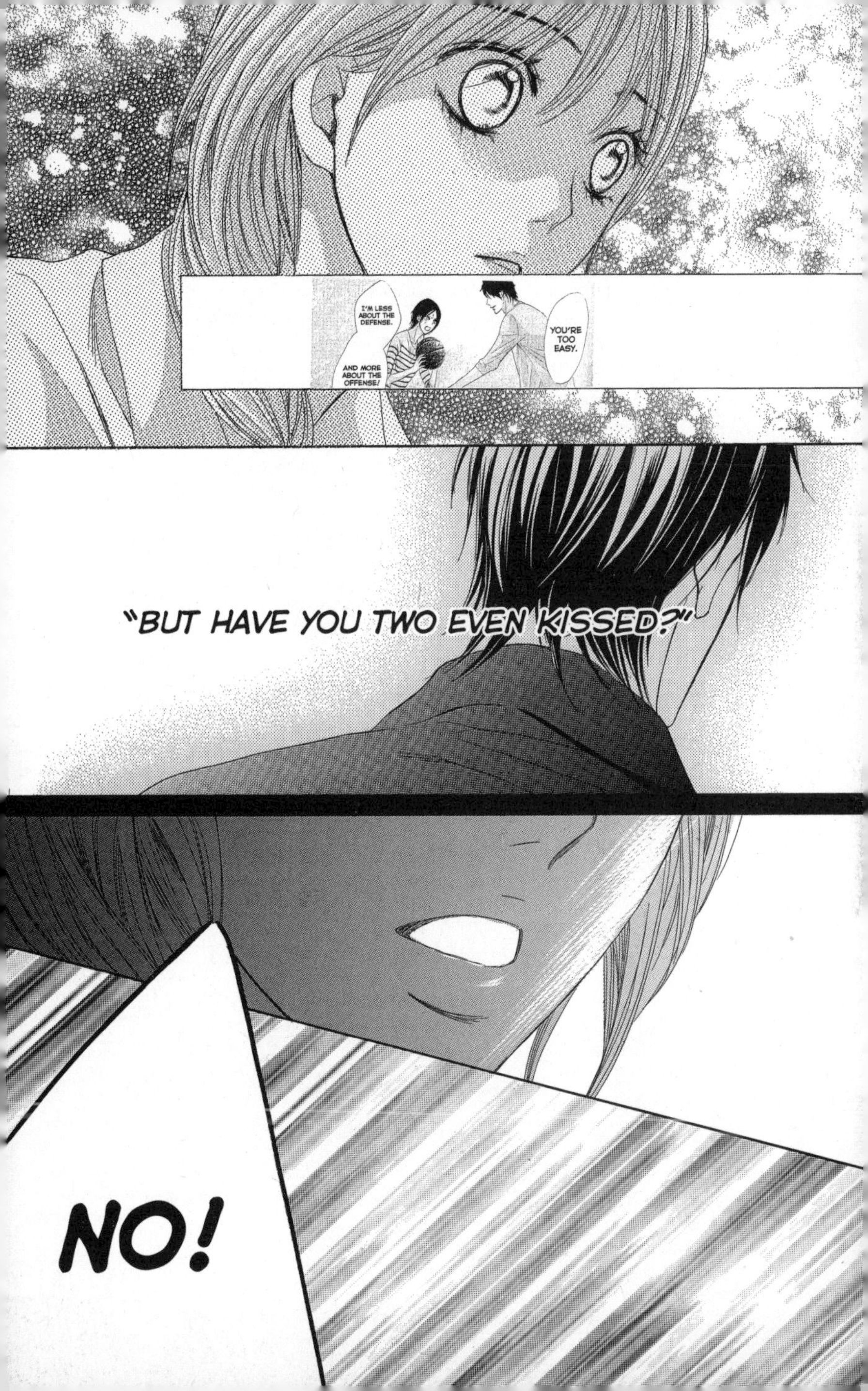
YOU'RE TOO EASY.
I'M LESS ABOUT THE DEFENSE.
AND MORE ABOUT THE OFFENSE!
"BUT HAVE YOU TWO EVEN KISSED?"
NO!

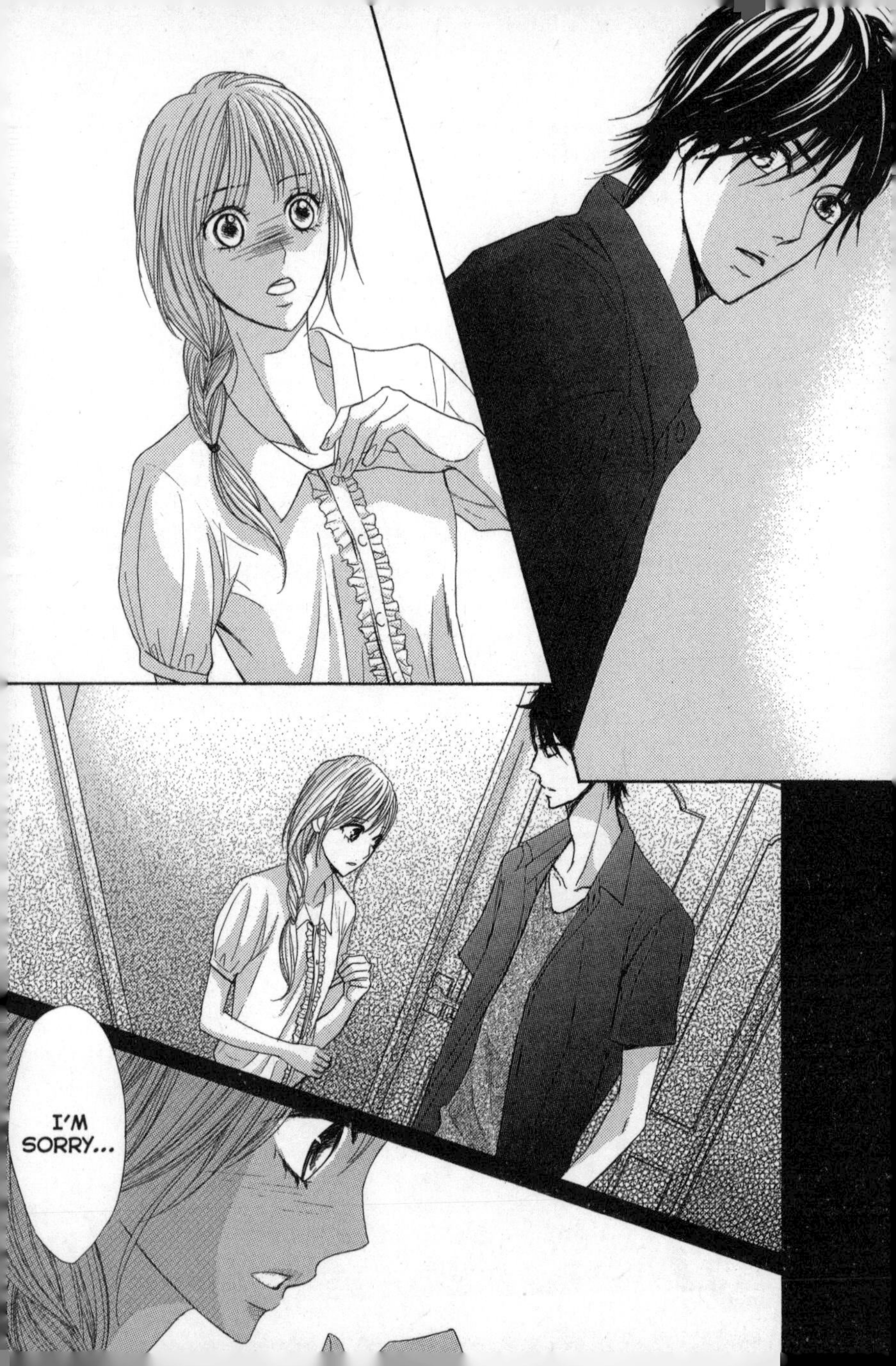
I'M SORRY...

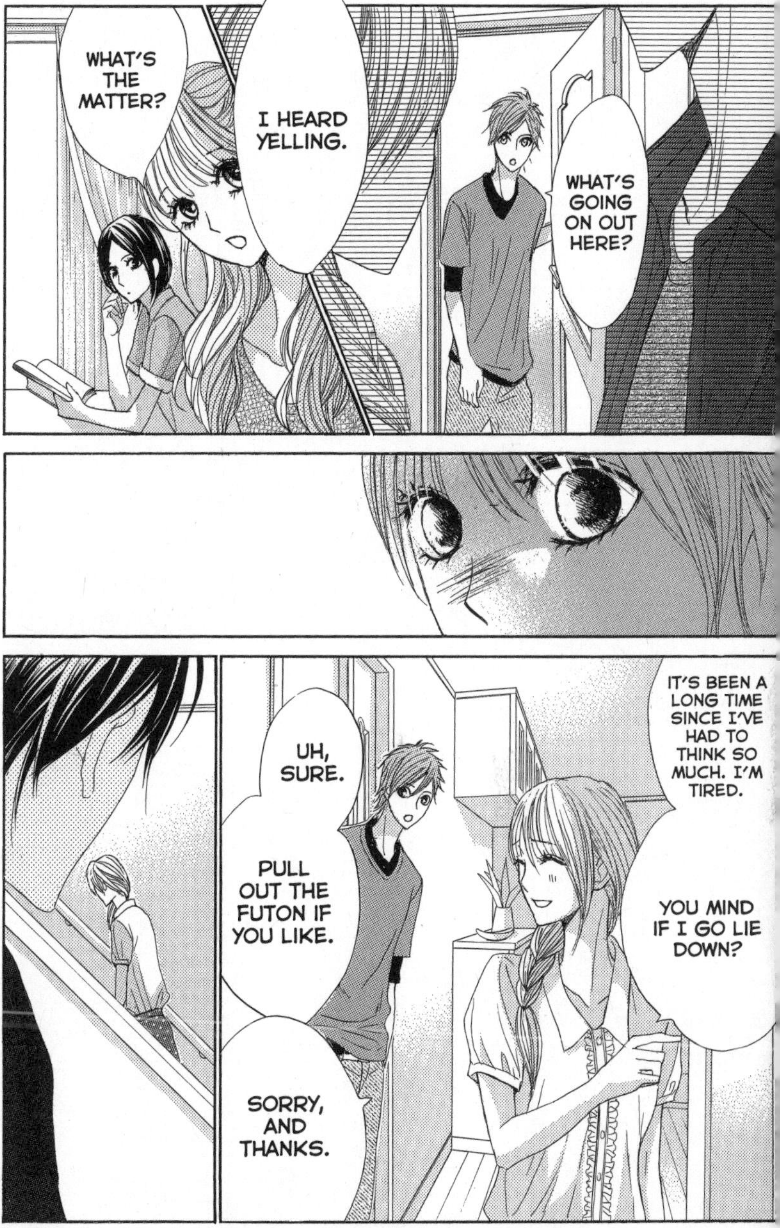
WHAT'S GOING ON OUT HERE?
I HEARD YELLING.
WHAT'S THE MATTER?
IT'S BEEN A LONG TIME SINCE I'VE HAD TO THINK SO MUCH. I'M TIRED.
YOU MIND IF I GO LIE DOWN?
UH, SURE.
PULL OUT THE FUTON IF YOU LIKE.
SORRY, AND THANKS.

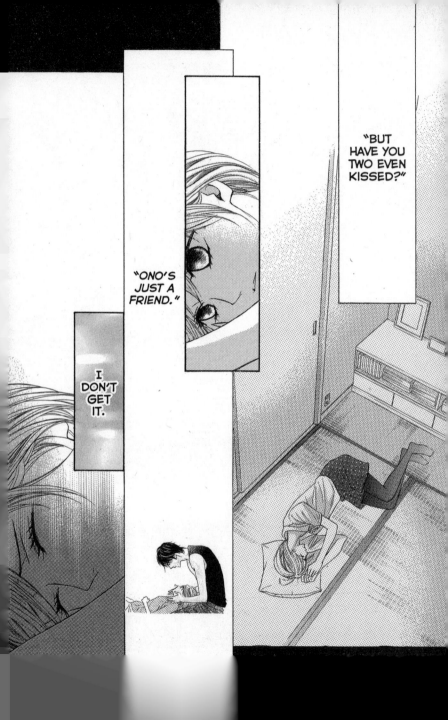

"BUT HAVE YOU TWO EVEN KISSED?"

"ONO'S JUST A FRIEND."

I DON'T GET IT.

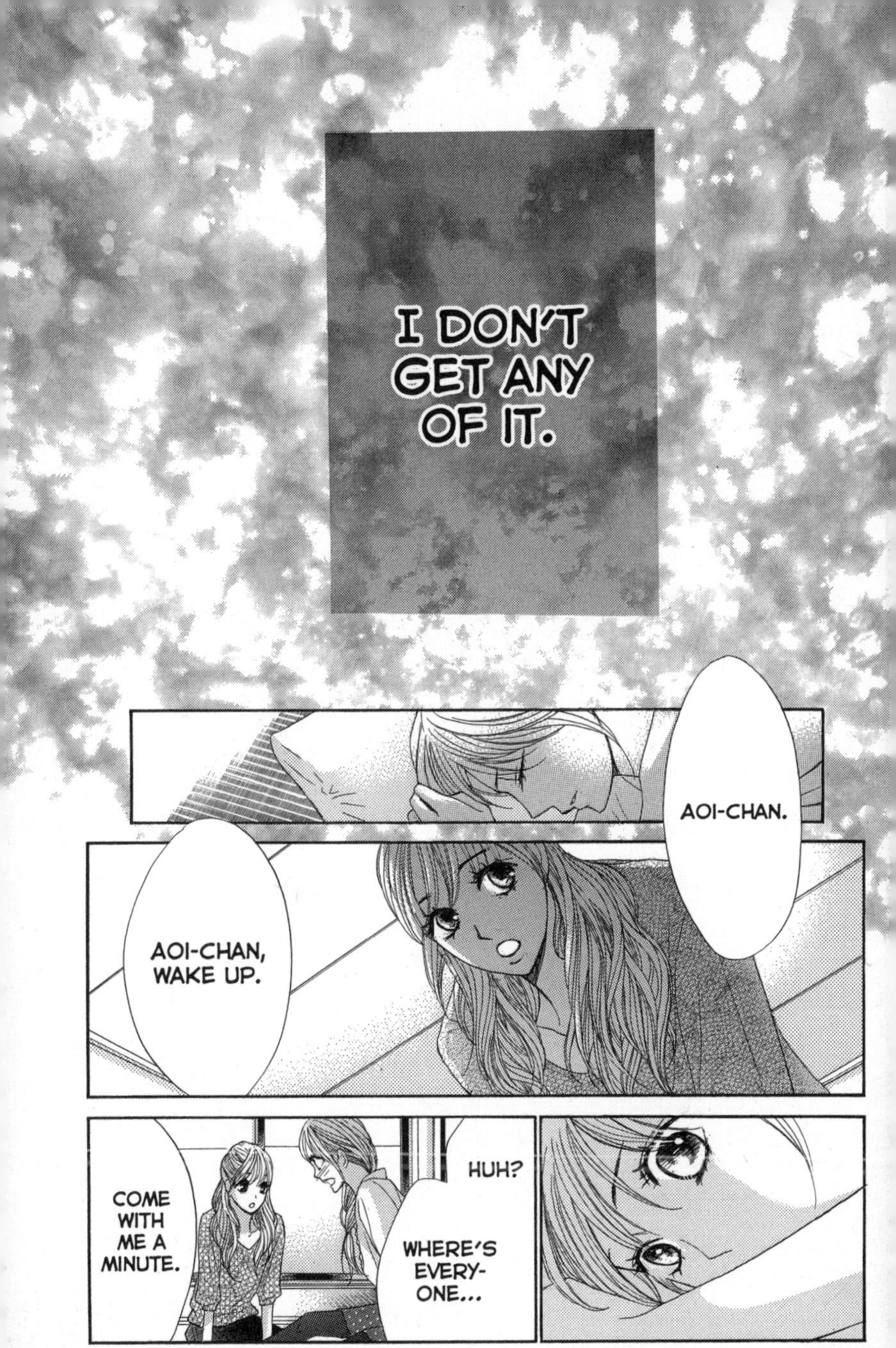
I DON'T GET ANY OF IT.
AOI-CHAN.
AOI-CHAN, WAKE UP.
HUH?
WHERE'S EVERY-ONE...
COME WITH ME A MINUTE.

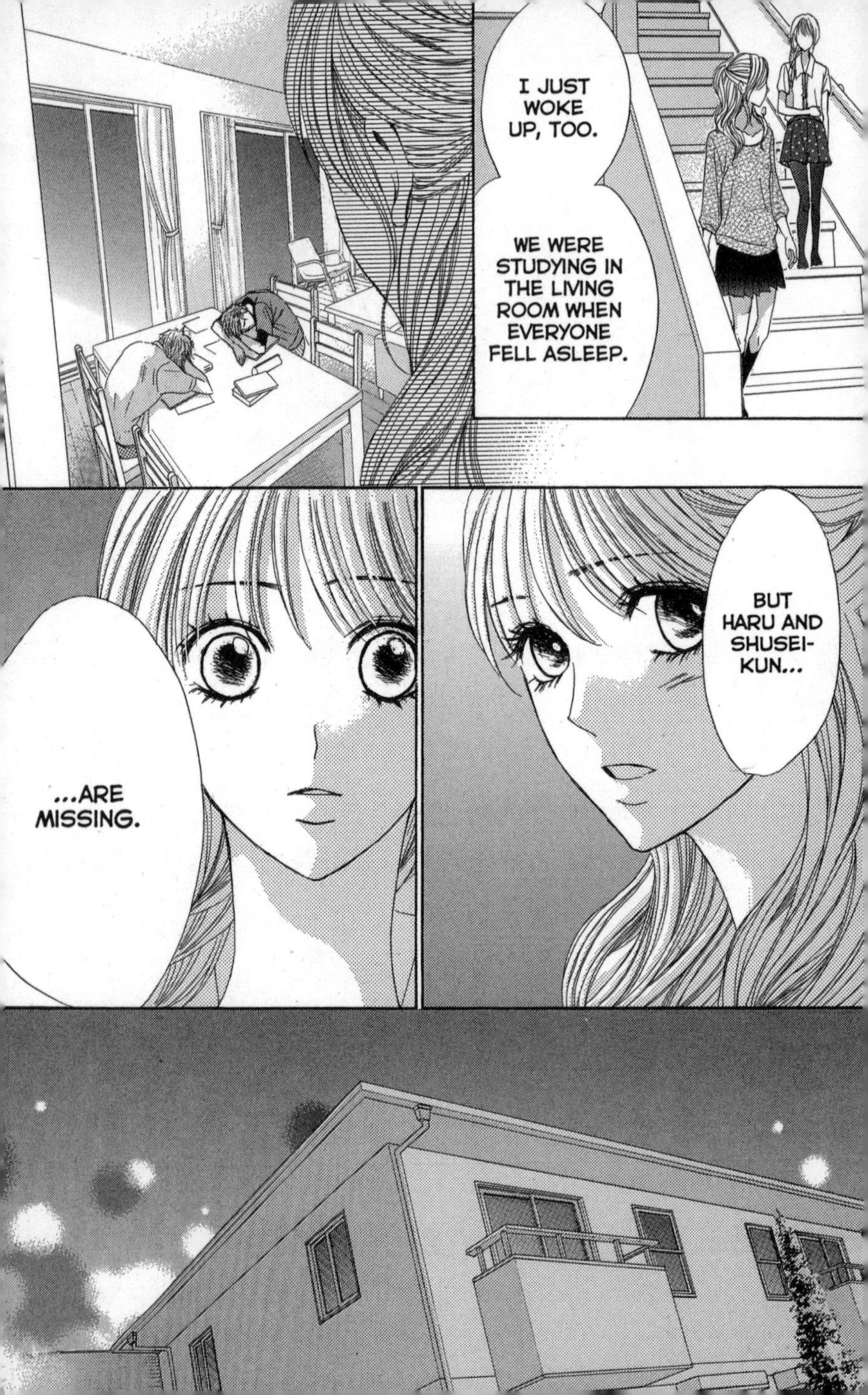
I JUST WOKE UP, TOO.
WE WERE STUDYING IN THE LIVING ROOM WHEN EVERYONE FELL ASLEEP.
BUT HARU AND SHUSEI-KUN...
...ARE MISSING.

L♥DK

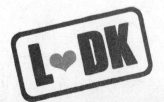

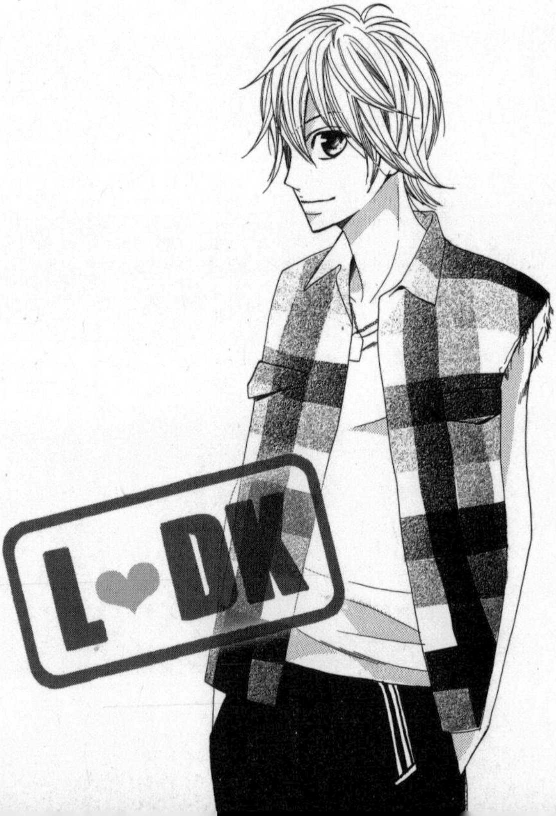
L♥DK

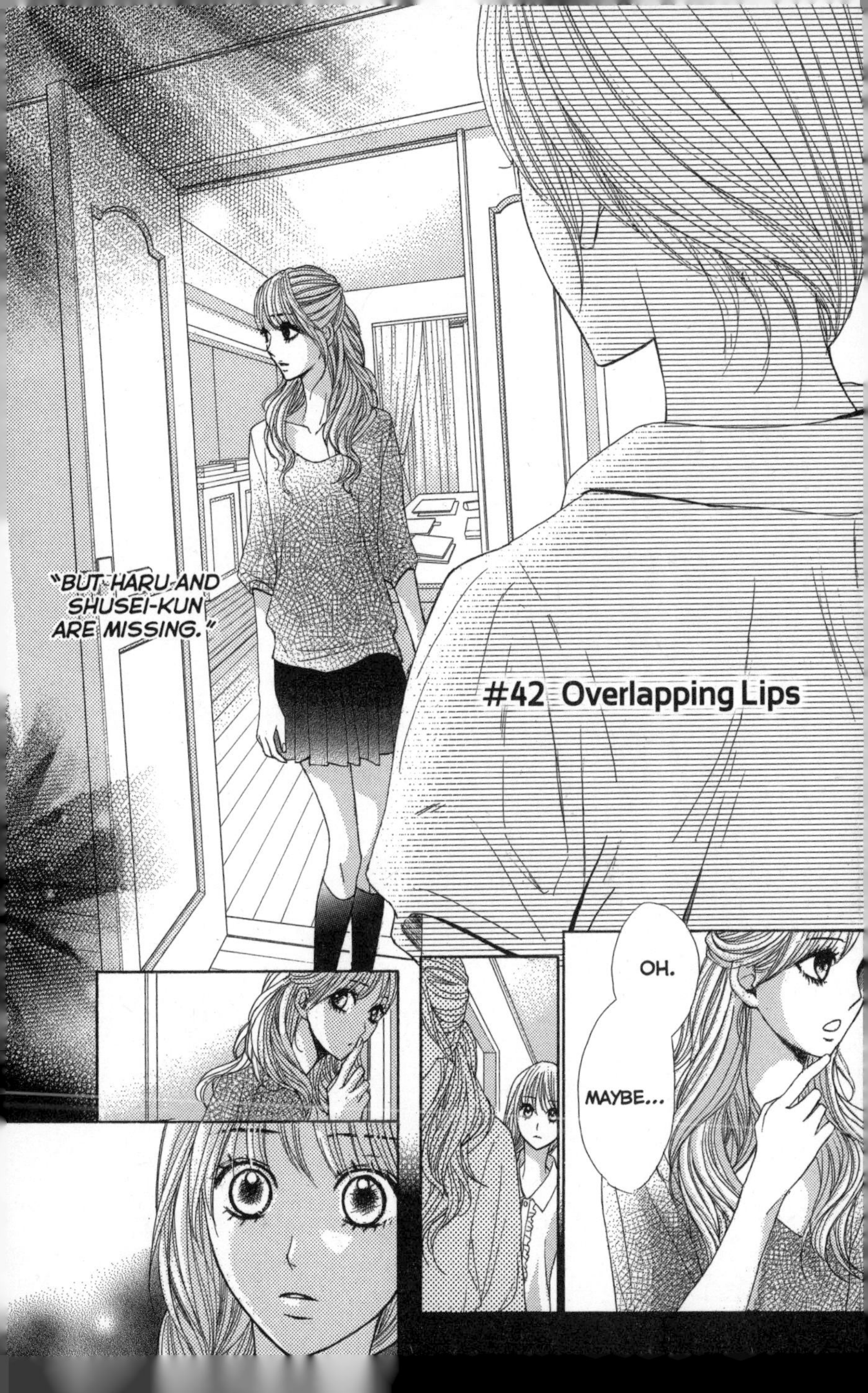
#42 Overlapping Lips
"BUT HARU AND SHUSEI-KUN ARE MISSING."
OH.
MAYBE...

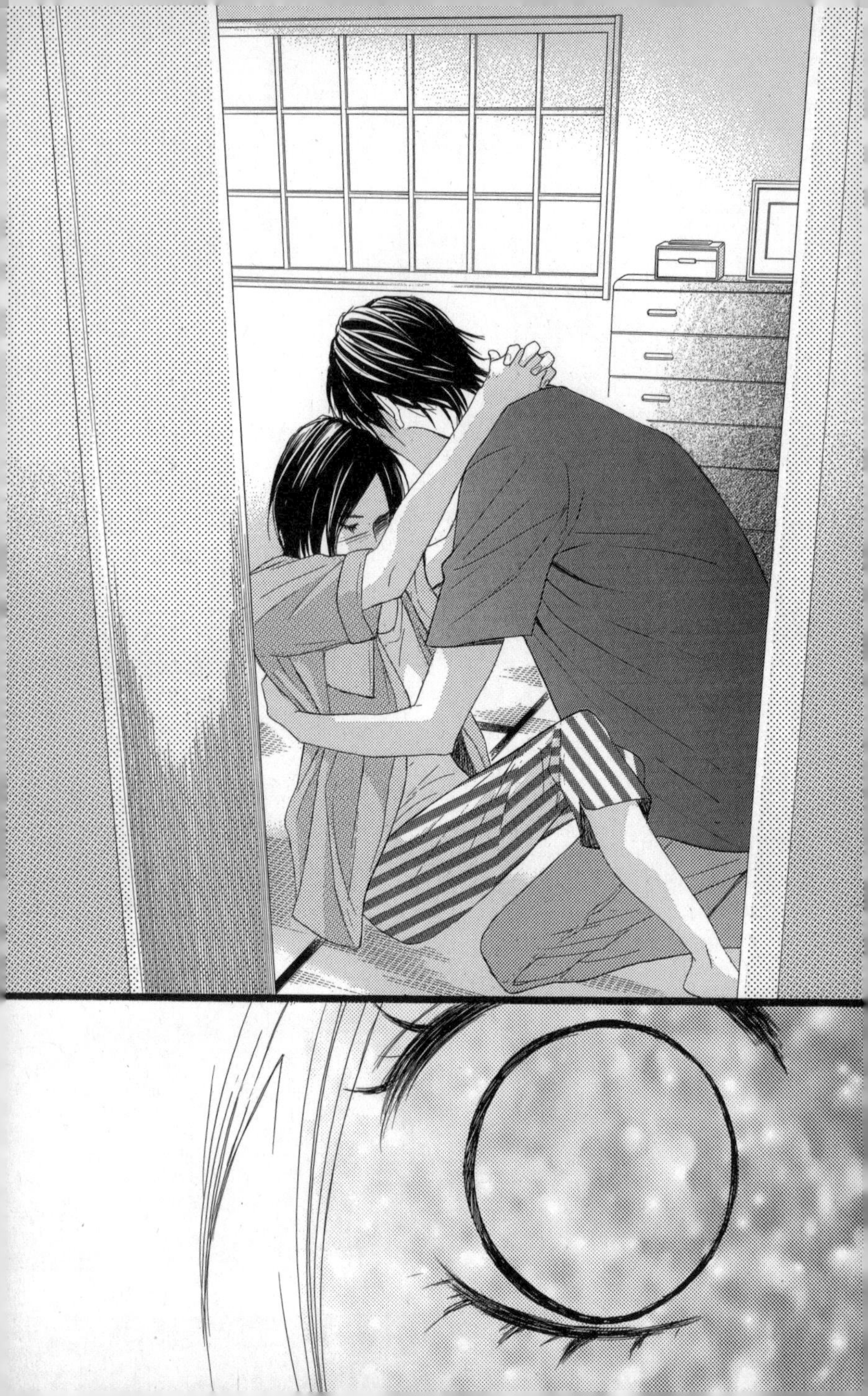

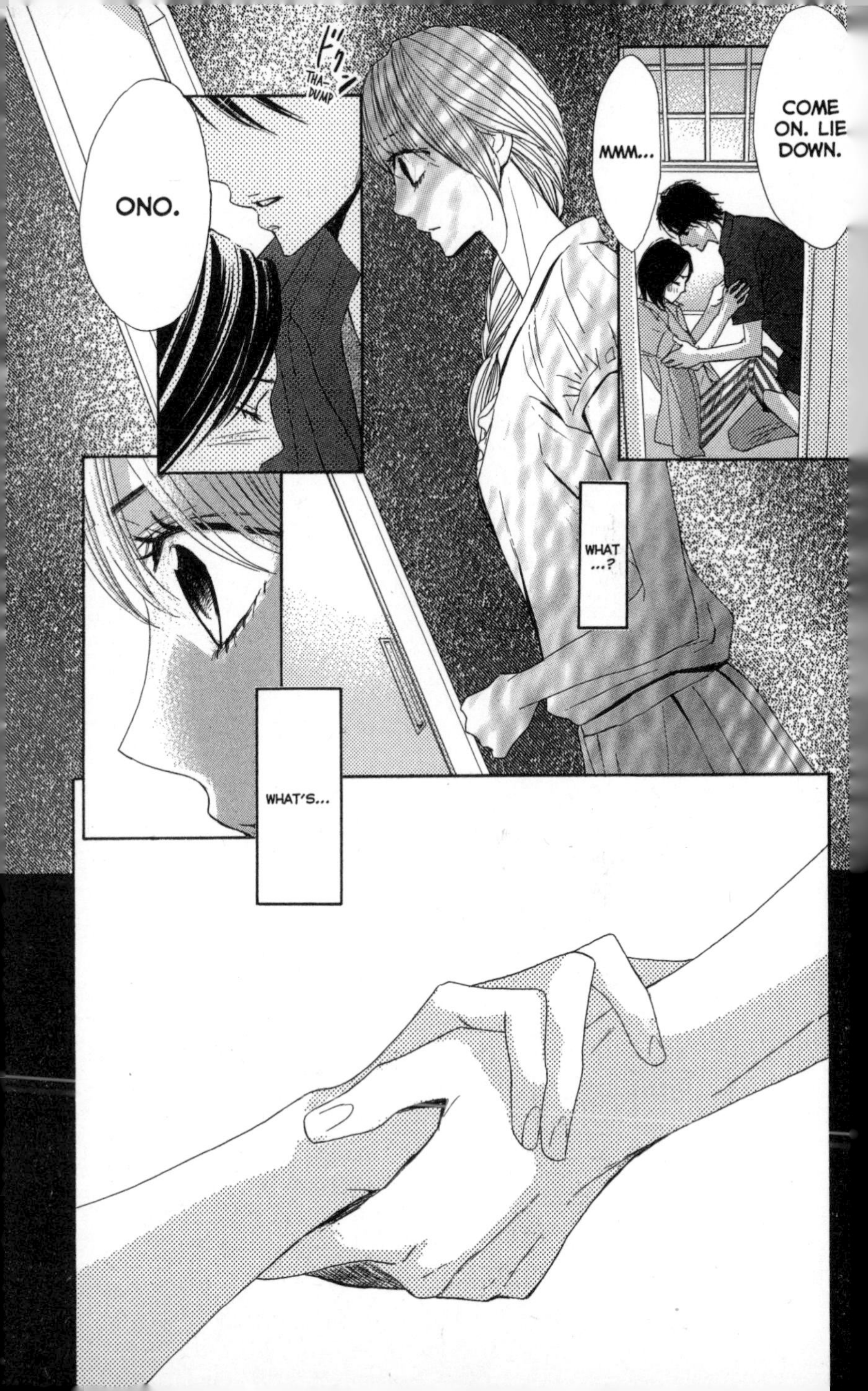

COME ON. LIE DOWN.
MMM...
ドクン
THA-DUMP
ONO.
WHAT...?
WHAT'S...

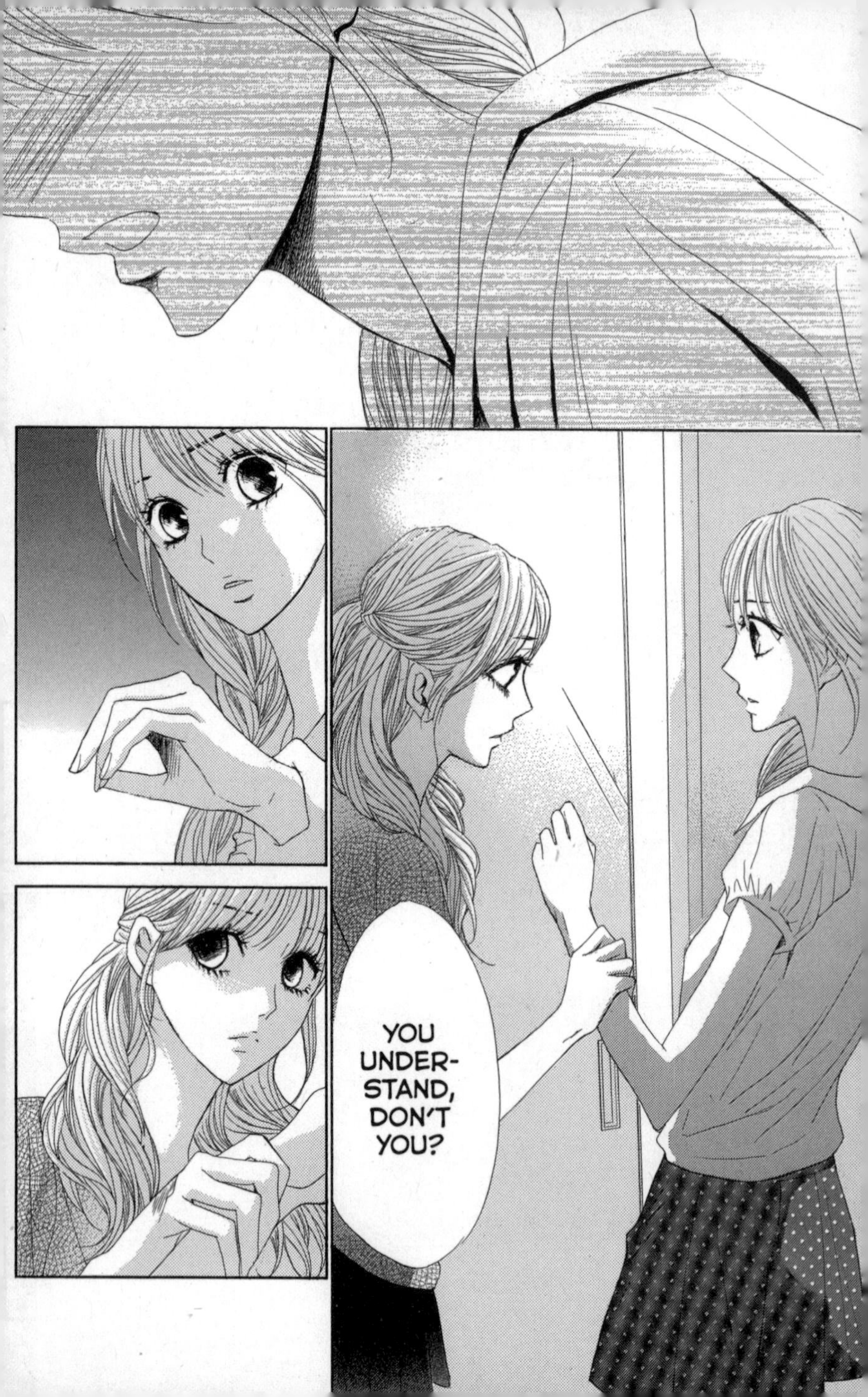
YOU UNDER-STAND, DON'T YOU?

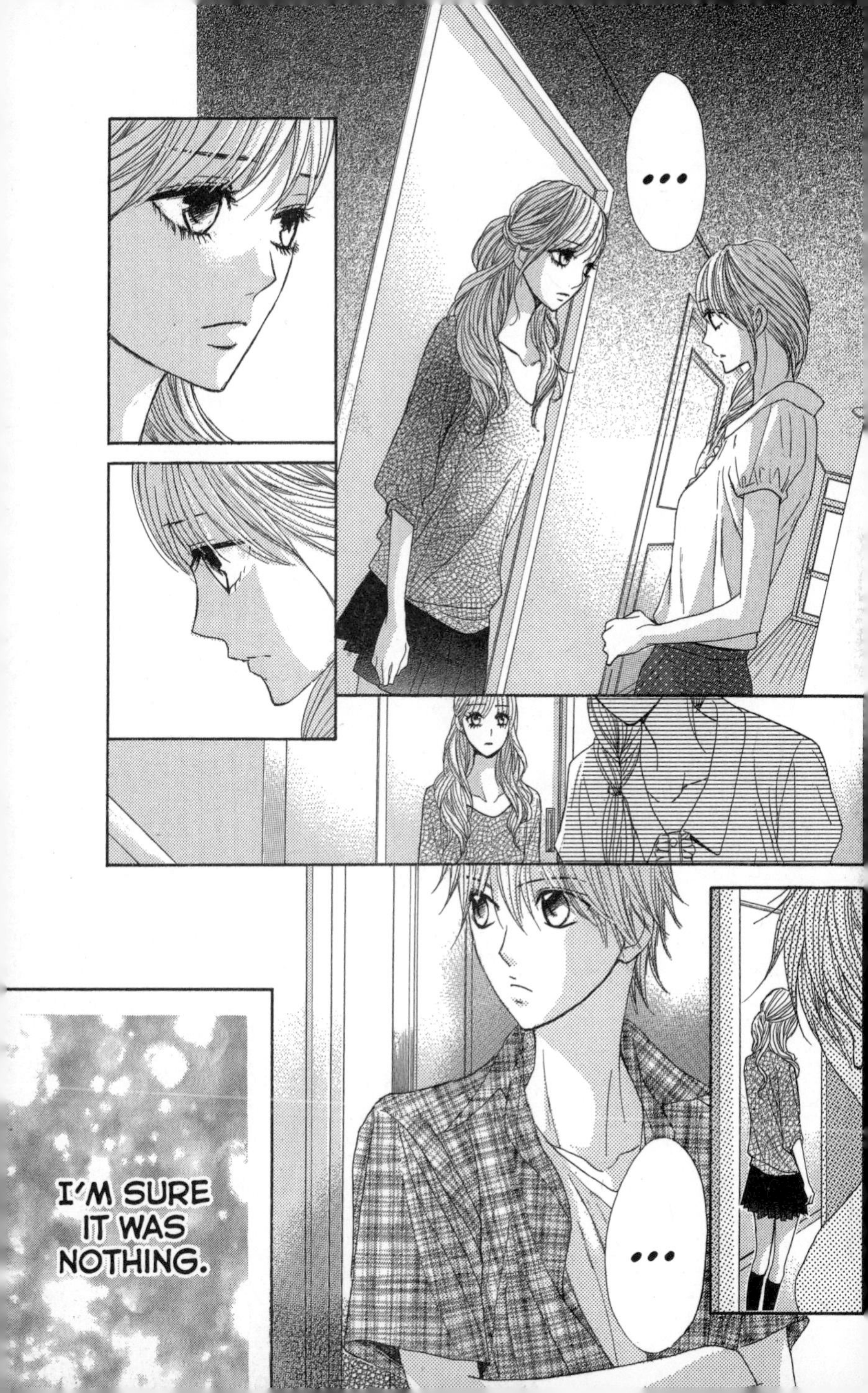
...
...
I'M SURE IT WAS NOTHING.

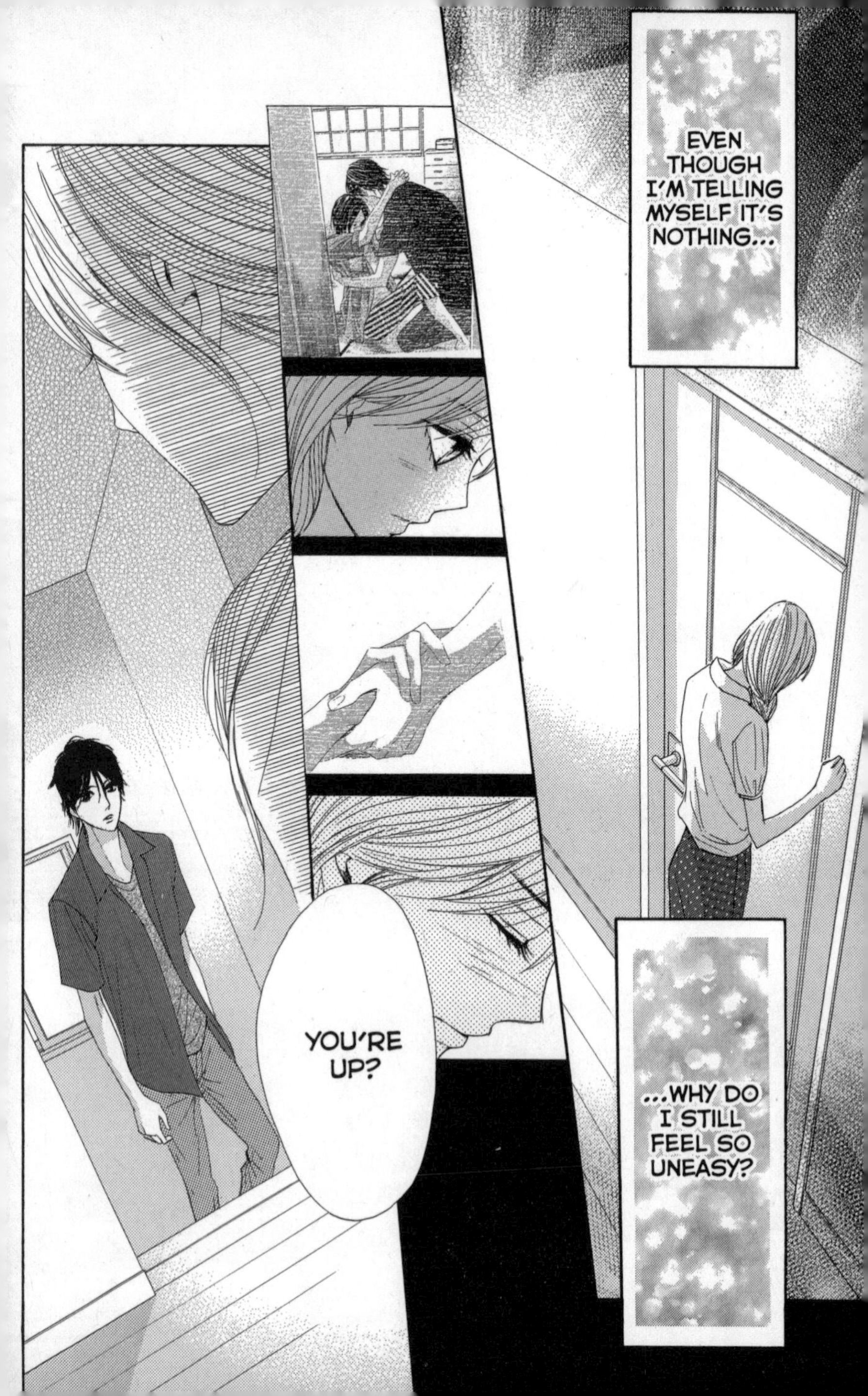
EVEN THOUGH I'M TELLING MYSELF IT'S NOTHING...
...WHY DO I STILL FEEL SO UNEASY?
YOU'RE UP?

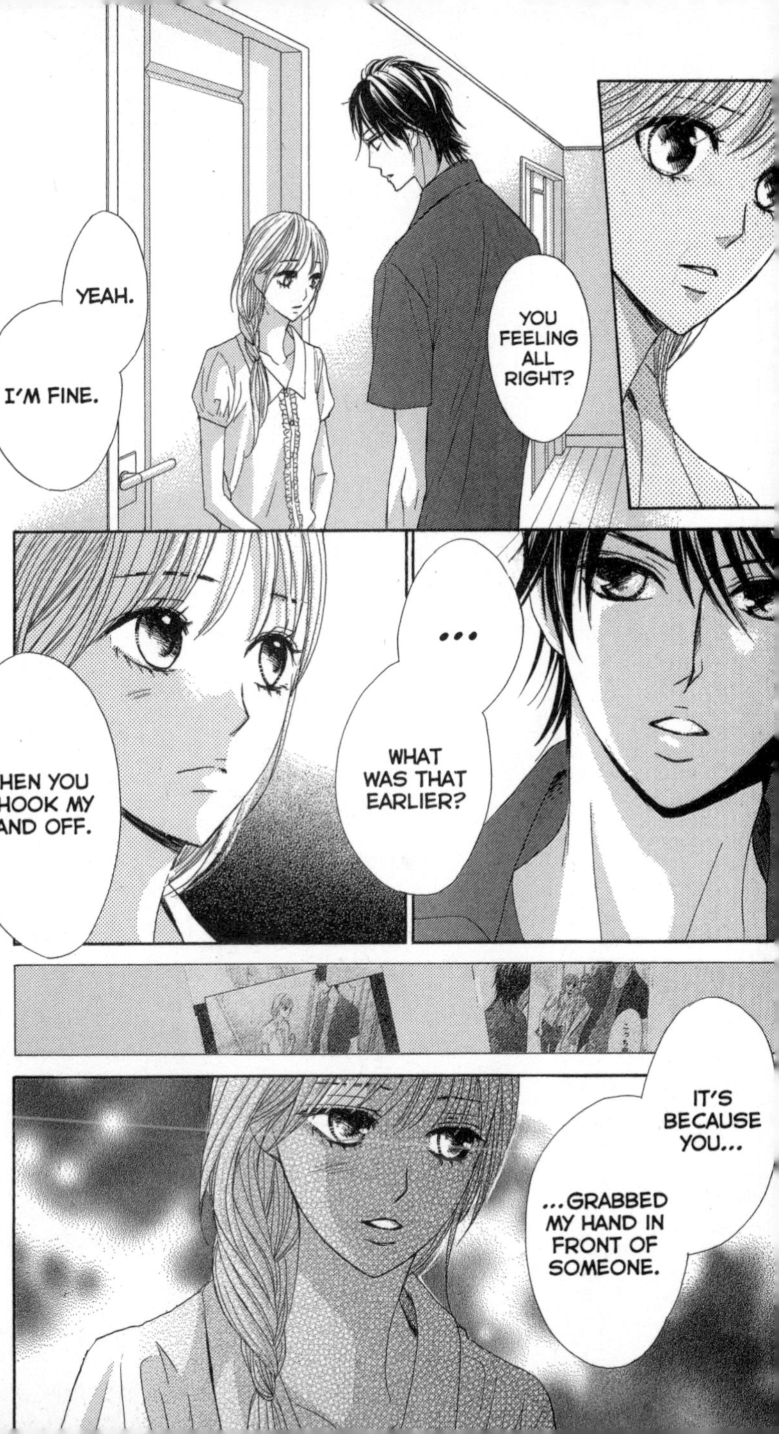
YOU FEELING ALL RIGHT?
YEAH.
I'M FINE.
...
WHAT WAS THAT EARLIER?
WHEN YOU SHOOK MY HAND OFF.
IT'S BECAUSE YOU...
...GRABBED MY HAND IN FRONT OF SOMEONE.

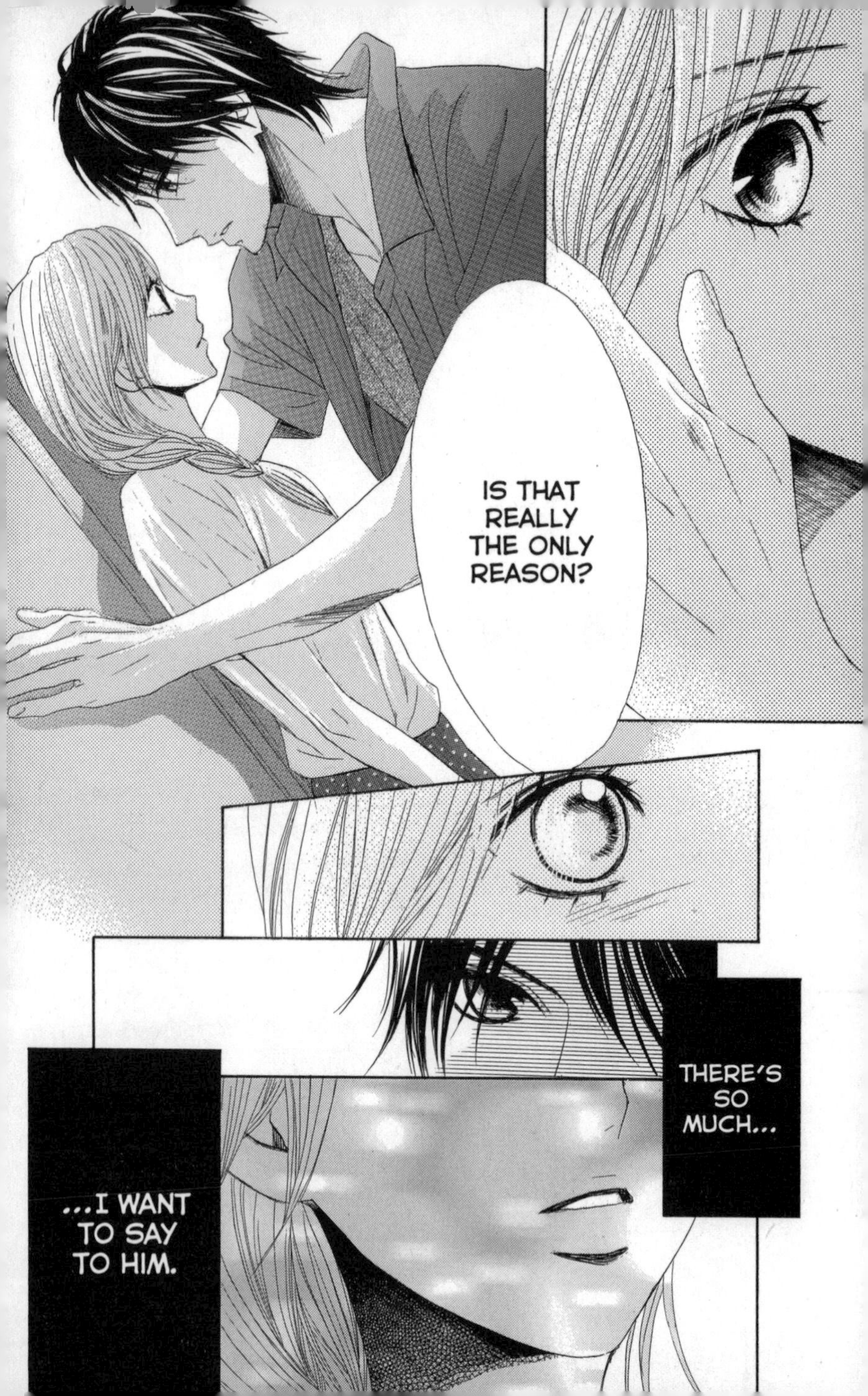
IS THAT REALLY THE ONLY REASON?
THERE'S SO MUCH...
...I WANT TO SAY TO HIM.

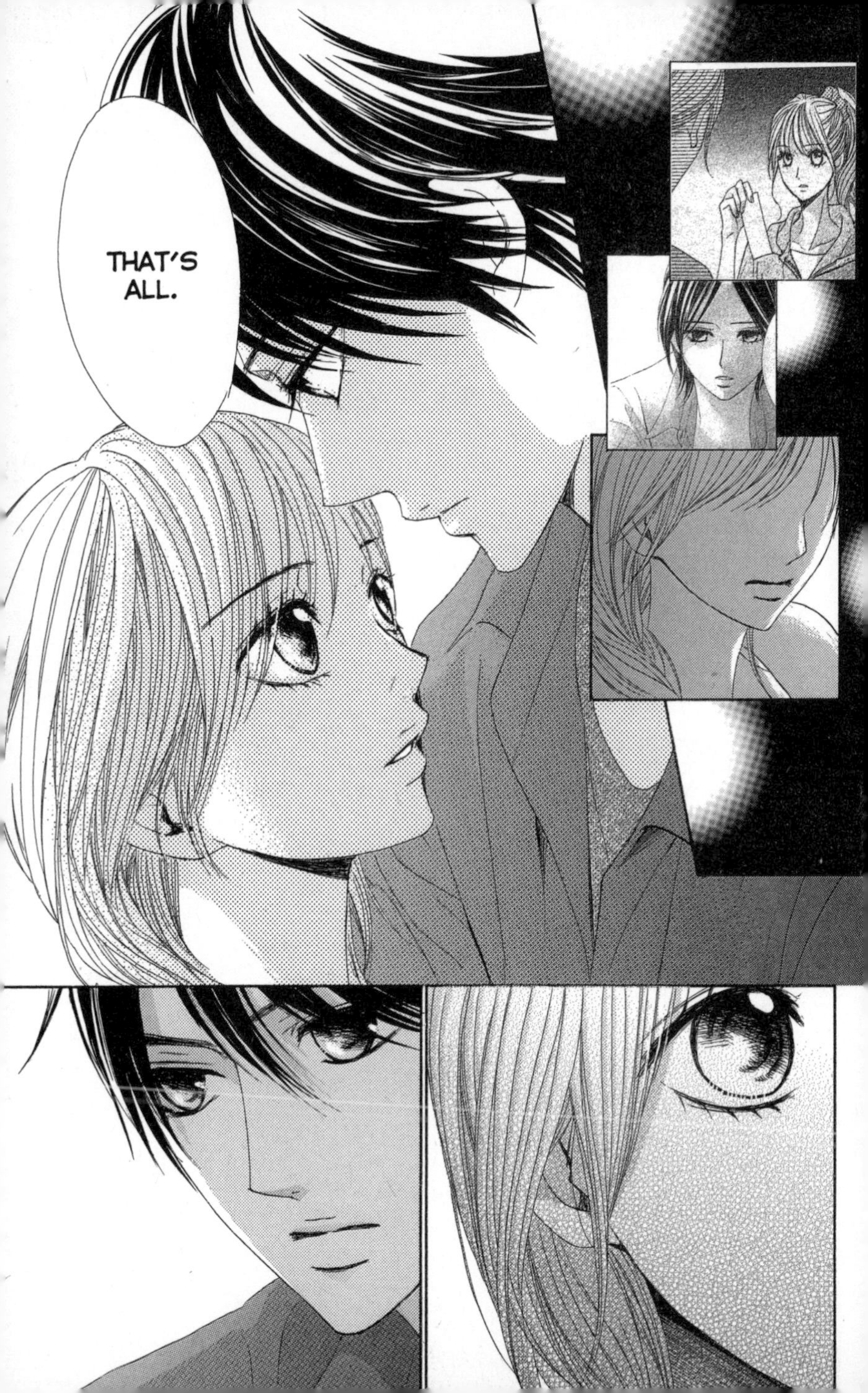
THAT'S ALL.

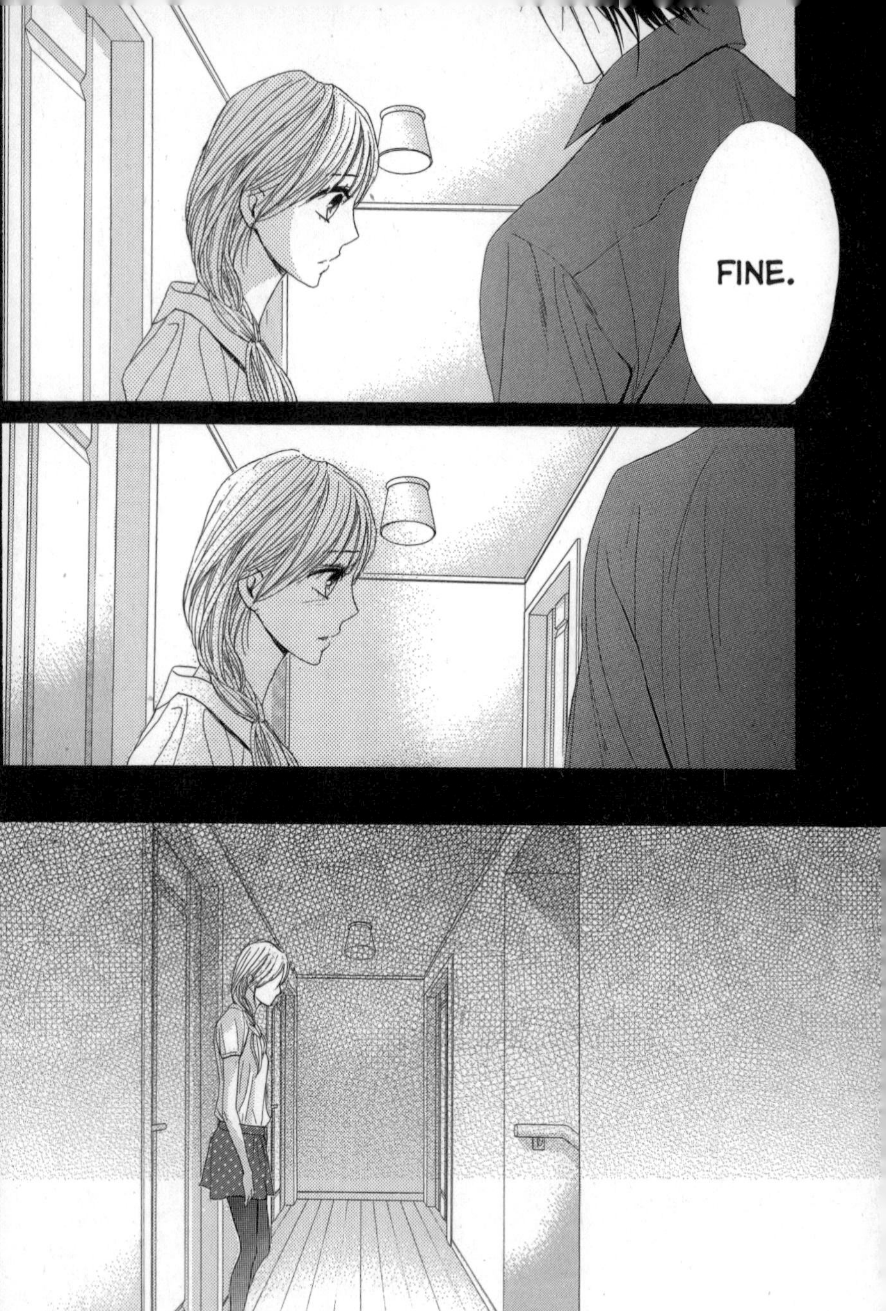
FINE.

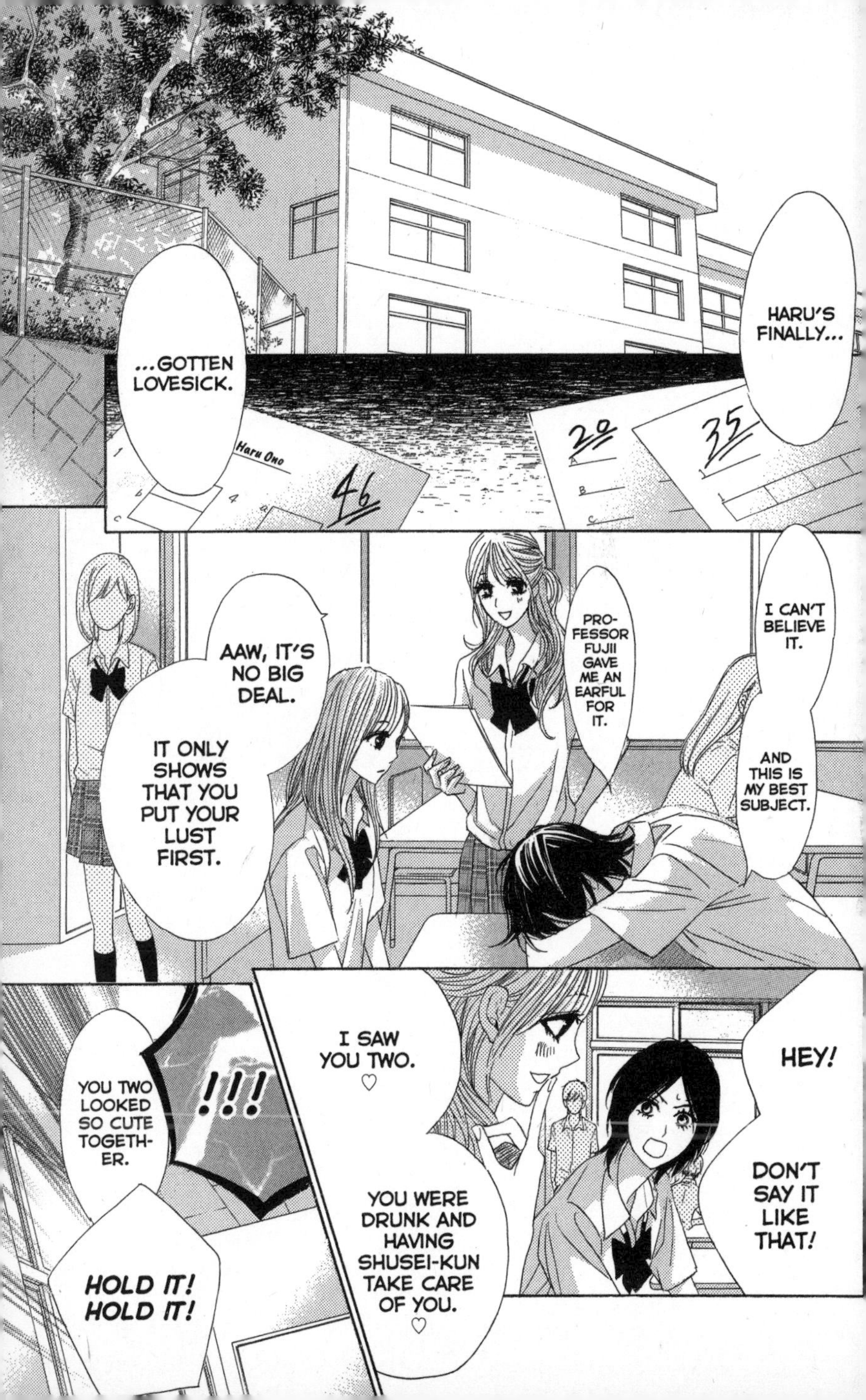
HARU'S FINALLY...
...GOTTEN LOVESICK.
35
20
Haru Ono
46
I CAN'T BELIEVE IT.
AND THIS IS MY BEST SUBJECT.
PRO-FESSOR FUJII GAVE ME AN EARFUL FOR IT.
AAW, IT'S NO BIG DEAL.
IT ONLY SHOWS THAT YOU PUT YOUR LUST FIRST.
I SAW YOU TWO. ♡
YOU WERE DRUNK AND HAVING SHUSEI-KUN TAKE CARE OF YOU. ♡
HEY!
DON'T SAY IT LIKE THAT!
YOU TWO LOOKED SO CUTE TOGETH-ER.
!!!
HOLD IT! HOLD IT!

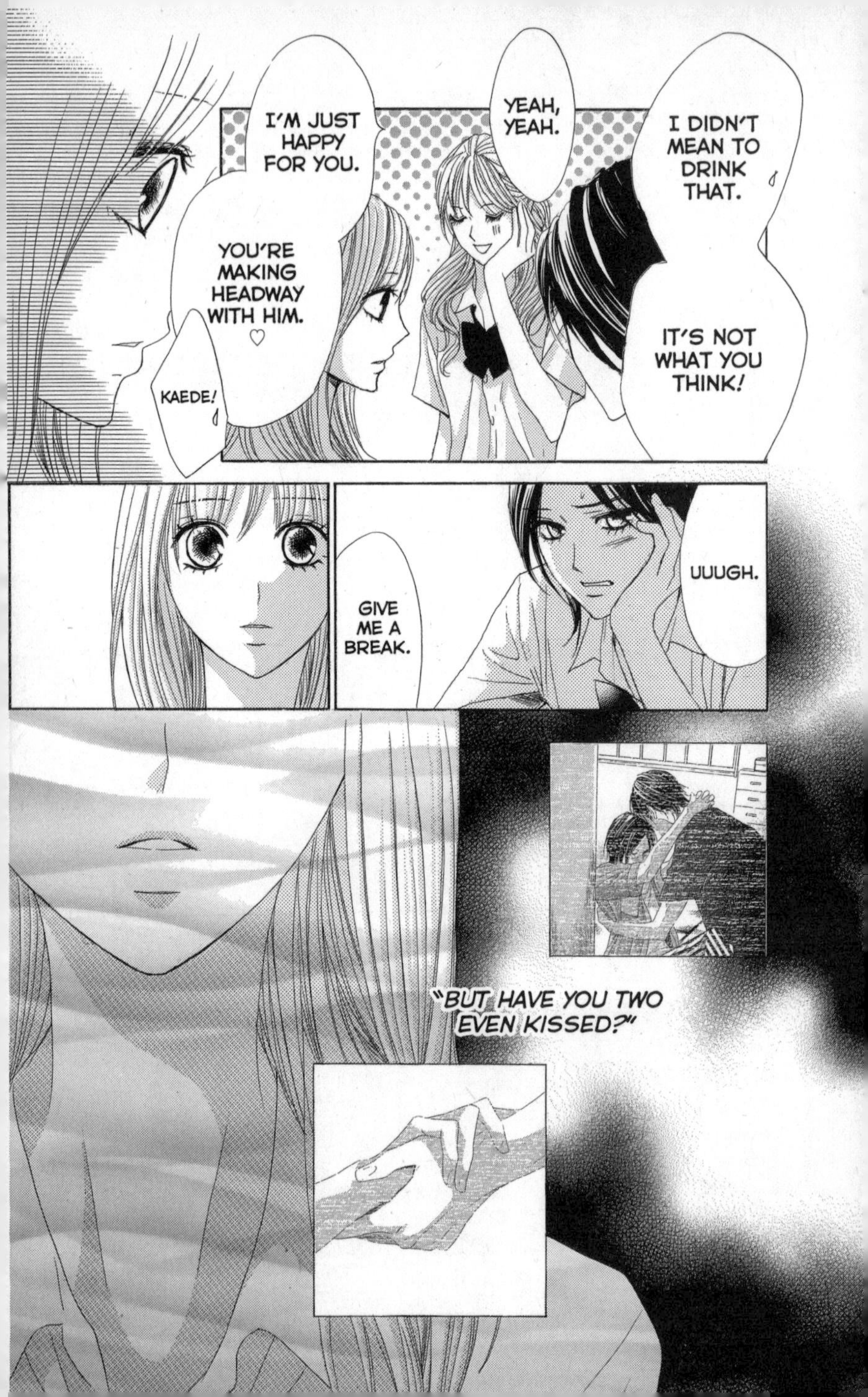
I DIDN'T MEAN TO DRINK THAT.
IT'S NOT WHAT YOU THINK!
YEAH, YEAH.
I'M JUST HAPPY FOR YOU.
YOU'RE MAKING HEADWAY WITH HIM. ♡
KAEDE!
UUUGH.
GIVE ME A BREAK.
"BUT HAVE YOU TWO EVEN KISSED?"

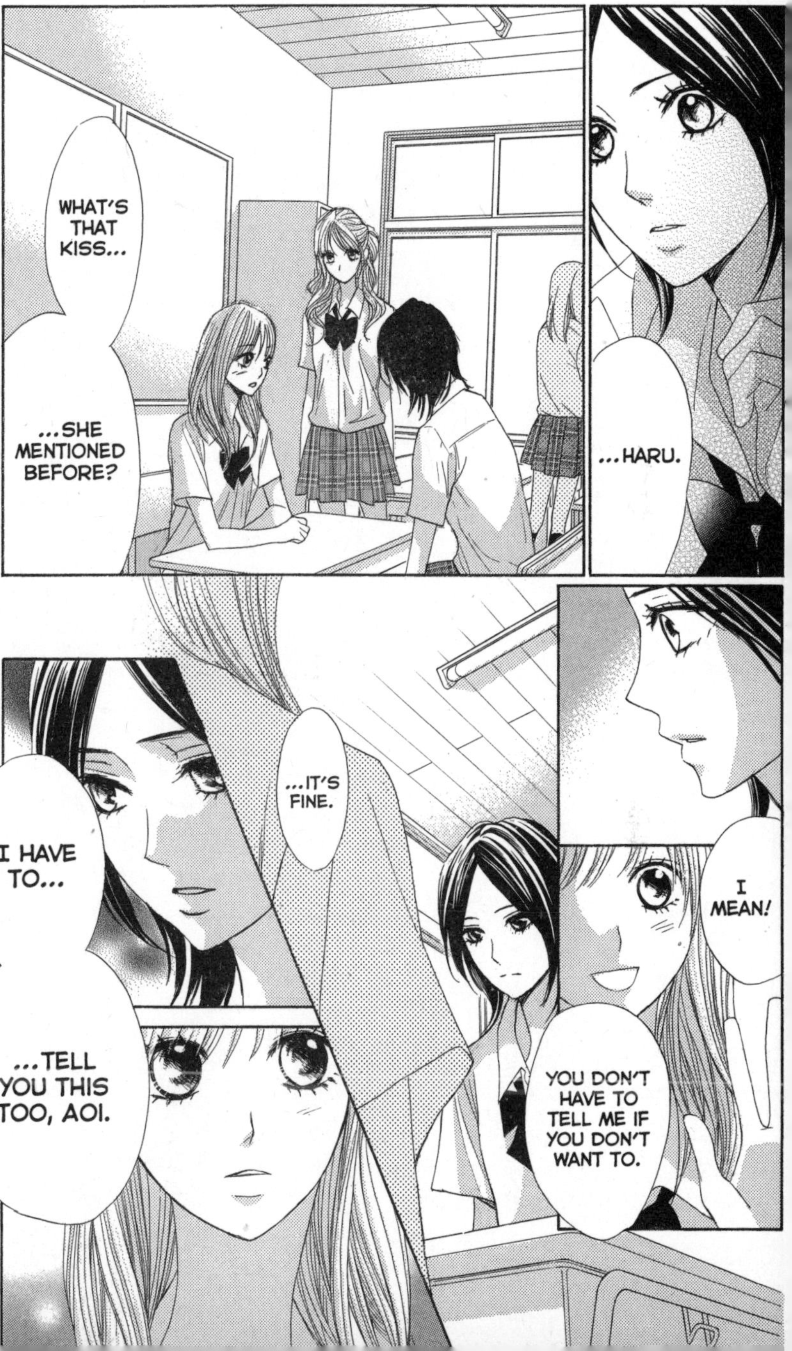
...HARU.
WHAT'S THAT KISS...
...SHE MENTIONED BEFORE?
I MEAN!
YOU DON'T HAVE TO TELL ME IF YOU DON'T WANT TO.
...IT'S FINE.
I HAVE TO...
...TELL YOU THIS TOO, AOI.

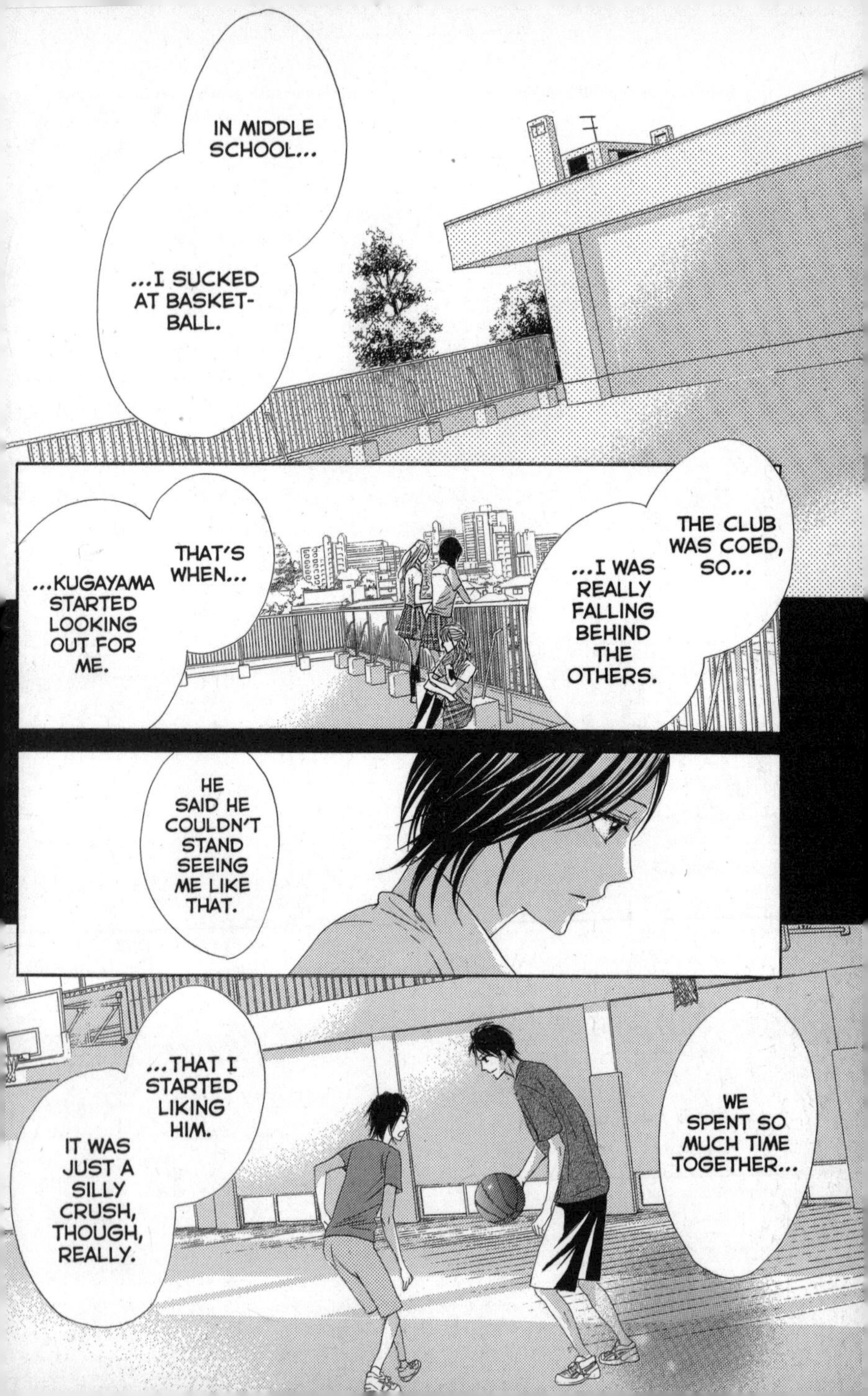

IN MIDDLE SCHOOL...
...I SUCKED AT BASKET-BALL.
THE CLUB WAS COED, SO...
...I WAS REALLY FALLING BEHIND THE OTHERS.
THAT'S WHEN...
...KUGAYAMA STARTED LOOKING OUT FOR ME.
HE SAID HE COULDN'T STAND SEEING ME LIKE THAT.
WE SPENT SO MUCH TIME TOGETHER...
...THAT I STARTED LIKING HIM.
IT WAS JUST A SILLY CRUSH, THOUGH, REALLY.

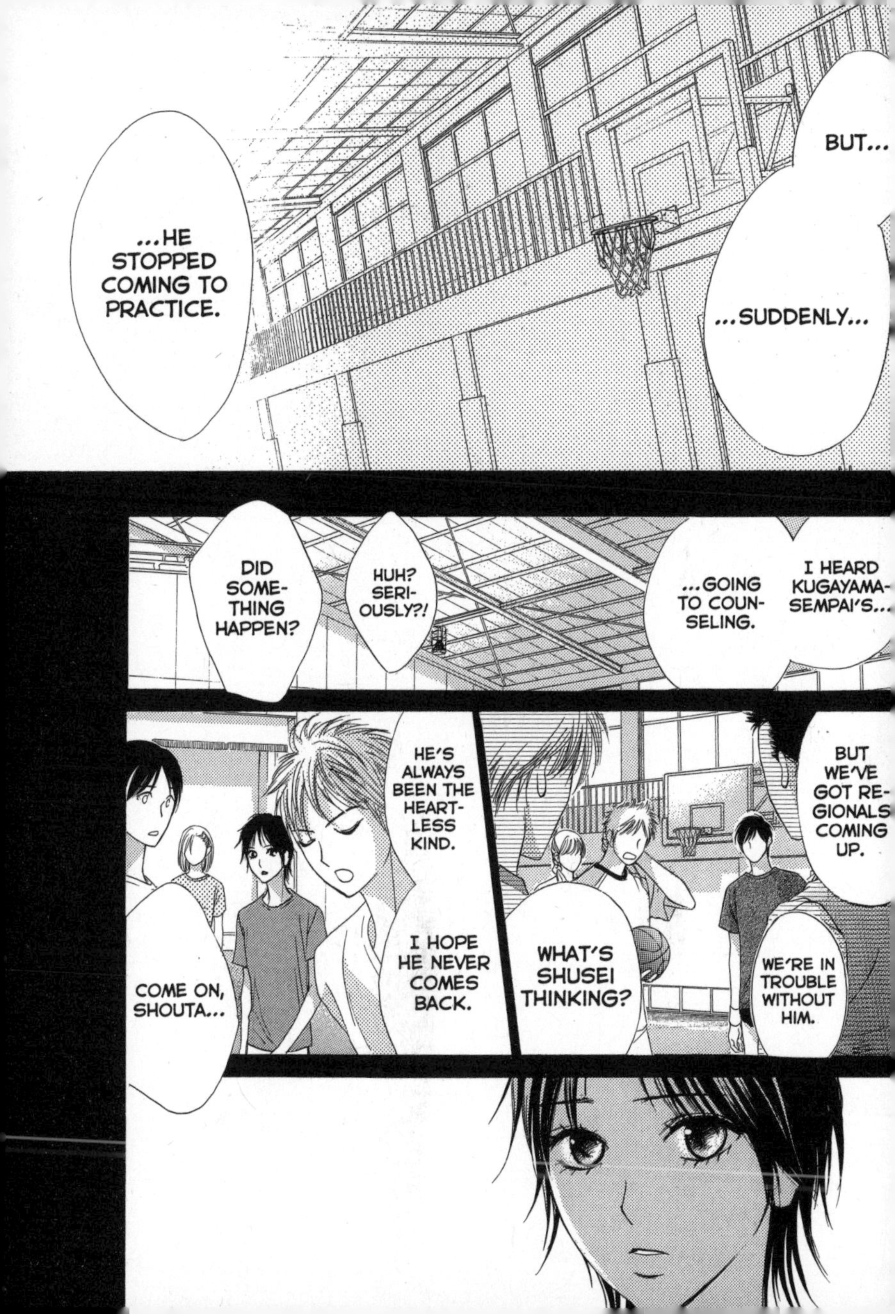
BUT...
...SUDDENLY...
...HE STOPPED COMING TO PRACTICE.
I HEARD KUGAYAMA-SEMPAI'S...
...GOING TO COUNSELING.
HUH? SERIOUSLY?!
DID SOMETHING HAPPEN?
BUT WE'VE GOT REGIONALS COMING UP.
WE'RE IN TROUBLE WITHOUT HIM.
WHAT'S SHUSEI THINKING?
HE'S ALWAYS BEEN THE HEARTLESS KIND.
I HOPE HE NEVER COMES BACK.
COME ON, SHOUTA...

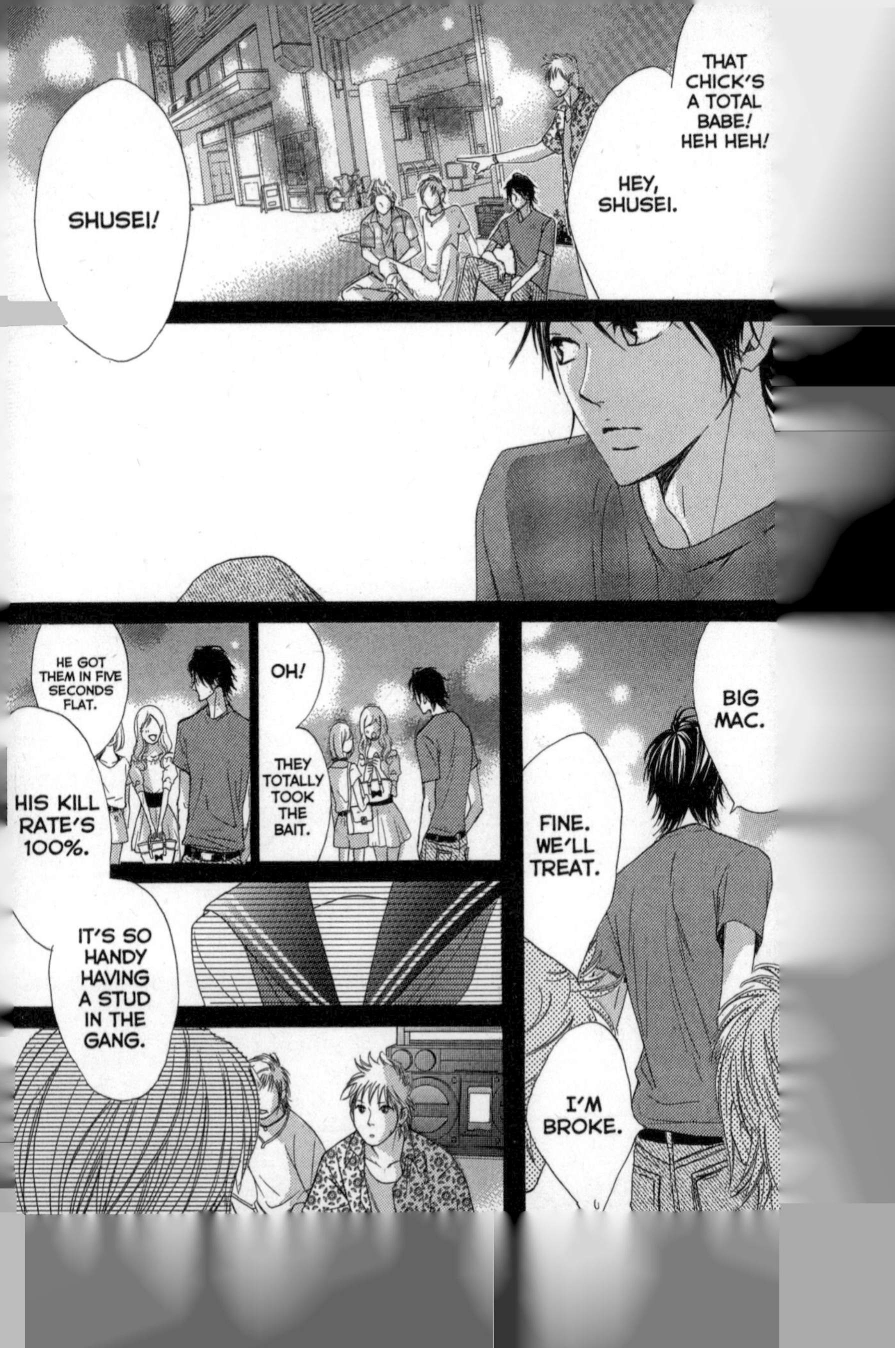
THAT CHICK'S A TOTAL BABE! HEH HEH!
HEY, SHUSEI.
SHUSEI!
BIG MAC.
FINE. WE'LL TREAT.
I'M BROKE.
OH!
THEY TOTALLY TOOK THE BAIT.
HE GOT THEM IN FIVE SECONDS FLAT.
HIS KILL RATE'S 100%.
IT'S SO HANDY HAVING A STUD IN THE GANG.

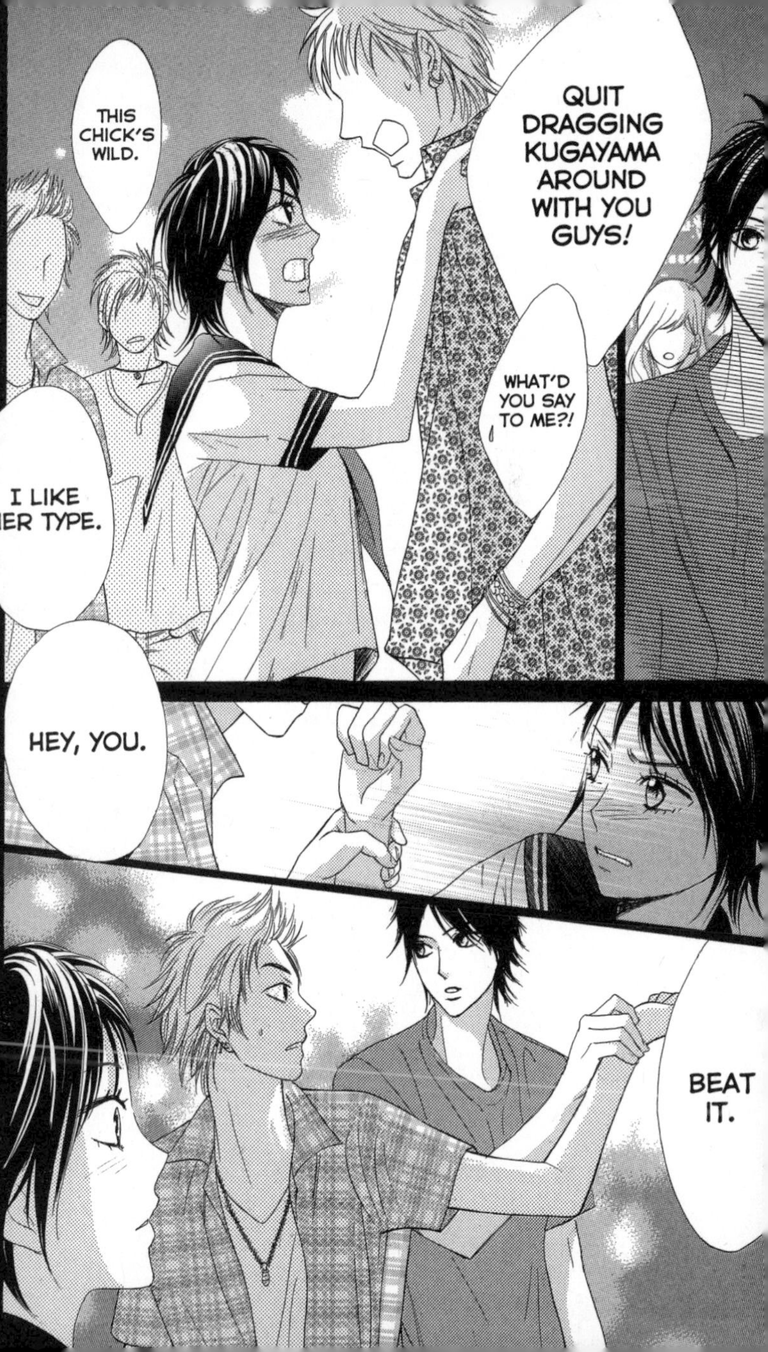
QUIT DRAGGING KUGAYAMA AROUND WITH YOU GUYS!
THIS CHICK'S WILD.
WHAT'D YOU SAY TO ME?!
I LIKE HER TYPE.
HEY, YOU.
BEAT IT.

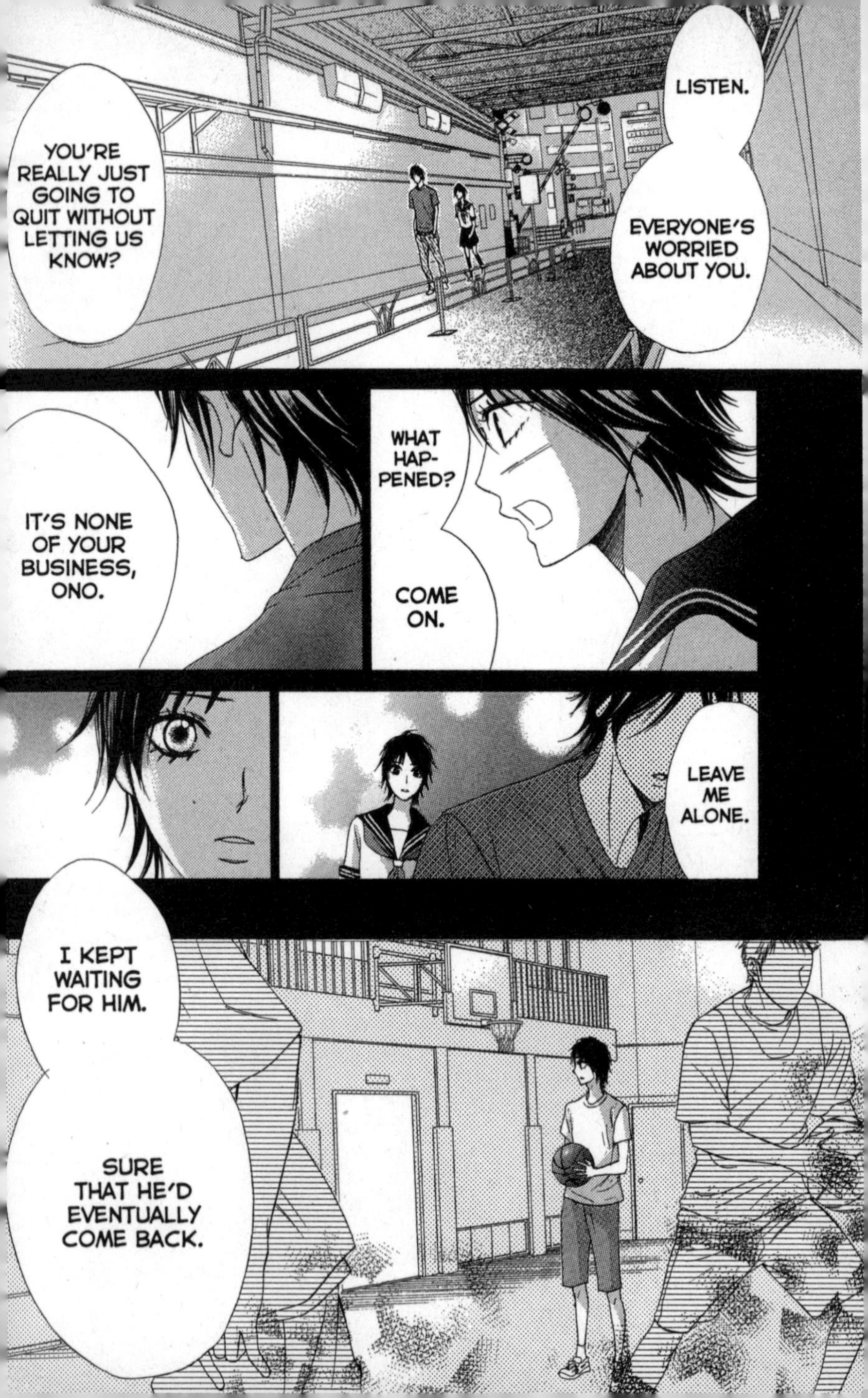
LISTEN.
EVERYONE'S WORRIED ABOUT YOU.
YOU'RE REALLY JUST GOING TO QUIT WITHOUT LETTING US KNOW?
WHAT HAP-PENED?
COME ON.
IT'S NONE OF YOUR BUSINESS, ONO.
LEAVE ME ALONE.
I KEPT WAITING FOR HIM.
SURE THAT HE'D EVENTUALLY COME BACK.

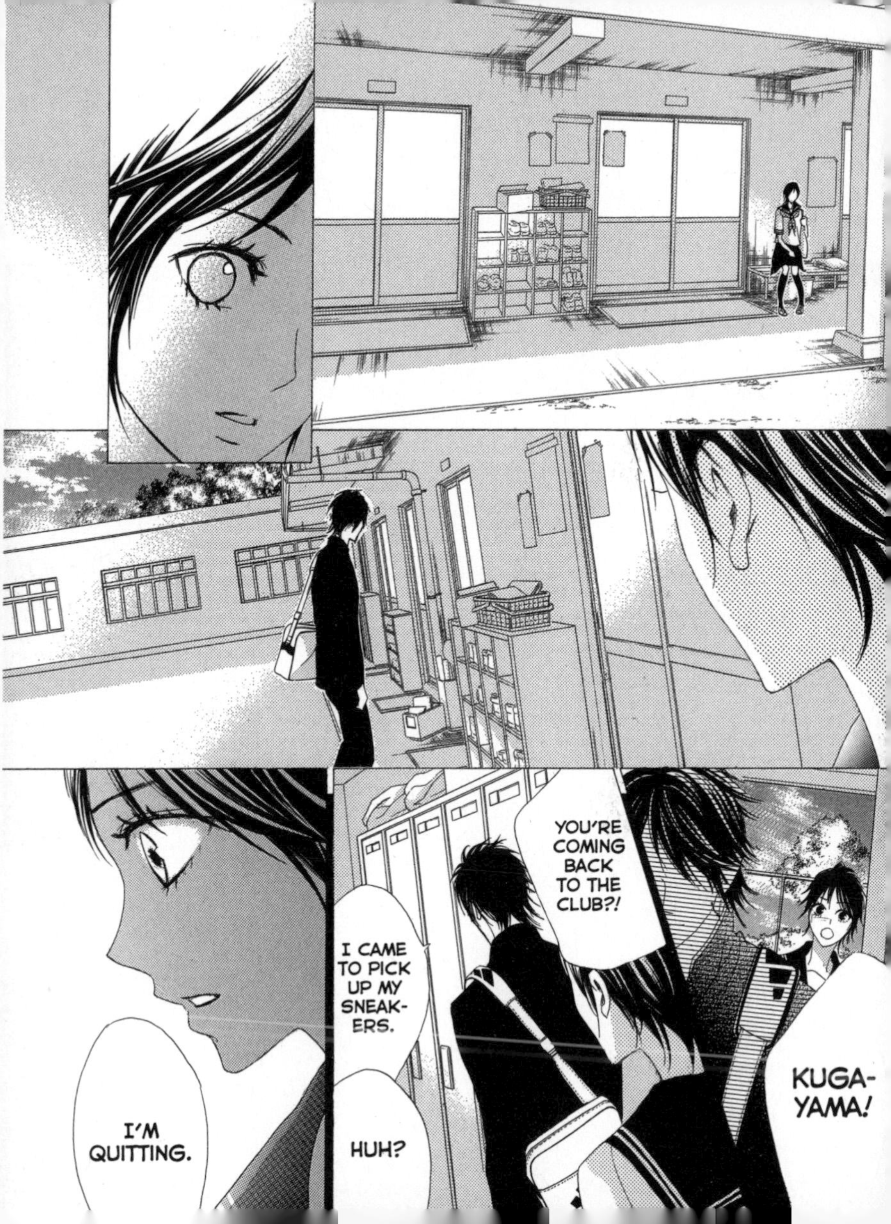
KUGA-YAMA!
YOU'RE COMING BACK TO THE CLUB?!
I CAME TO PICK UP MY SNEAKERS.
HUH?
I'M QUITTING.

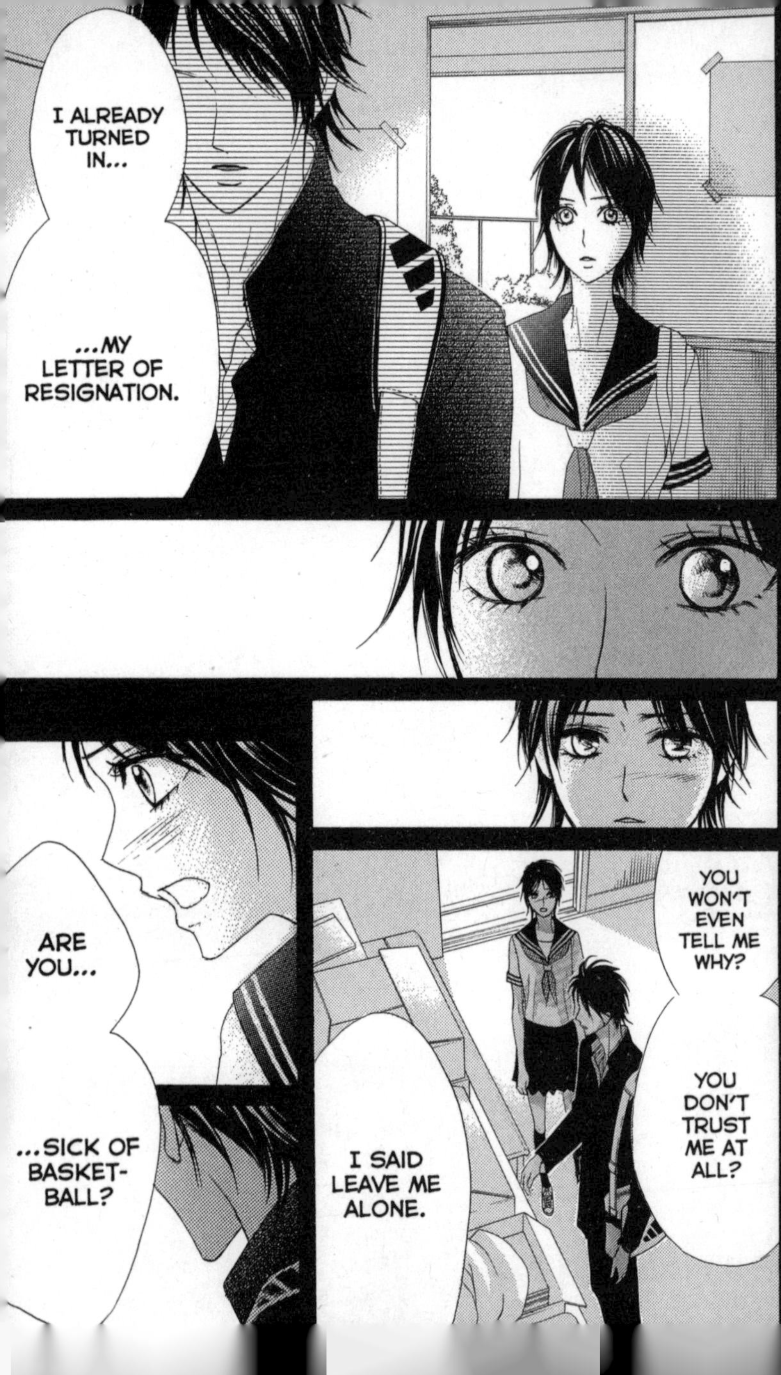
I ALREADY TURNED IN...
...MY LETTER OF RESIGNATION.
YOU WON'T EVEN TELL ME WHY?
YOU DON'T TRUST ME AT ALL?
I SAID LEAVE ME ALONE.
ARE YOU...
...SICK OF BASKET-BALL?

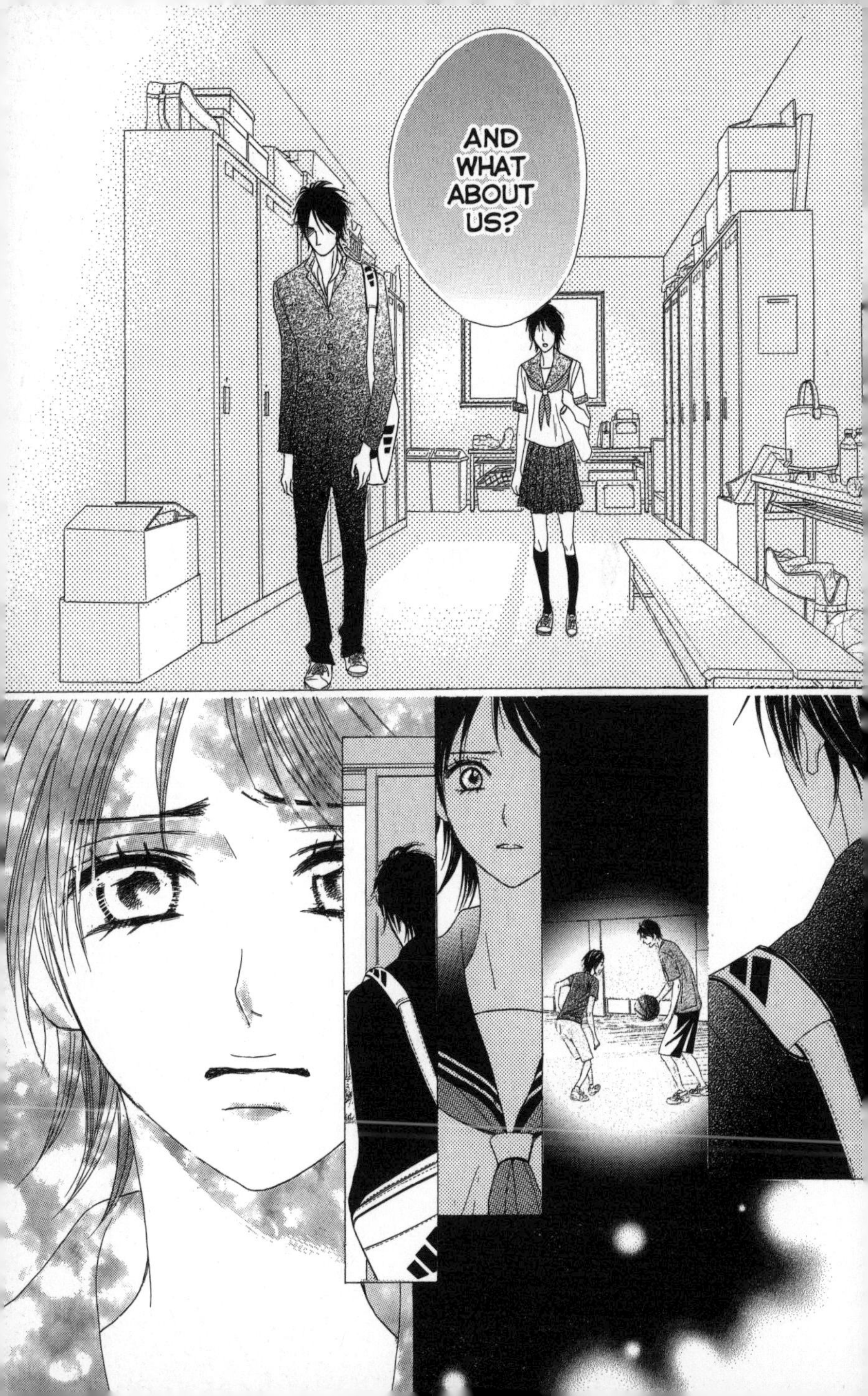
AND WHAT ABOUT US?

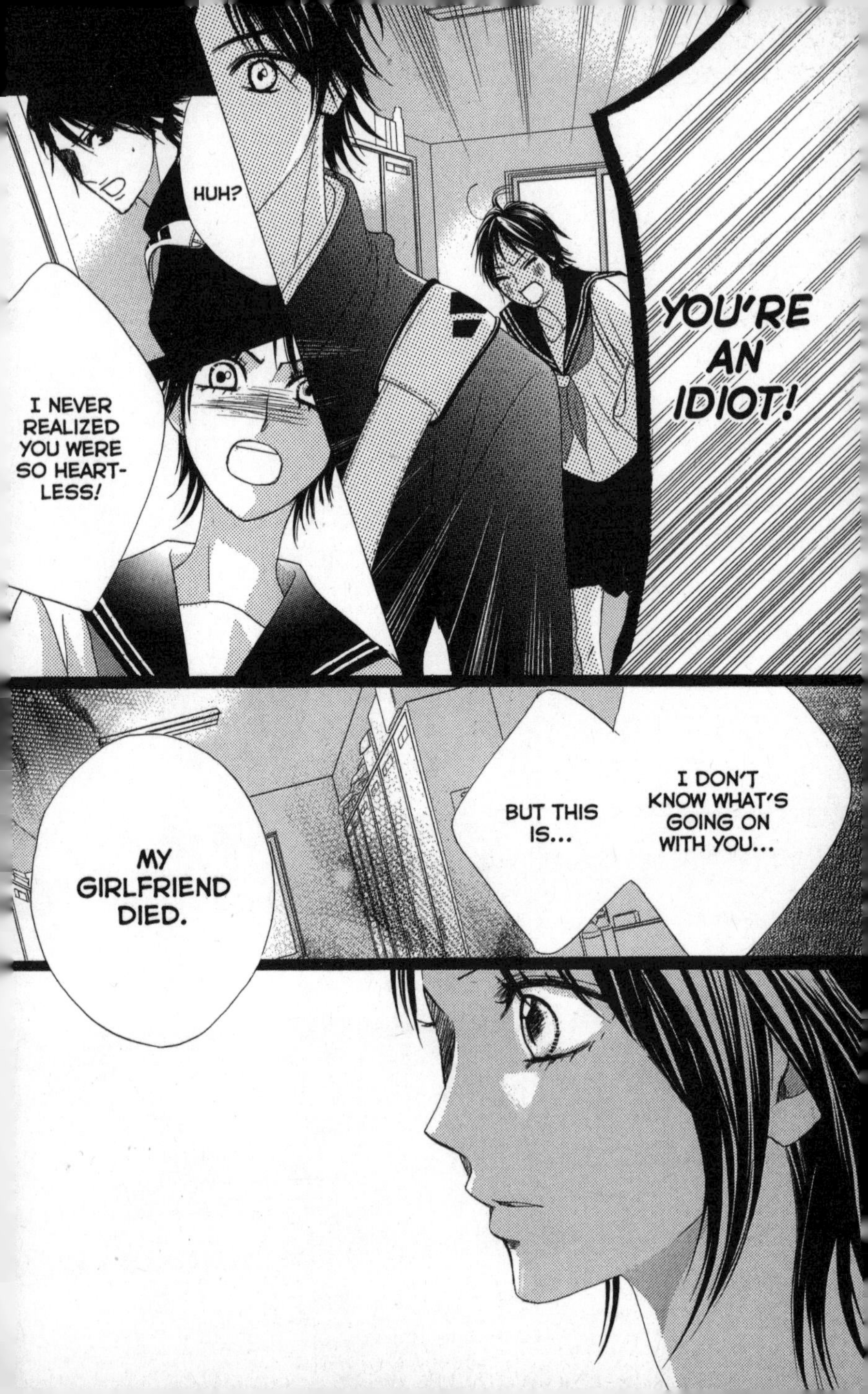
YOU'RE AN IDIOT!
HUH?
I NEVER REALIZED YOU WERE SO HEART-LESS!
I DON'T KNOW WHAT'S GOING ON WITH YOU...
BUT THIS IS...
MY GIRLFRIEND DIED.

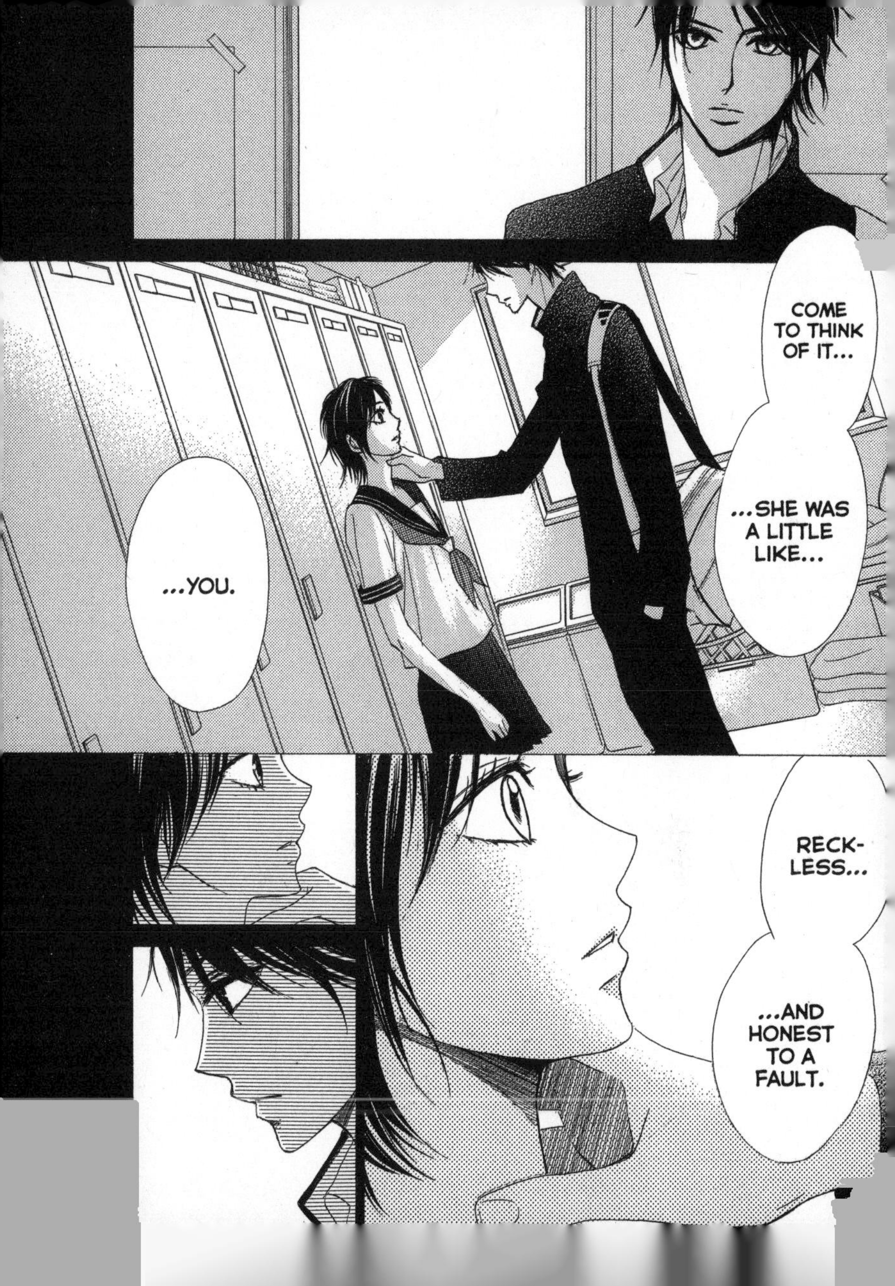
COME TO THINK OF IT...
...SHE WAS A LITTLE LIKE...
...YOU.
RECK-LESS...
...AND HONEST TO A FAULT.

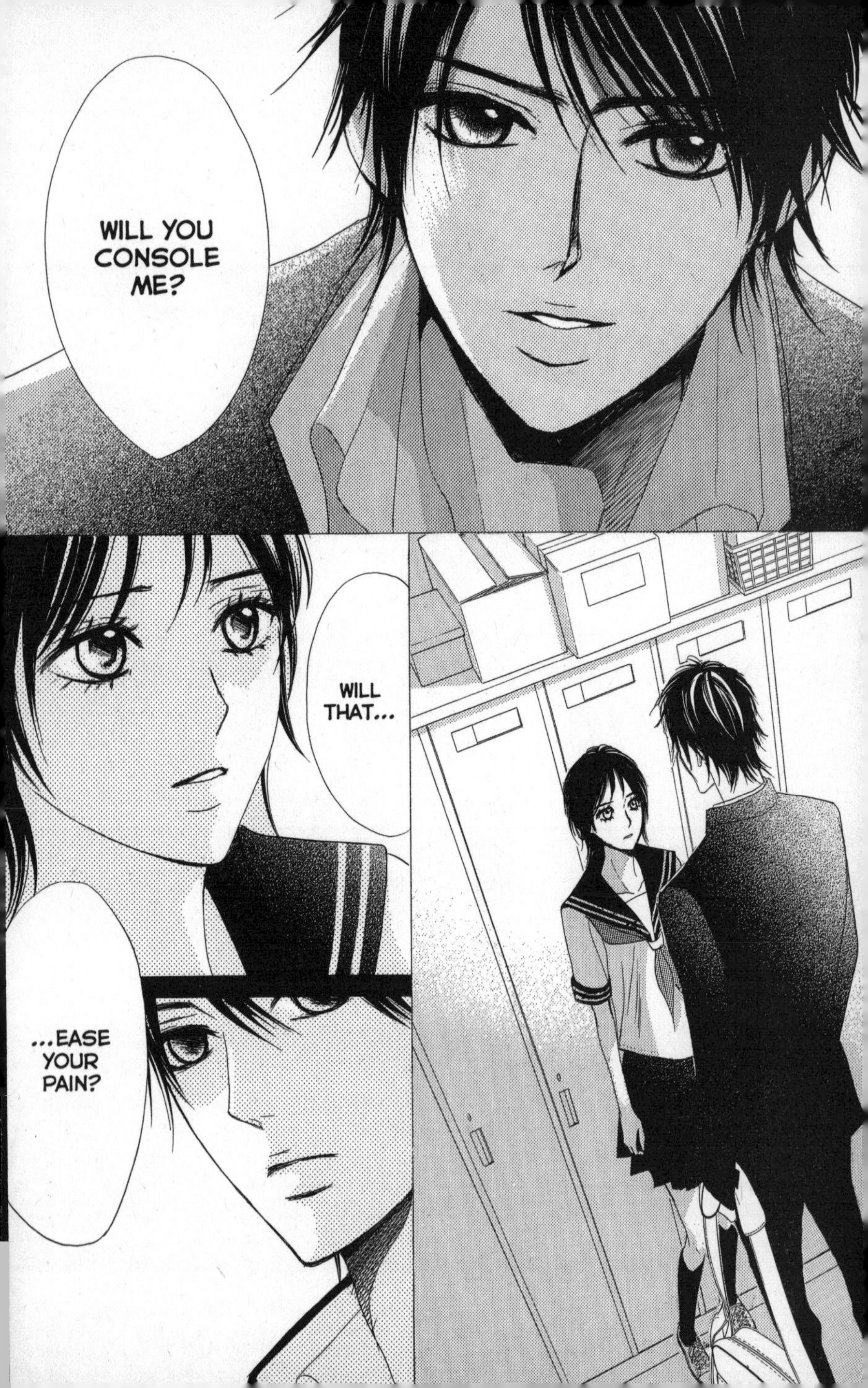
WILL YOU CONSOLE ME?
WILL THAT...
...EASE YOUR PAIN?

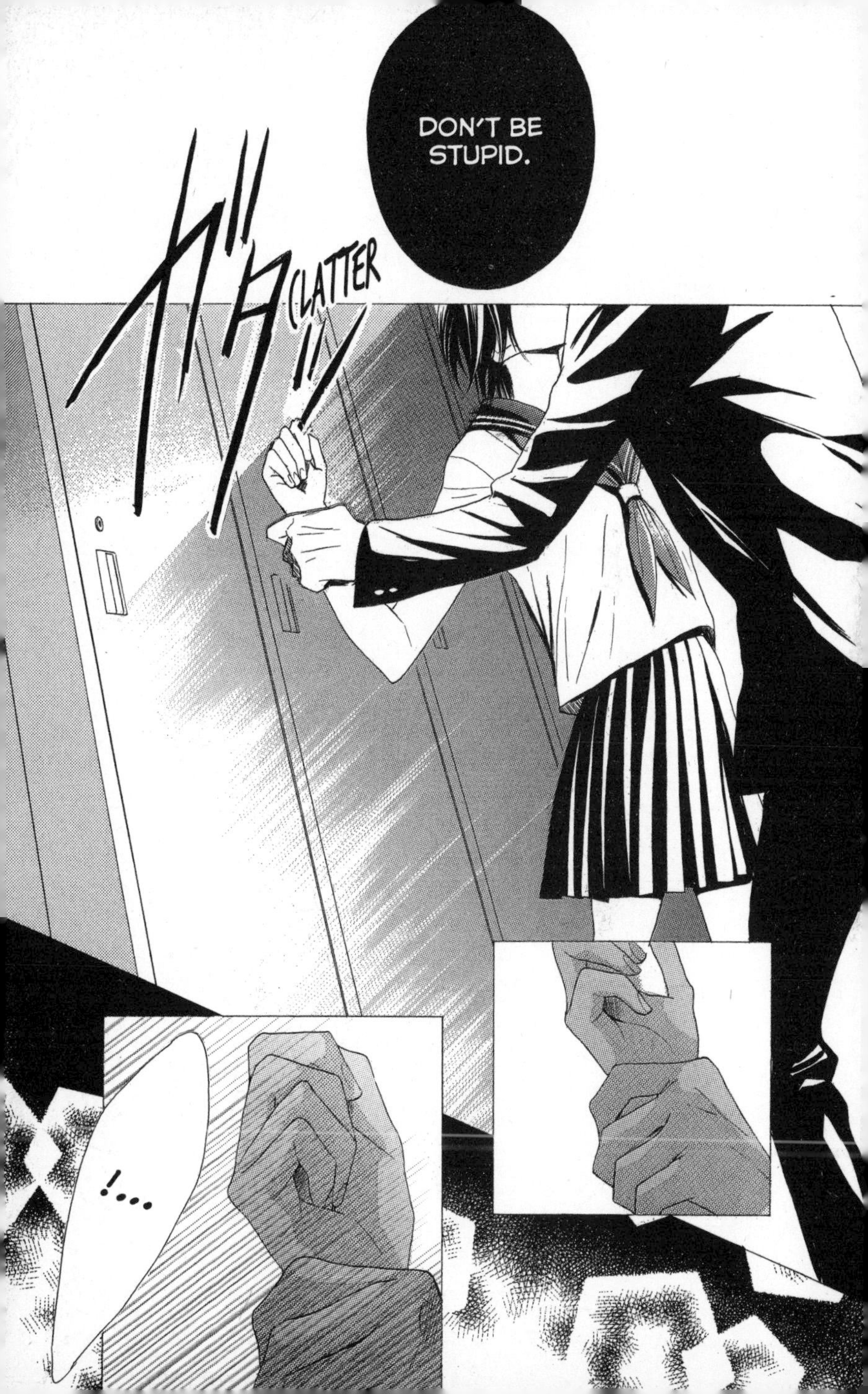
DON'T BE STUPID.
CLATTER
!...

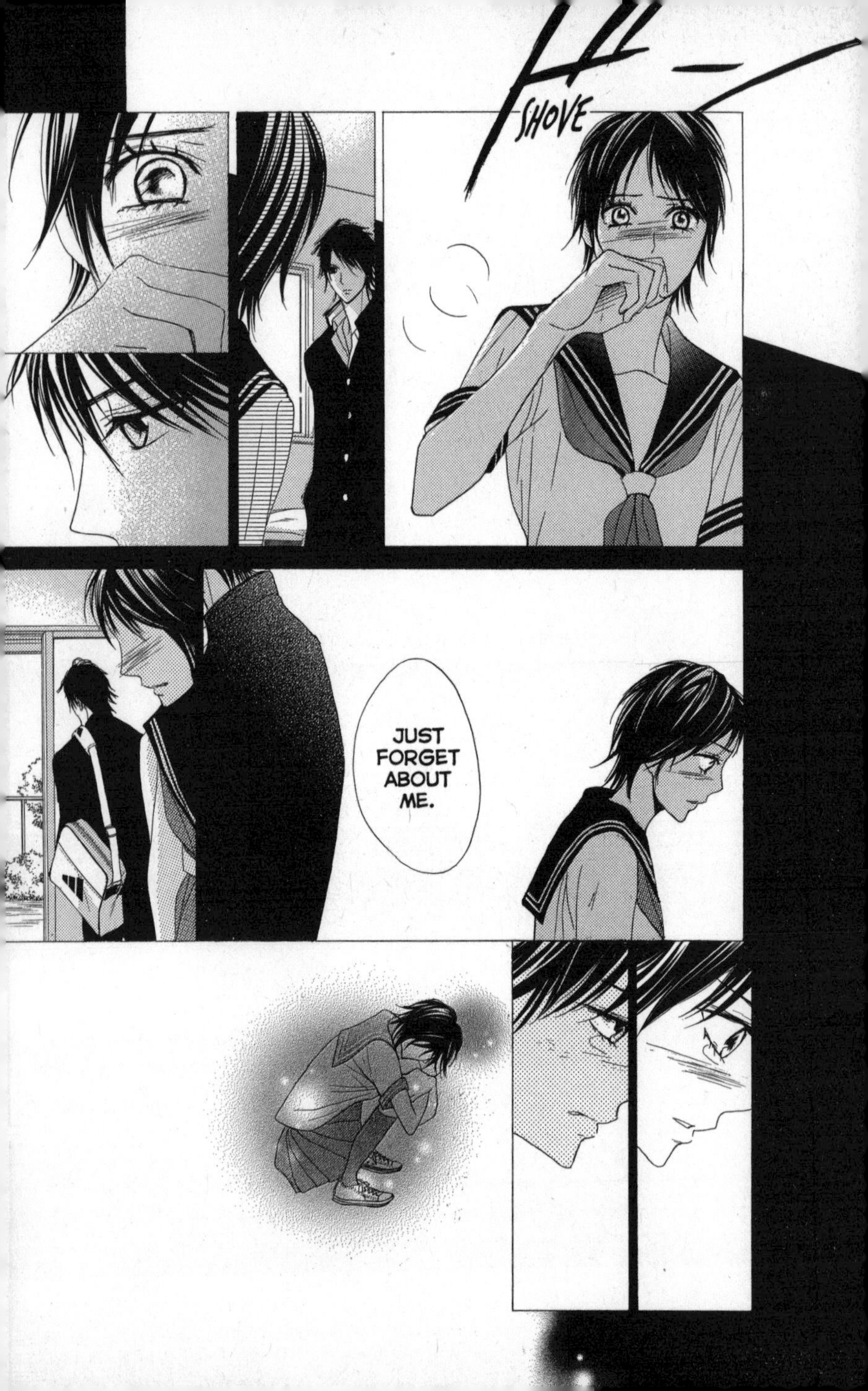
SHOVE
JUST FORGET ABOUT ME.

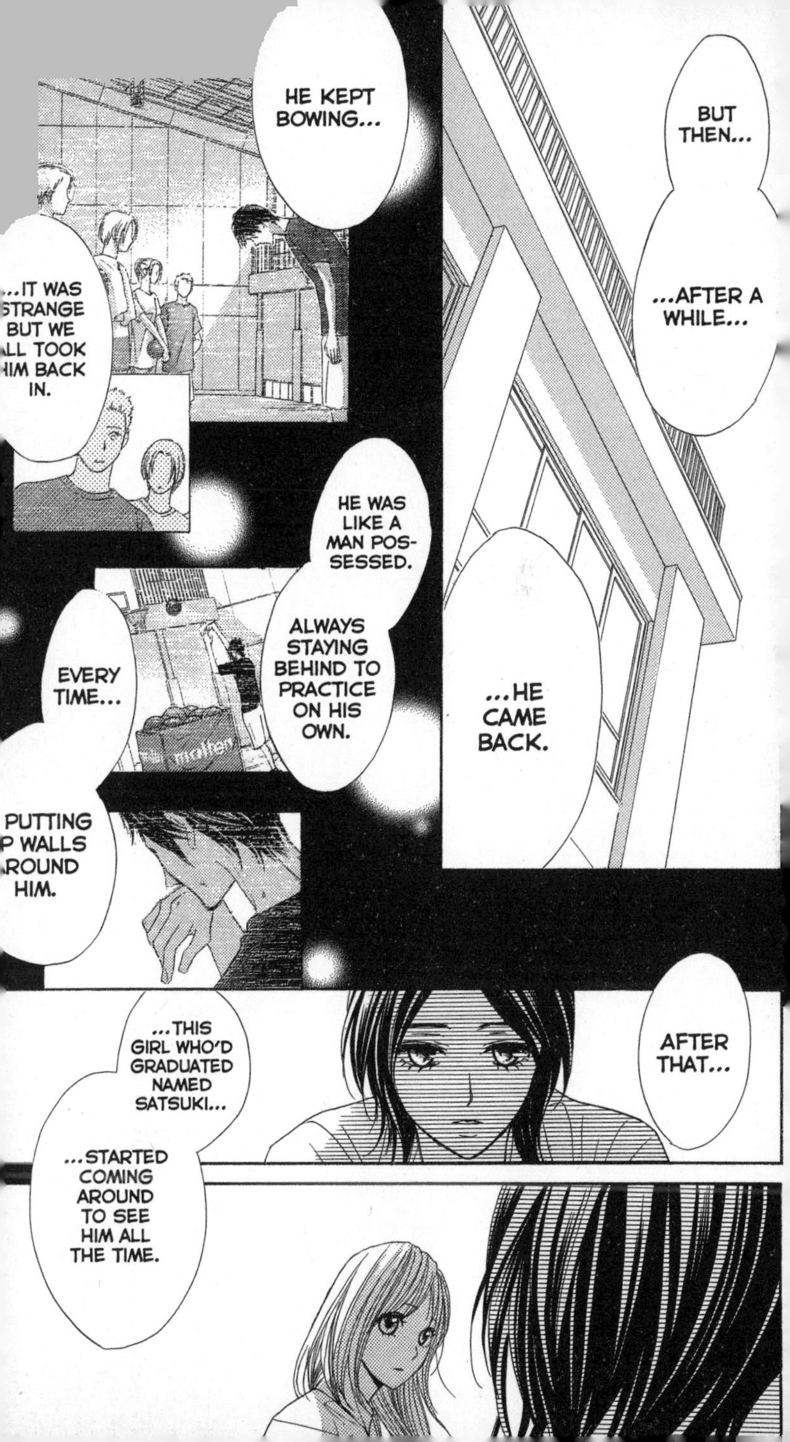
BUT THEN...
...AFTER A WHILE...
...HE CAME BACK.
HE KEPT BOWING...
...IT WAS STRANGE BUT WE LL TOOK IM BACK IN.
HE WAS LIKE A MAN POS-SESSED.
ALWAYS STAYING BEHIND TO PRACTICE ON HIS OWN.
EVERY TIME...
PUTTING P WALLS ROUND HIM.
AFTER THAT...
...THIS GIRL WHO'D GRADUATED NAMED SATSUKI...
...STARTED COMING AROUND TO SEE HIM ALL THE TIME.

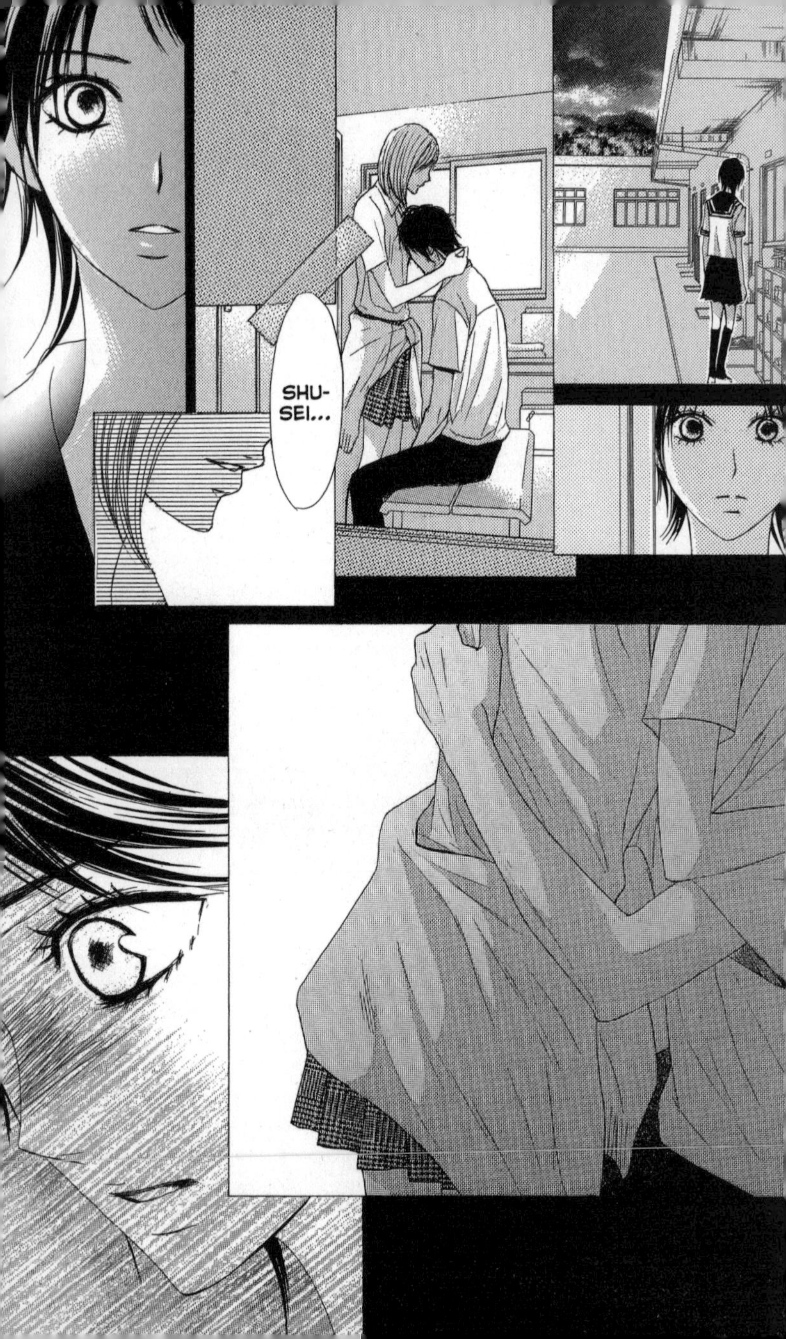
SHU-
SEI...

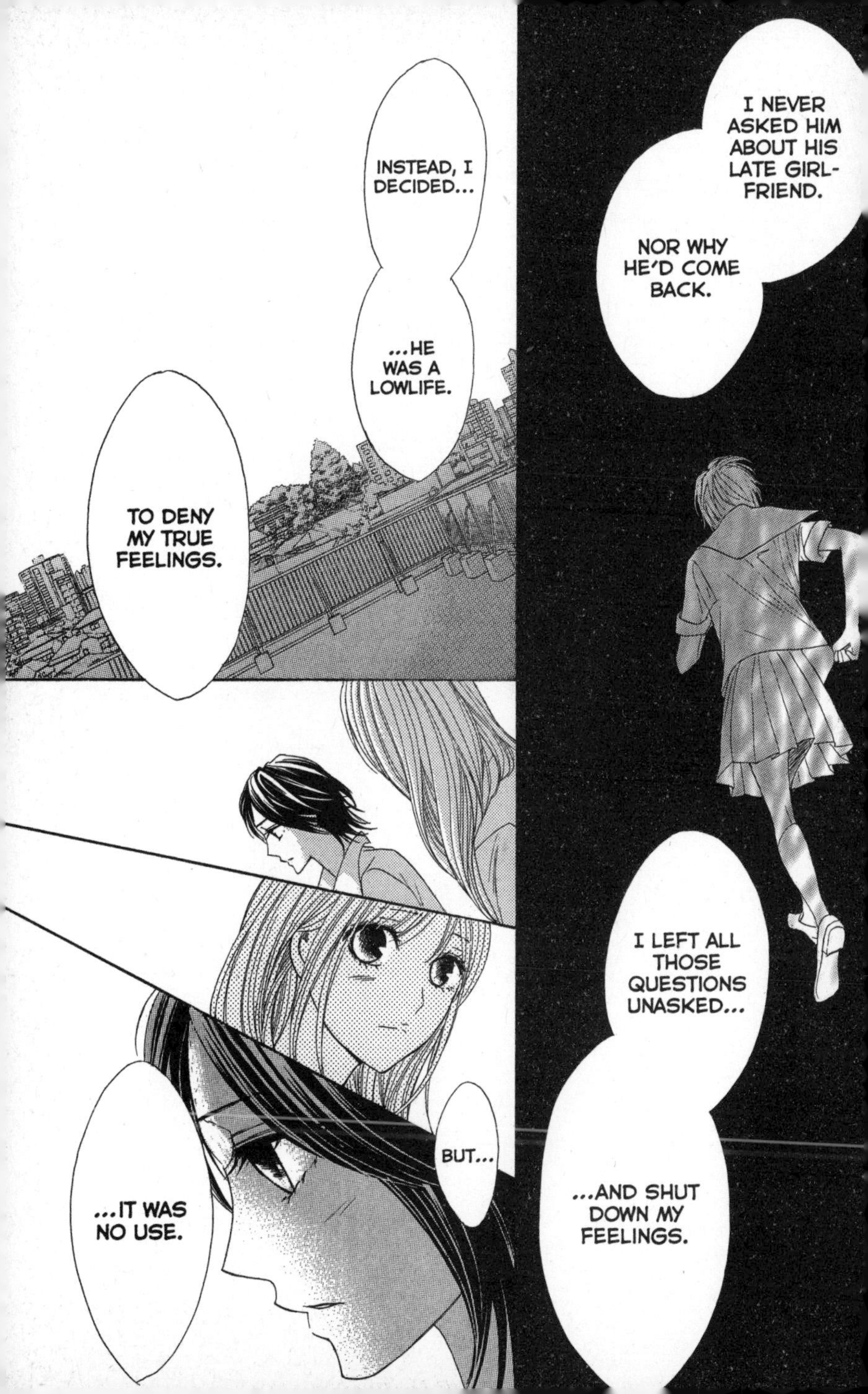
I NEVER ASKED HIM ABOUT HIS LATE GIRL-FRIEND.
NOR WHY HE'D COME BACK.
I LEFT ALL THOSE QUESTIONS UNASKED...
...AND SHUT DOWN MY FEELINGS.
INSTEAD, I DECIDED...
...HE WAS A LOWLIFE.
TO DENY MY TRUE FEELINGS.
BUT...
...IT WAS NO USE.

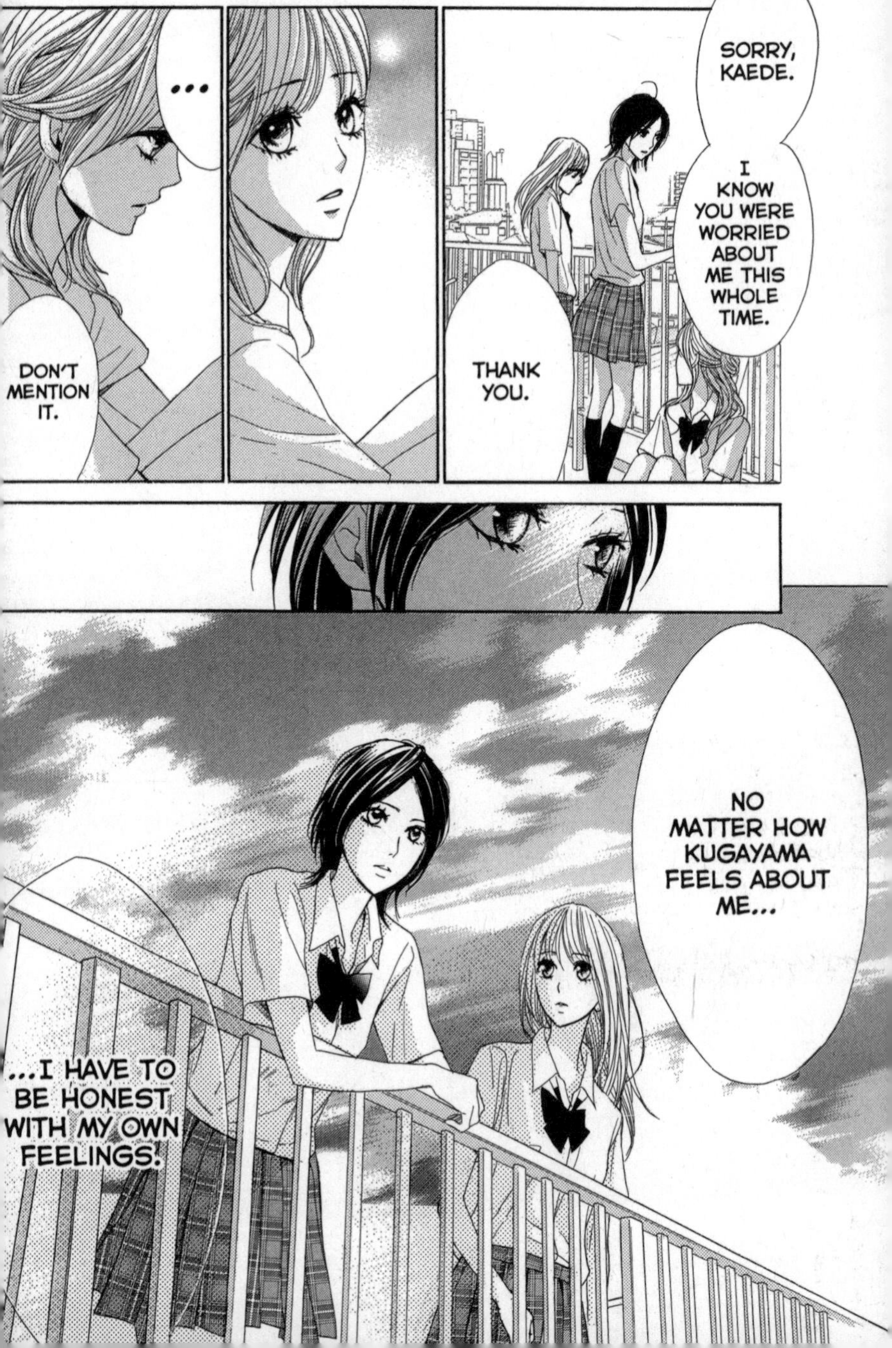
SORRY, KAEDE.
I KNOW YOU WERE WORRIED ABOUT ME THIS WHOLE TIME.
THANK YOU.
...
DON'T MENTION IT.
NO MATTER HOW KUGAYAMA FEELS ABOUT ME...
...I HAVE TO BE HONEST WITH MY OWN FEELINGS!

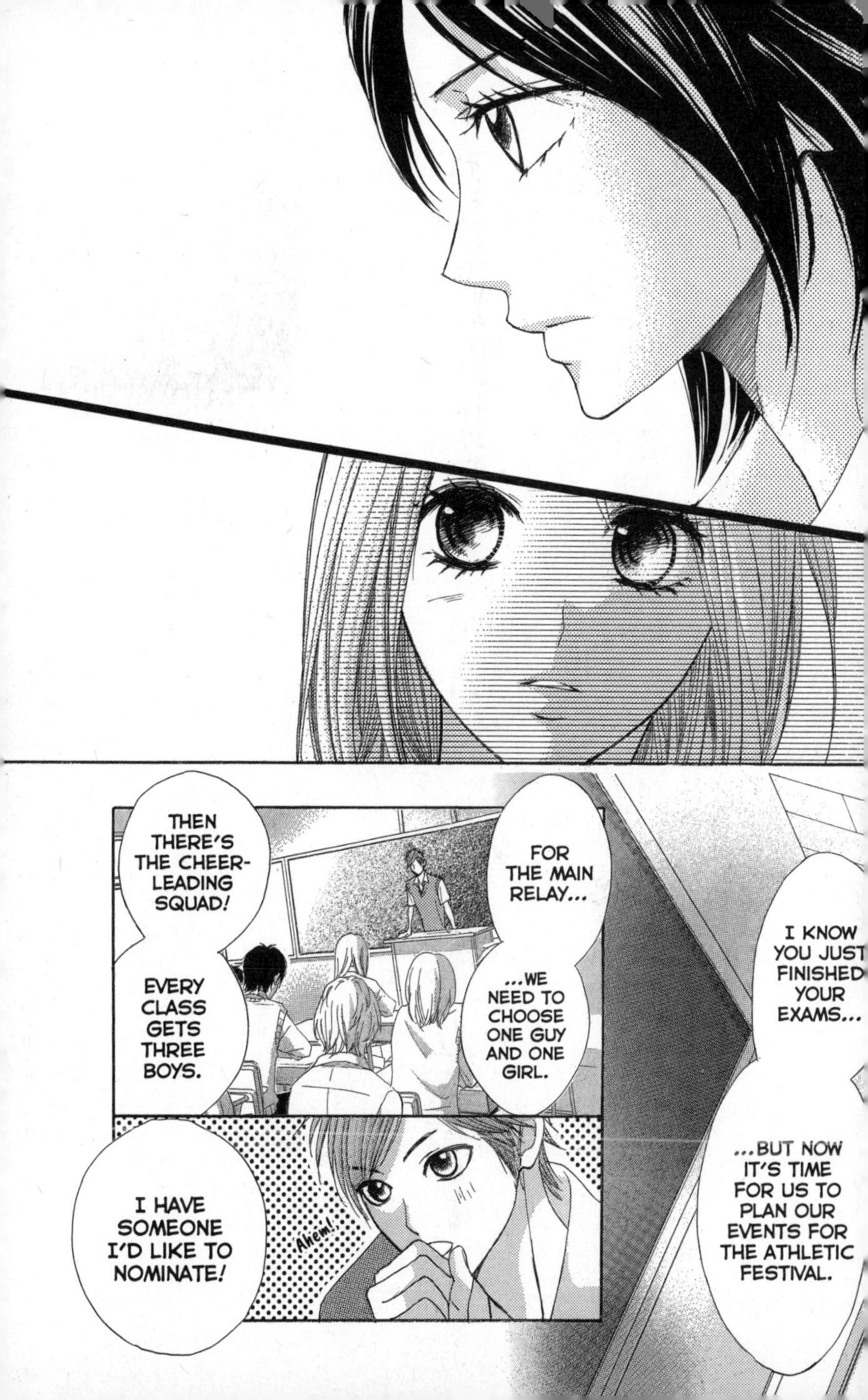
I KNOW YOU JUST FINISHED YOUR EXAMS...
...BUT NOW IT'S TIME FOR US TO PLAN OUR EVENTS FOR THE ATHLETIC FESTIVAL.
FOR THE MAIN RELAY...
...WE NEED TO CHOOSE ONE GUY AND ONE GIRL.
THEN THERE'S THE CHEER-LEADING SQUAD!
EVERY CLASS GETS THREE BOYS.
Ahem!
I HAVE SOMEONE I'D LIKE TO NOMINATE!

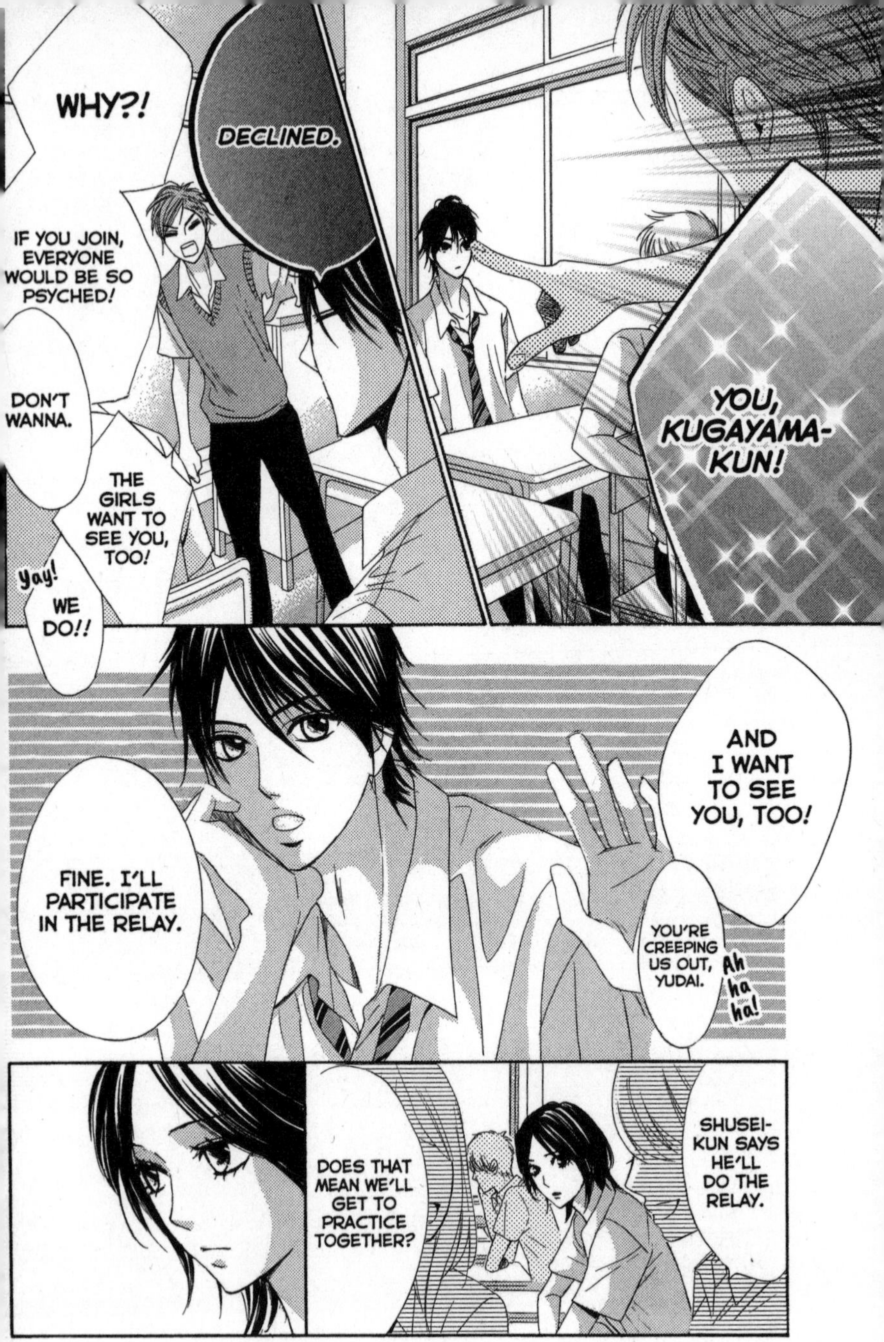
YOU, KUGAYAMA-KUN!
DECLINED.
WHY?!
IF YOU JOIN, EVERYONE WOULD BE SO PSYCHED!
DON'T WANNA.
THE GIRLS WANT TO SEE YOU, TOO!
Yay!
WE DO!!
AND I WANT TO SEE YOU, TOO!
Ah ha ha!
YOU'RE CREEPING US OUT, YUDAI.
FINE. I'LL PARTICIPATE IN THE RELAY.
SHUSEI-KUN SAYS HE'LL DO THE RELAY.
DOES THAT MEAN WE'LL GET TO PRACTICE TOGETHER?

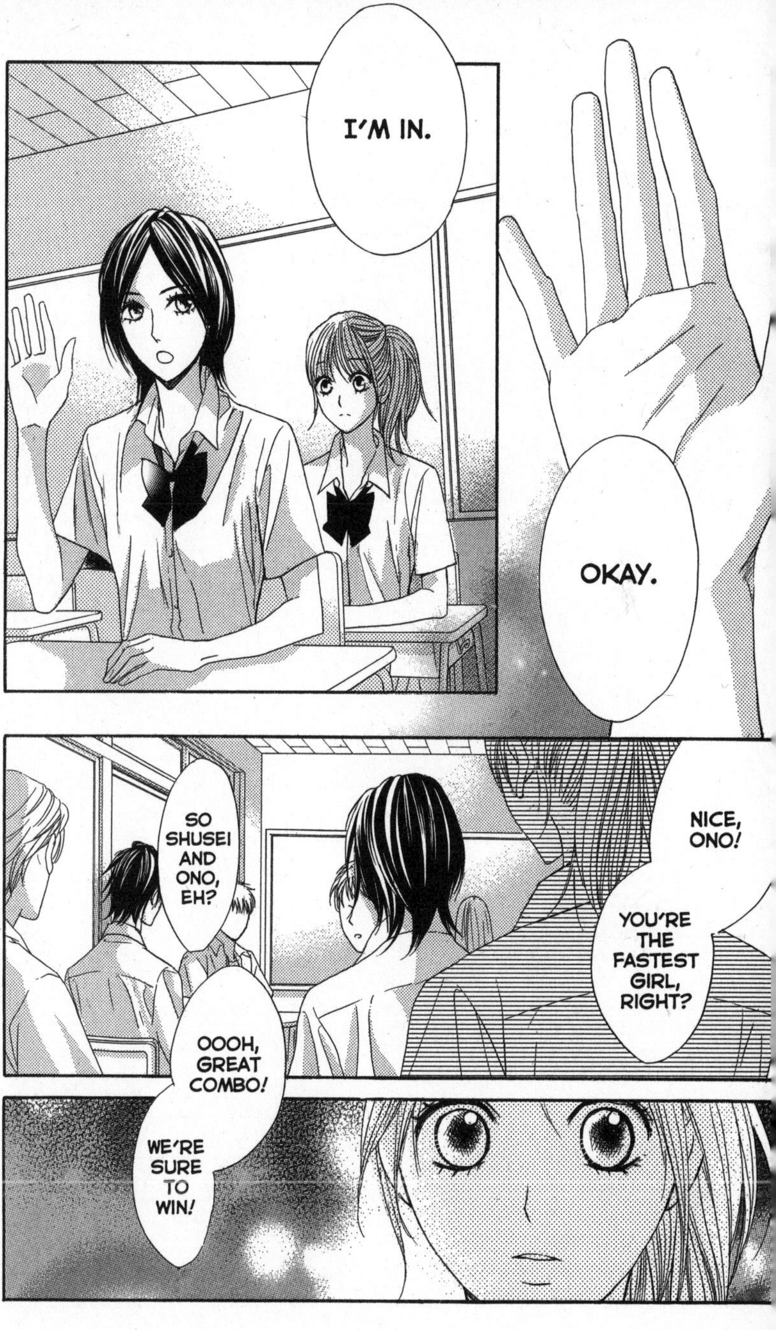
I'M IN.
OKAY.
NICE, ONO!
YOU'RE THE FASTEST GIRL, RIGHT?
SO SHUSEI AND ONO, EH?
OOOH, GREAT COMBO!
WE'RE SURE TO WIN!

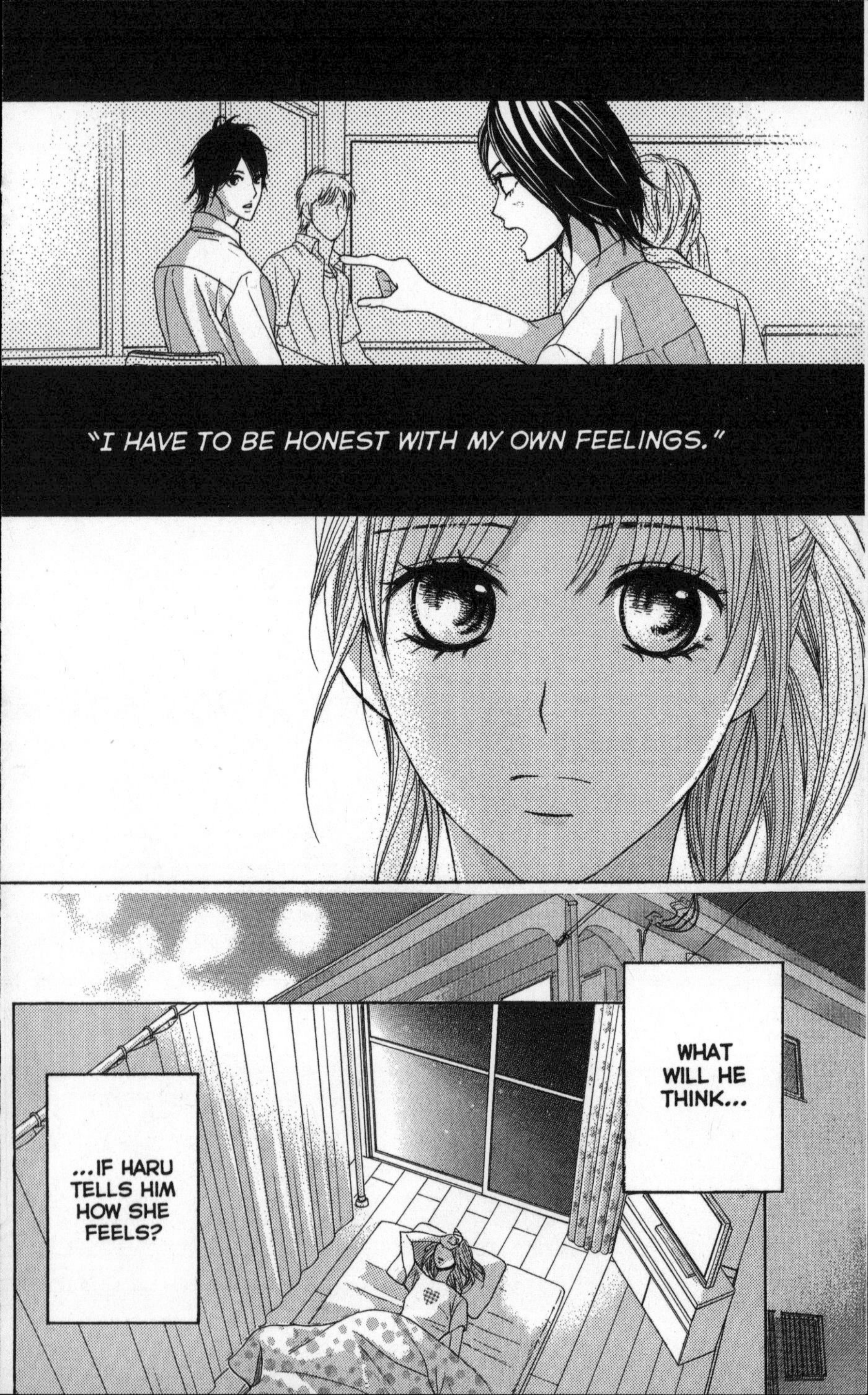
"I HAVE TO BE HONEST WITH MY OWN FEELINGS."
WHAT WILL HE THINK...
...IF HARU TELLS HIM HOW SHE FEELS?

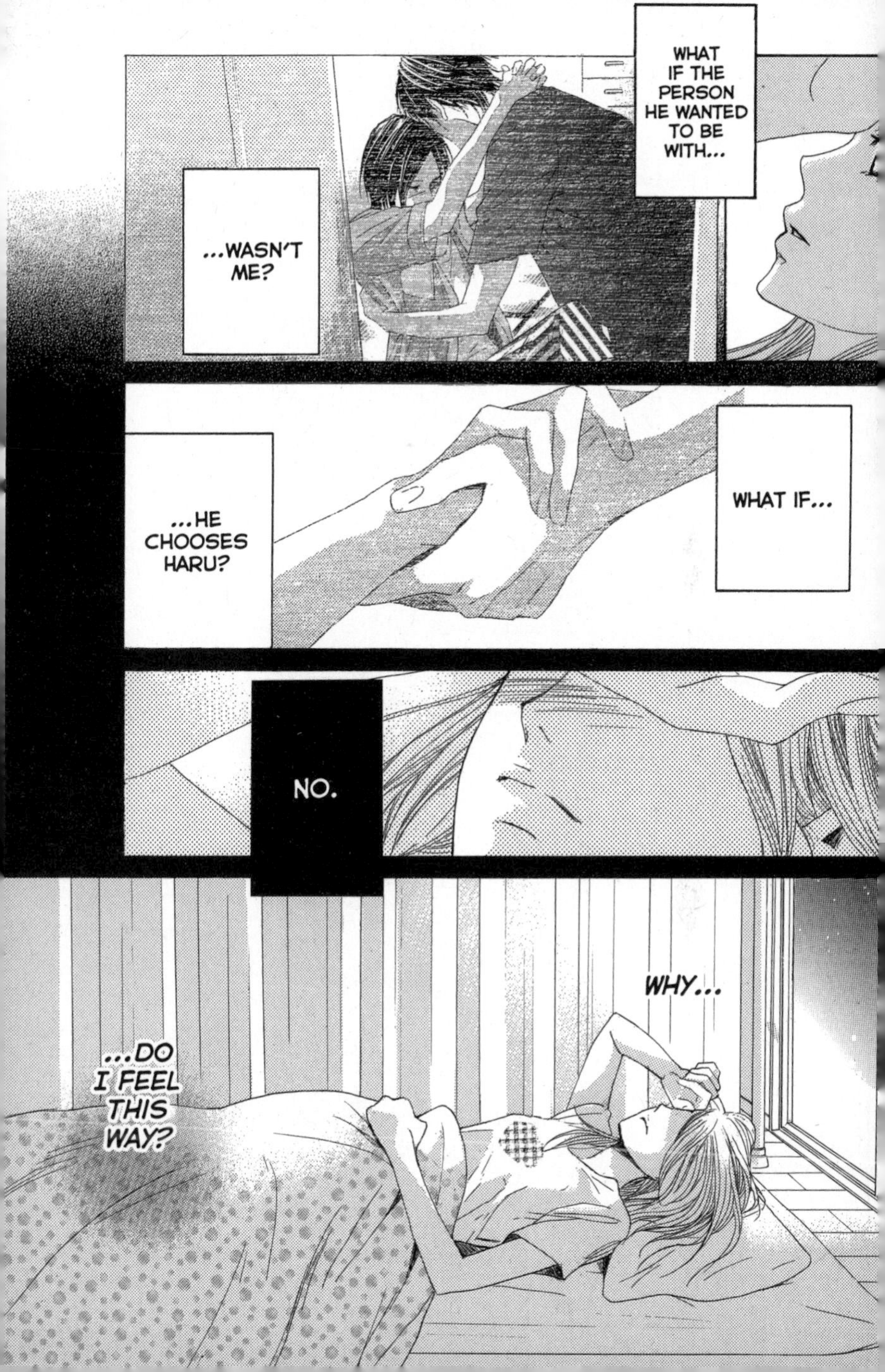
WHAT IF THE PERSON HE WANTED TO BE WITH...
...WASN'T ME?
WHAT IF...
...HE CHOOSES HARU?
NO.
WHY...
...DO I FEEL THIS WAY?

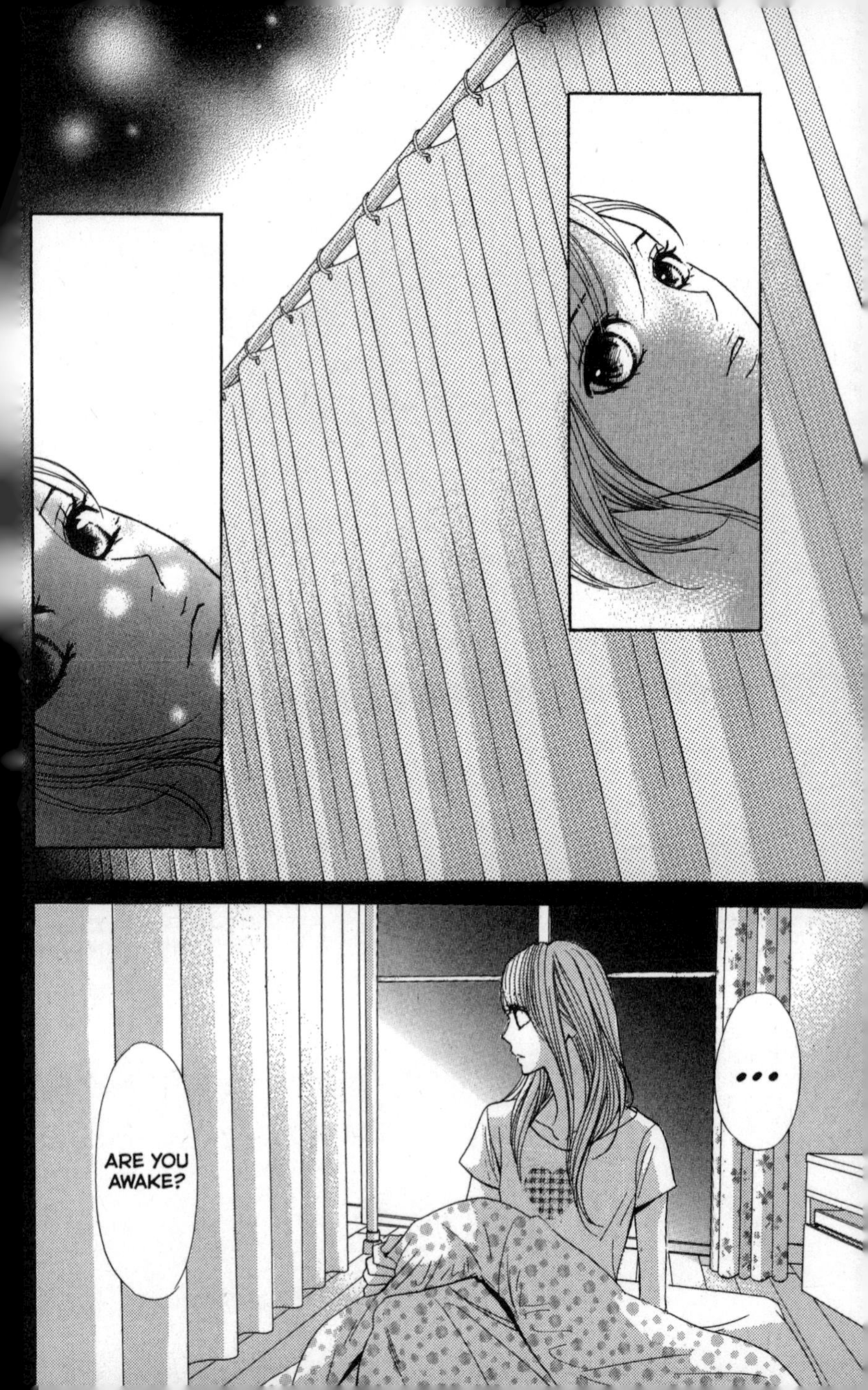
...
ARE YOU AWAKE?

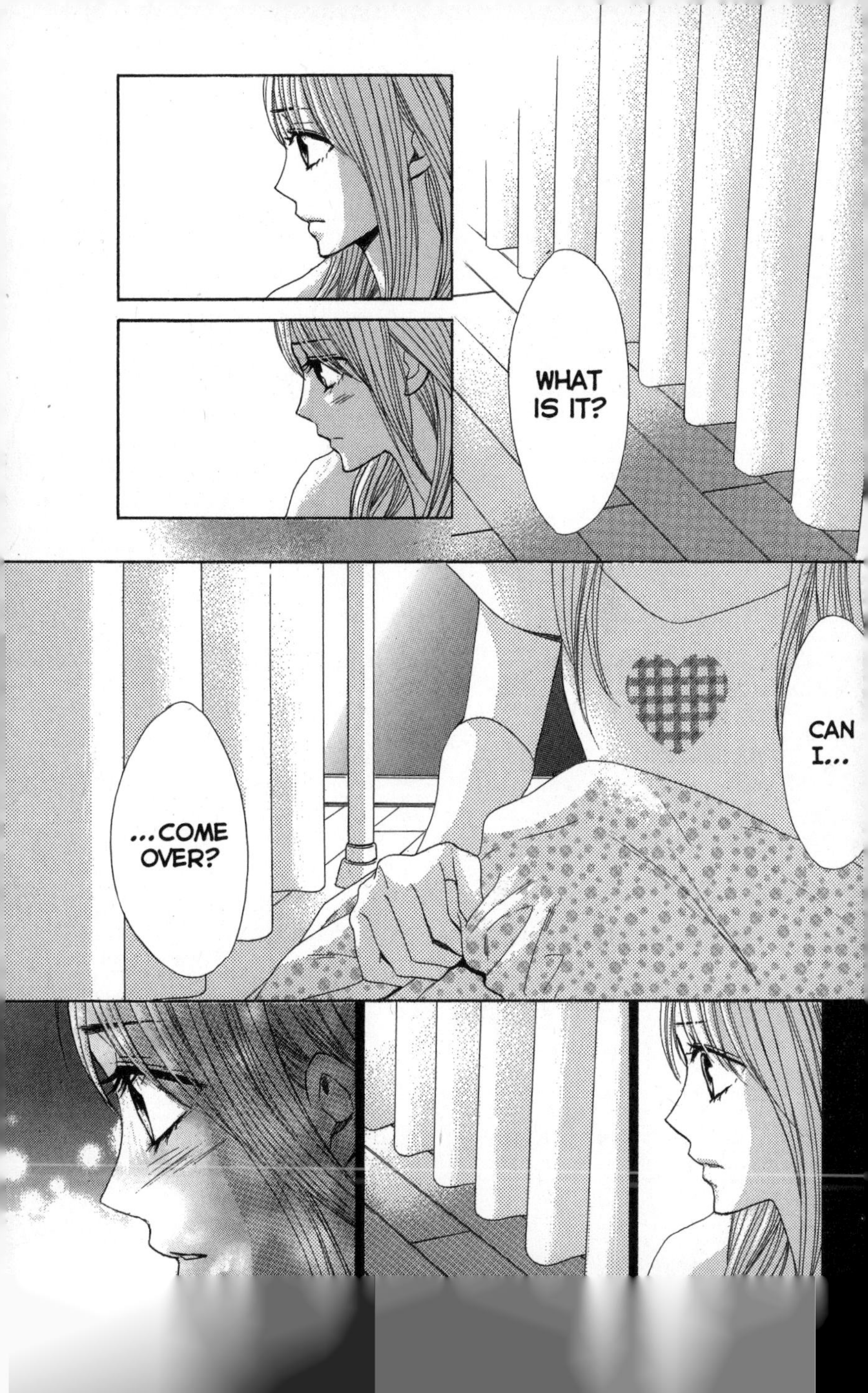
WHAT IS IT?
CAN I...
...COME OVER?

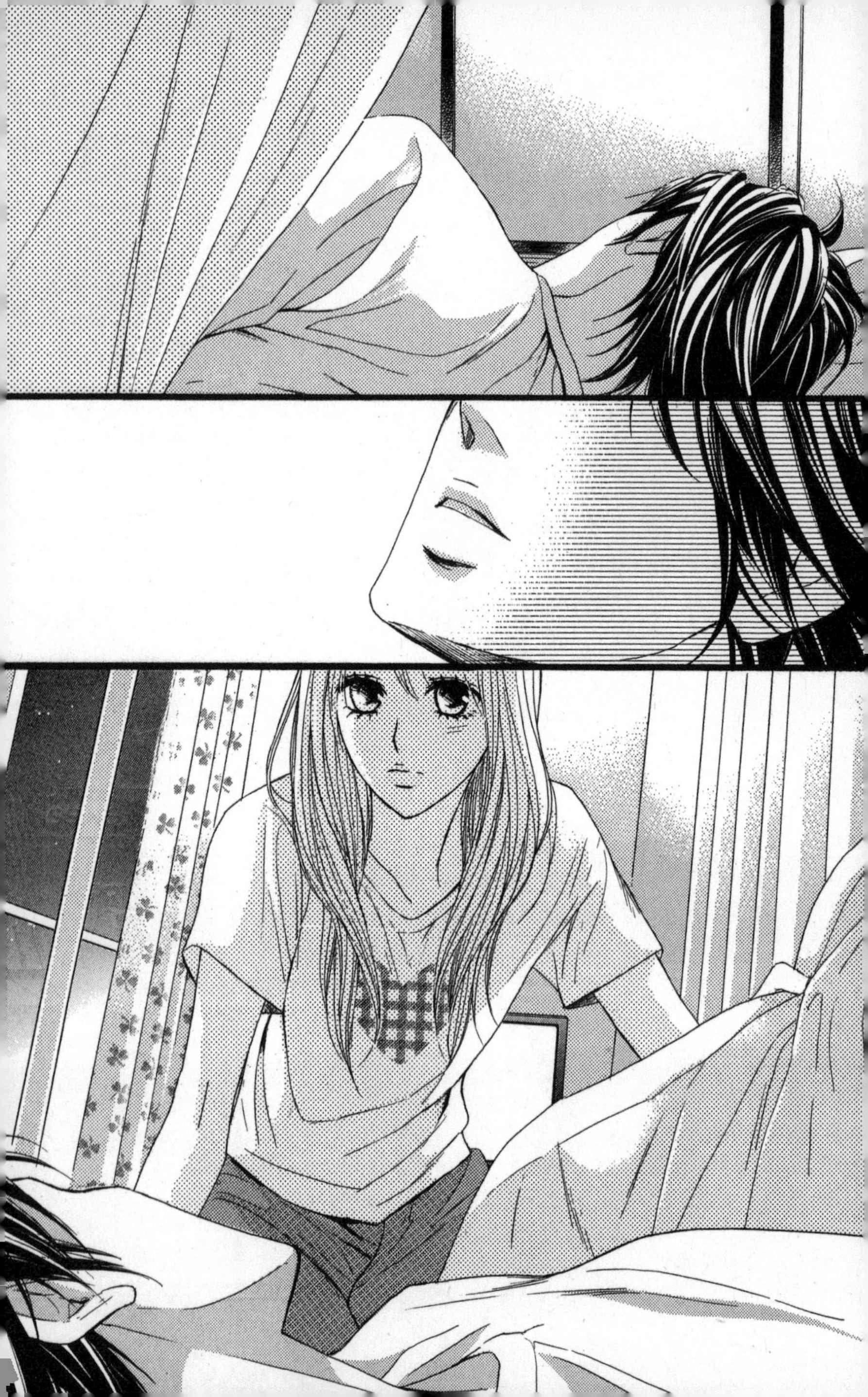

L♥DK

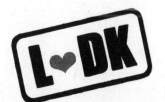

#43 Wounds and Bonds

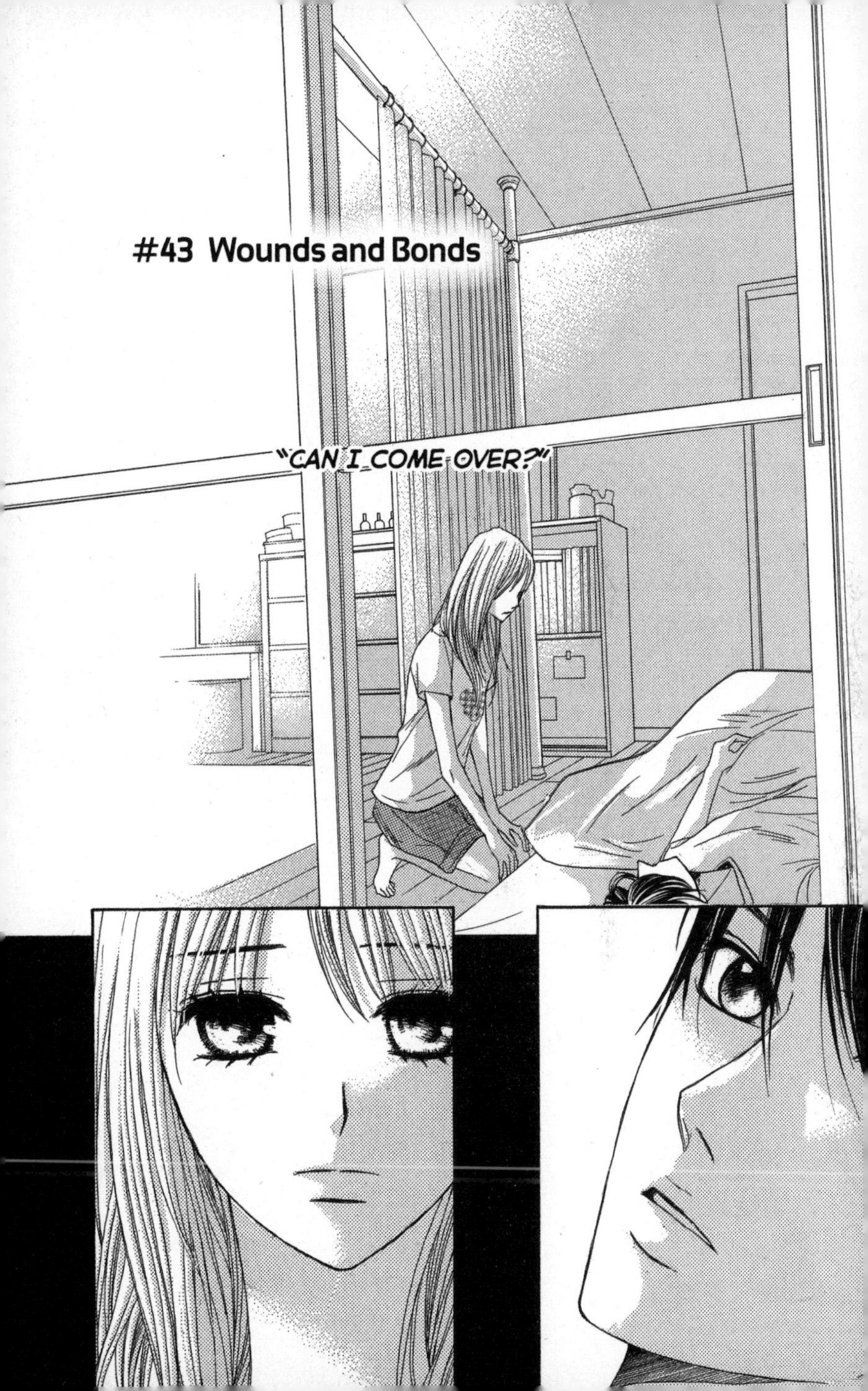
"CAN I COME OVER?"

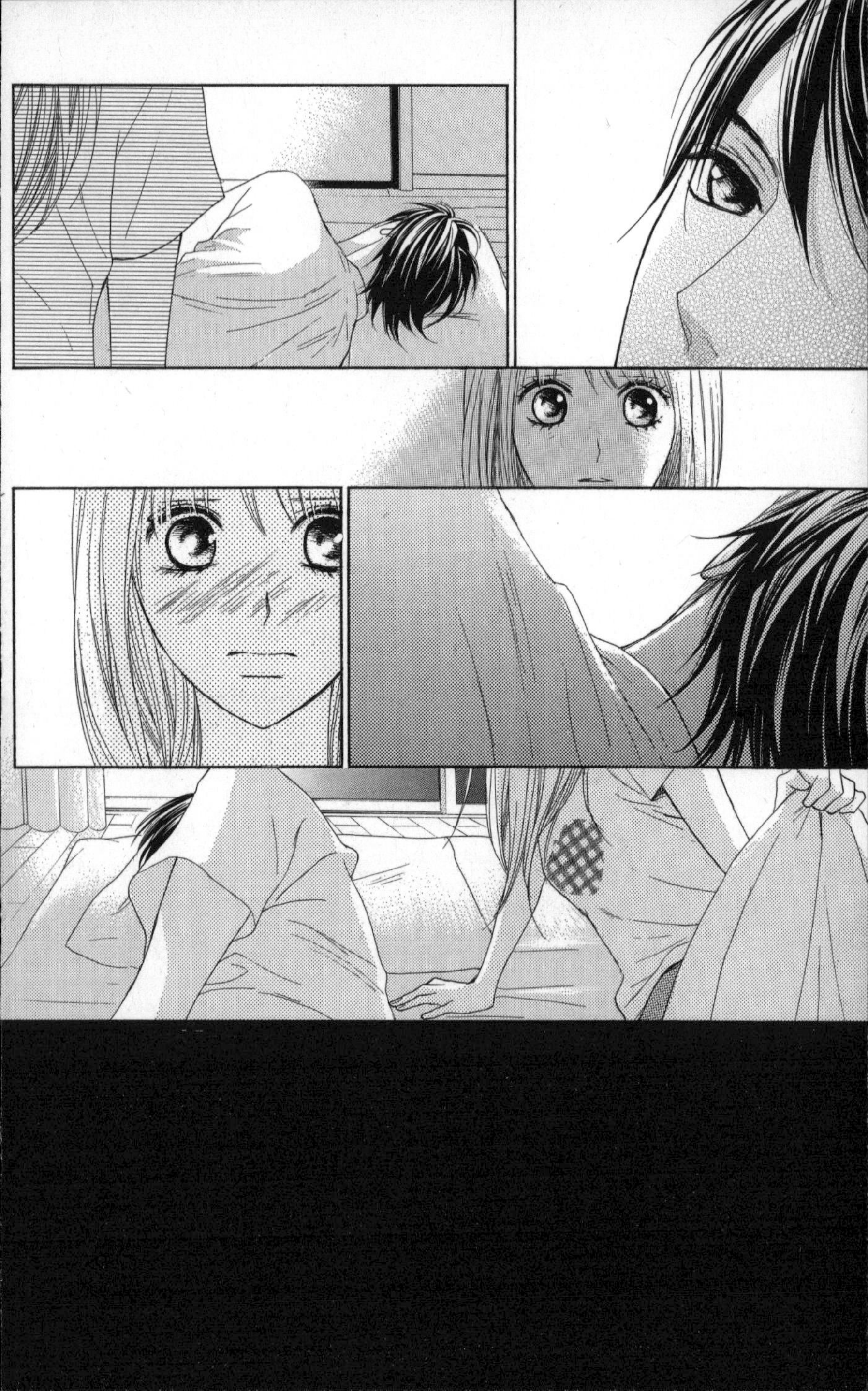

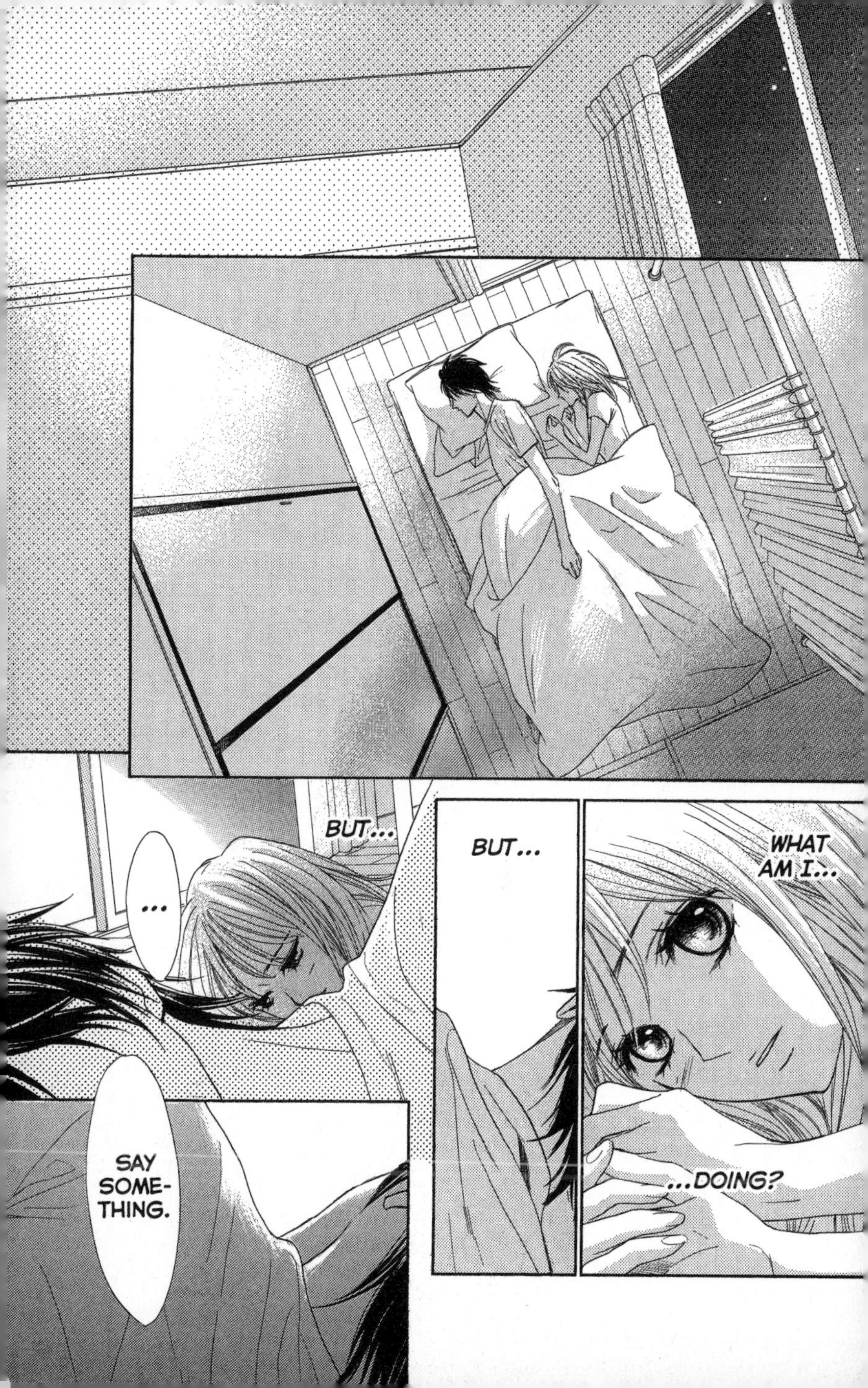
WHAT AM I...
...DOING?
BUT...
BUT...
...
SAY SOMETHING.

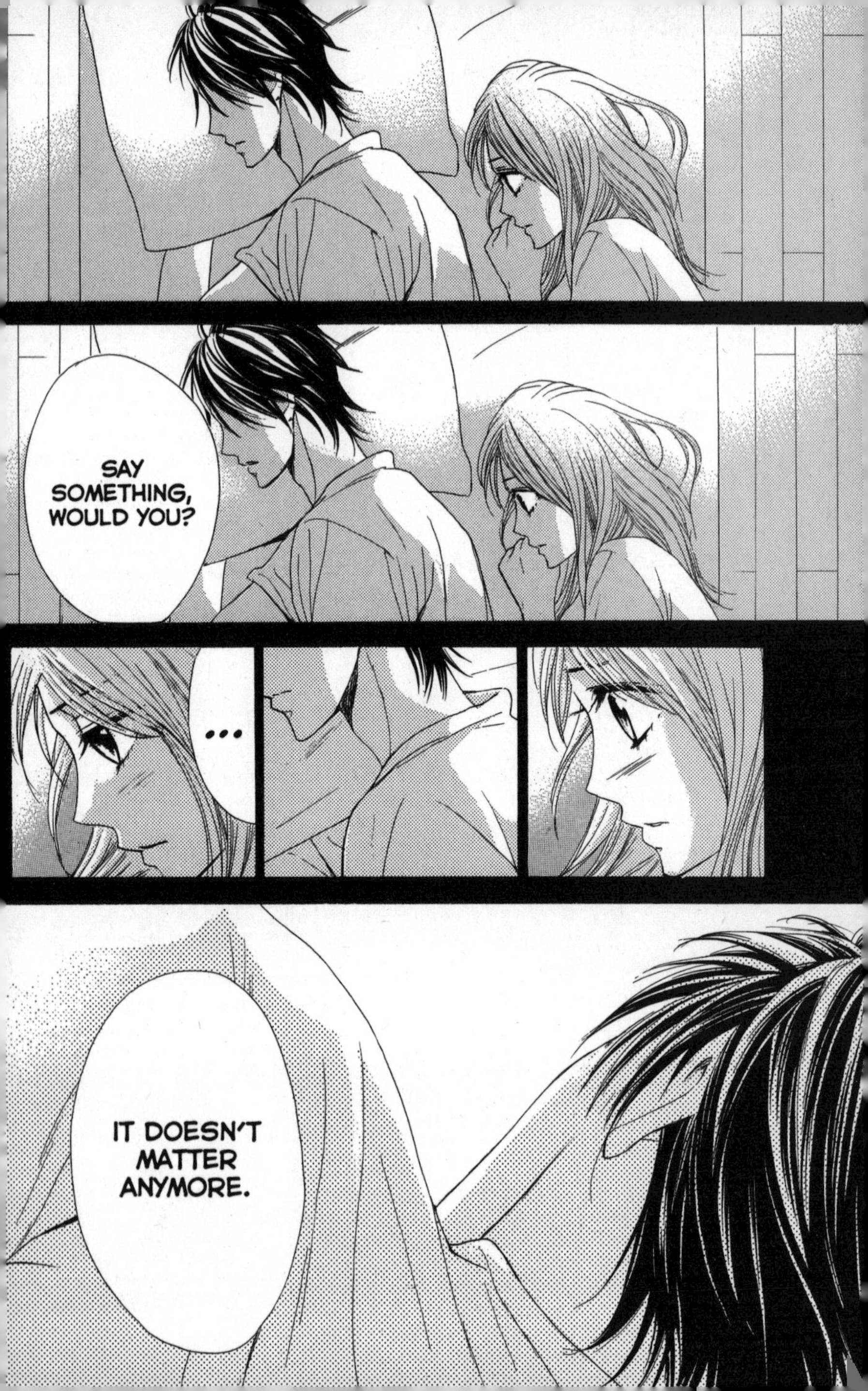
SAY SOMETHING, WOULD YOU?
...
IT DOESN'T MATTER ANYMORE.

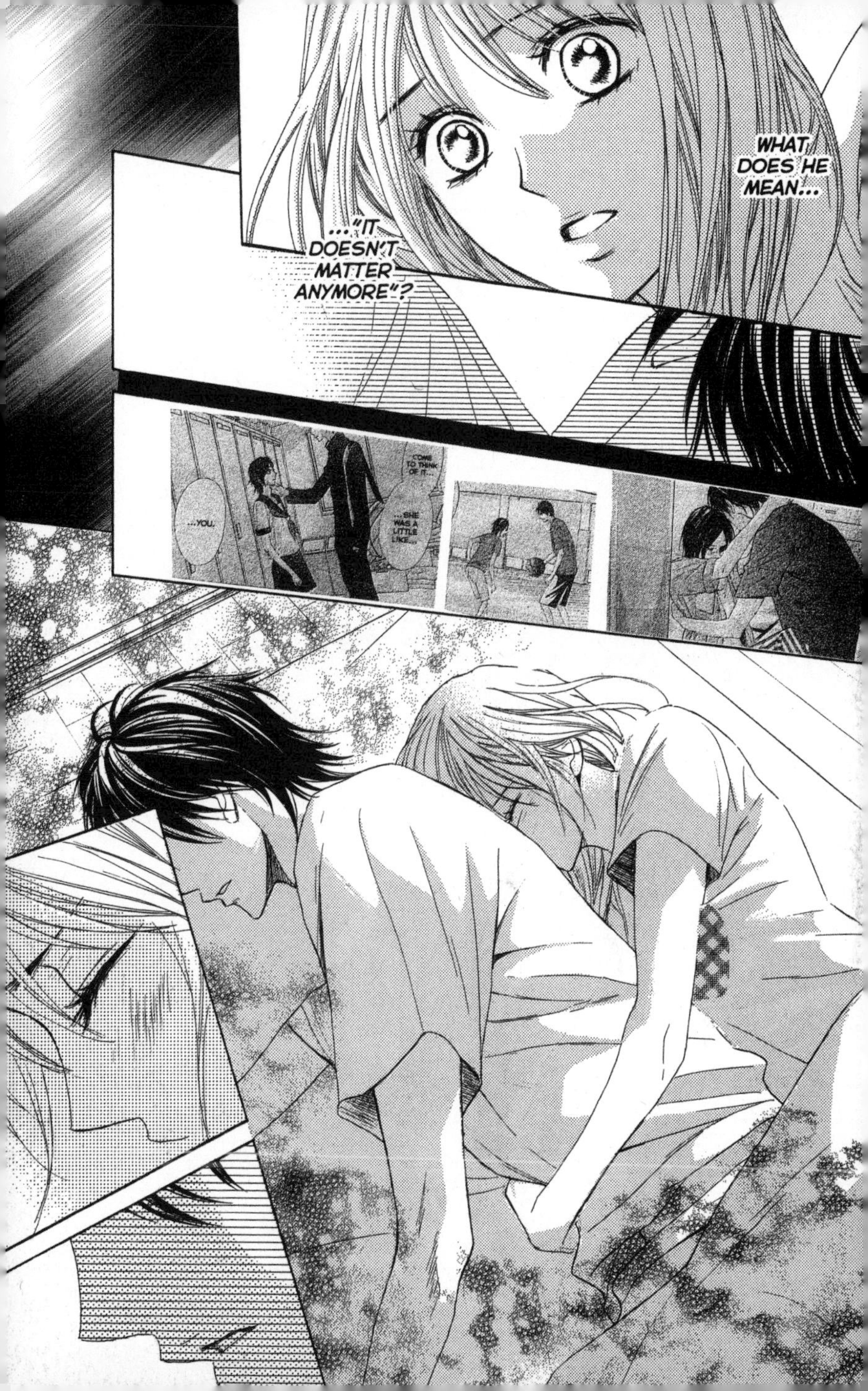
WHAT DOES HE MEAN...
..."IT DOESN'T MATTER ANYMORE"?
COME TO THINK OF IT...
...SHE WAS A LITTLE LIKE...
...YOU.

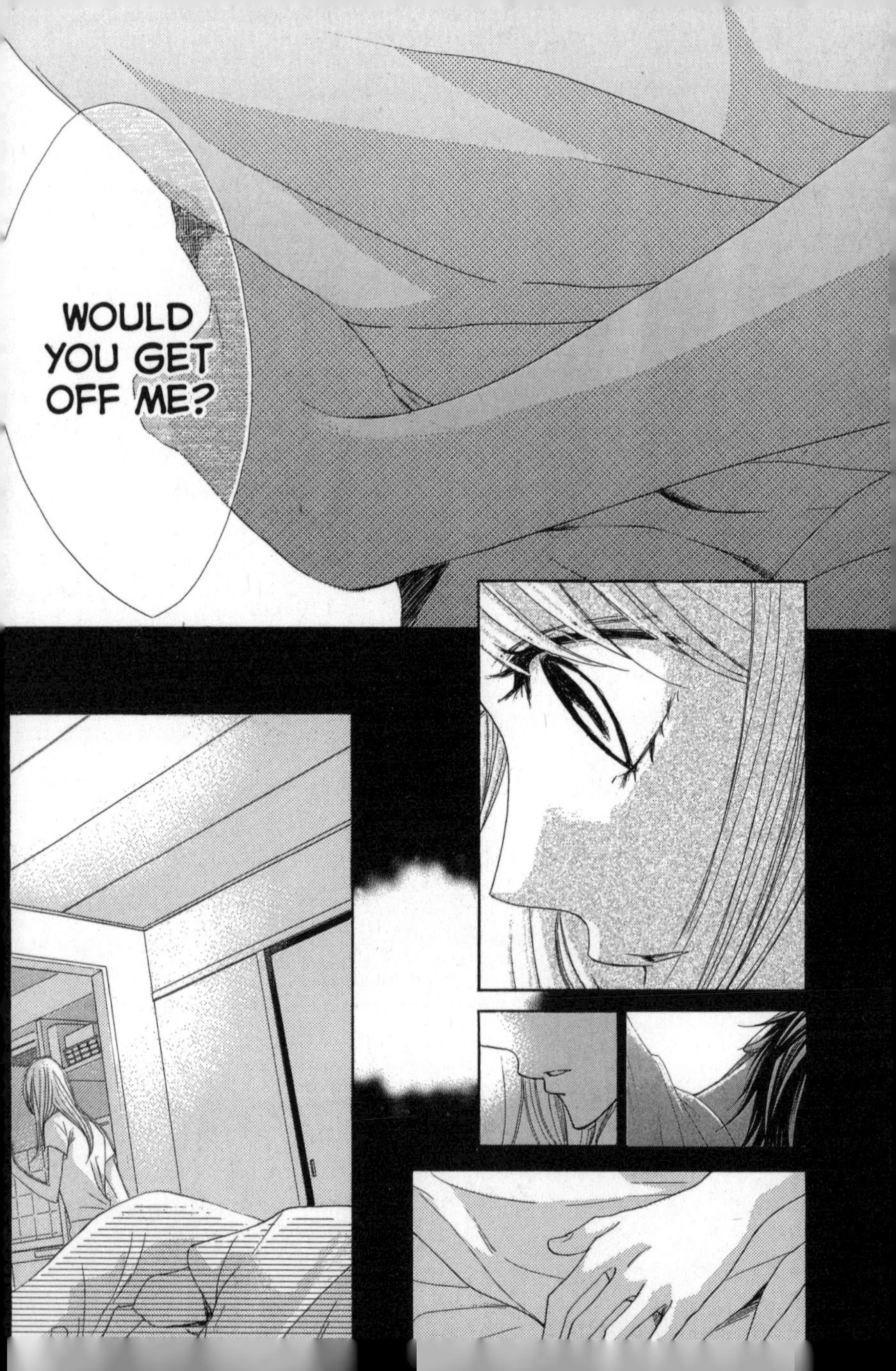
WOULD YOU GET OFF ME?

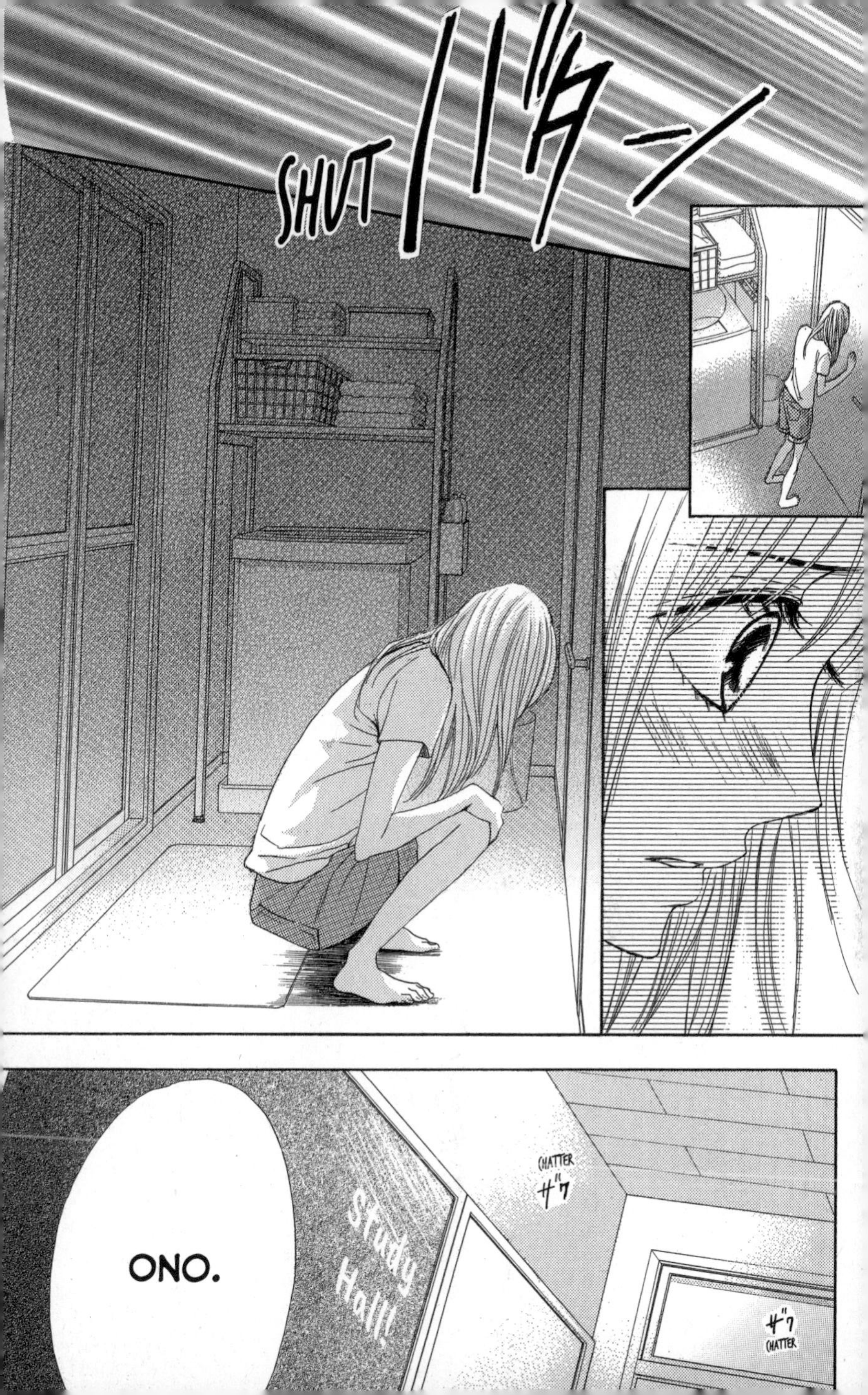
SHUT
バタ−ン
CHATTER
ザワ
Study Hall!
ONO.
ザワ
CHATTER

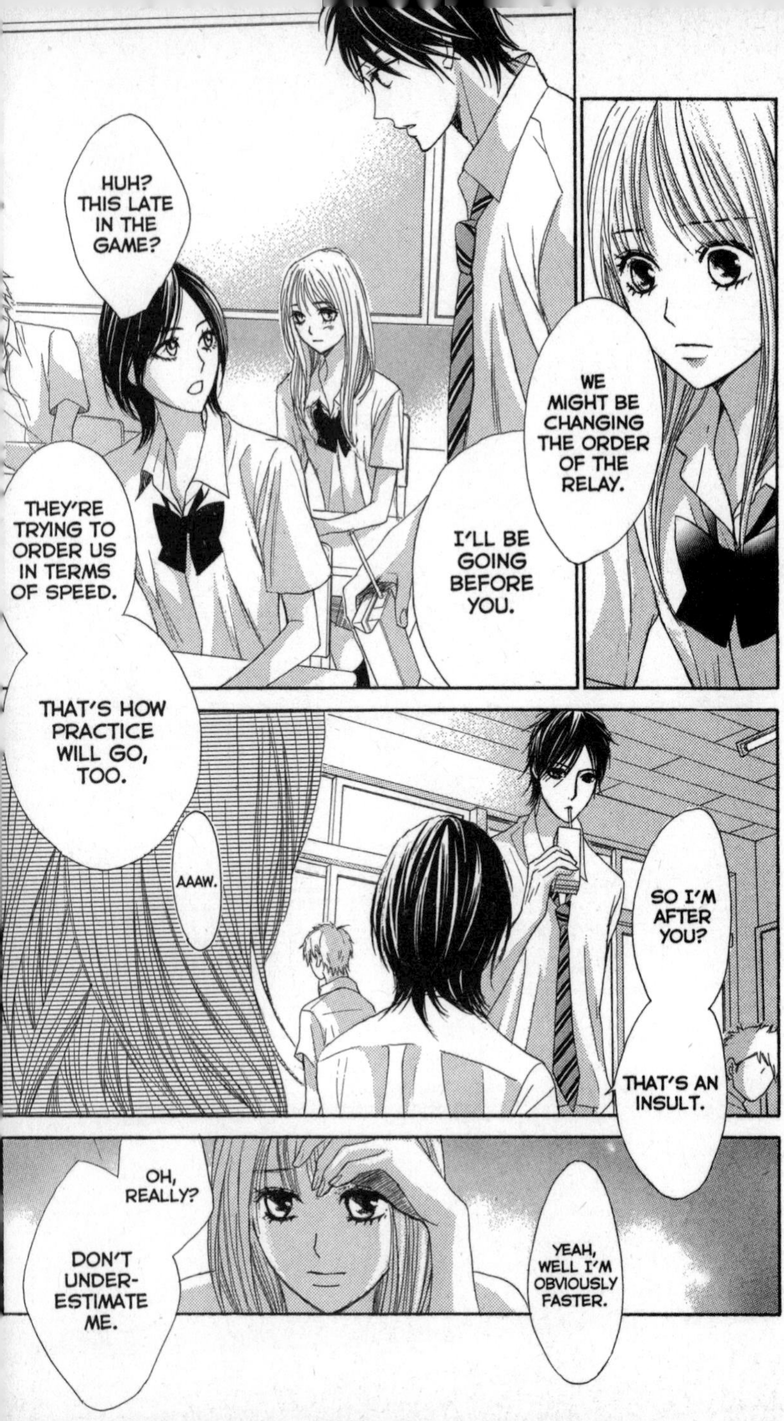
WE MIGHT BE CHANGING THE ORDER OF THE RELAY.
I'LL BE GOING BEFORE YOU.
HUH? THIS LATE IN THE GAME?
THEY'RE TRYING TO ORDER US IN TERMS OF SPEED.
THAT'S HOW PRACTICE WILL GO, TOO.
AAAW.
SO I'M AFTER YOU?
THAT'S AN INSULT.
YEAH, WELL I'M OBVIOUSLY FASTER.
OH, REALLY?
DON'T UNDER-ESTIMATE ME.

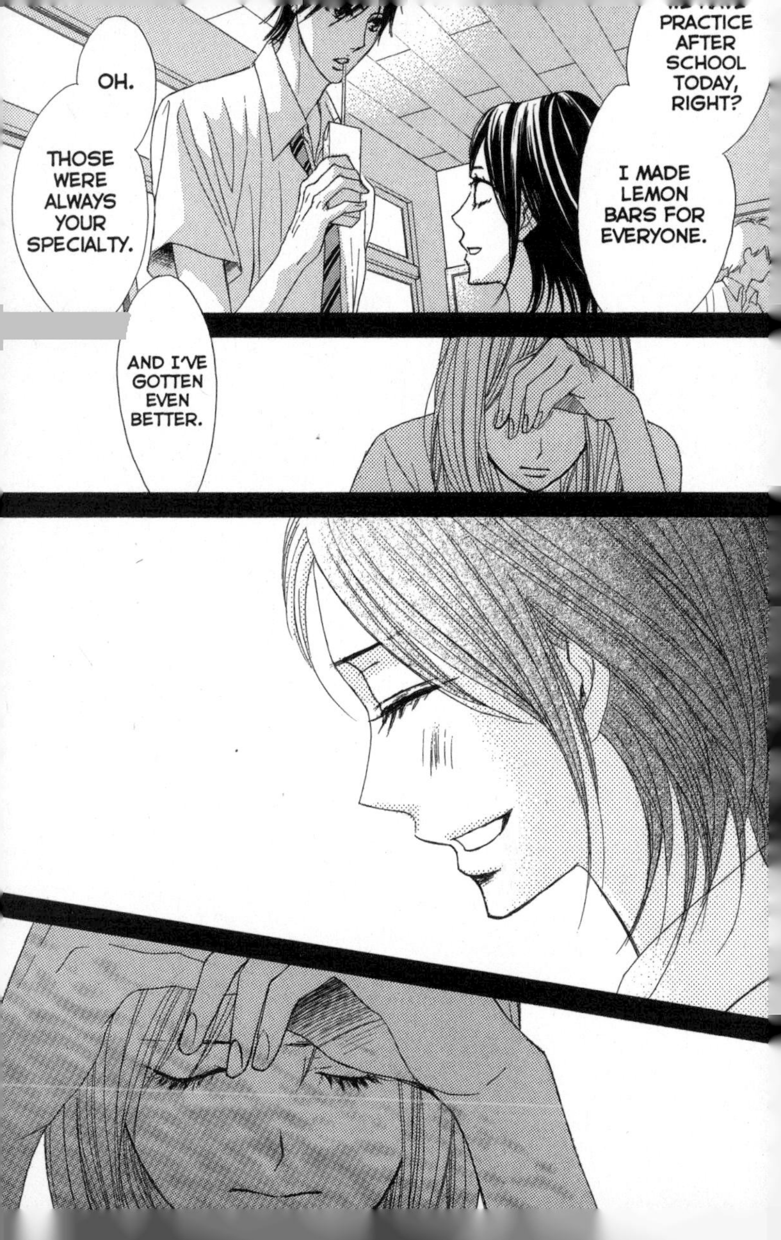
PRACTICE AFTER SCHOOL TODAY, RIGHT?
I MADE LEMON BARS FOR EVERYONE.
OH.
THOSE WERE ALWAYS YOUR SPECIALTY.
AND I'VE GOTTEN EVEN BETTER.

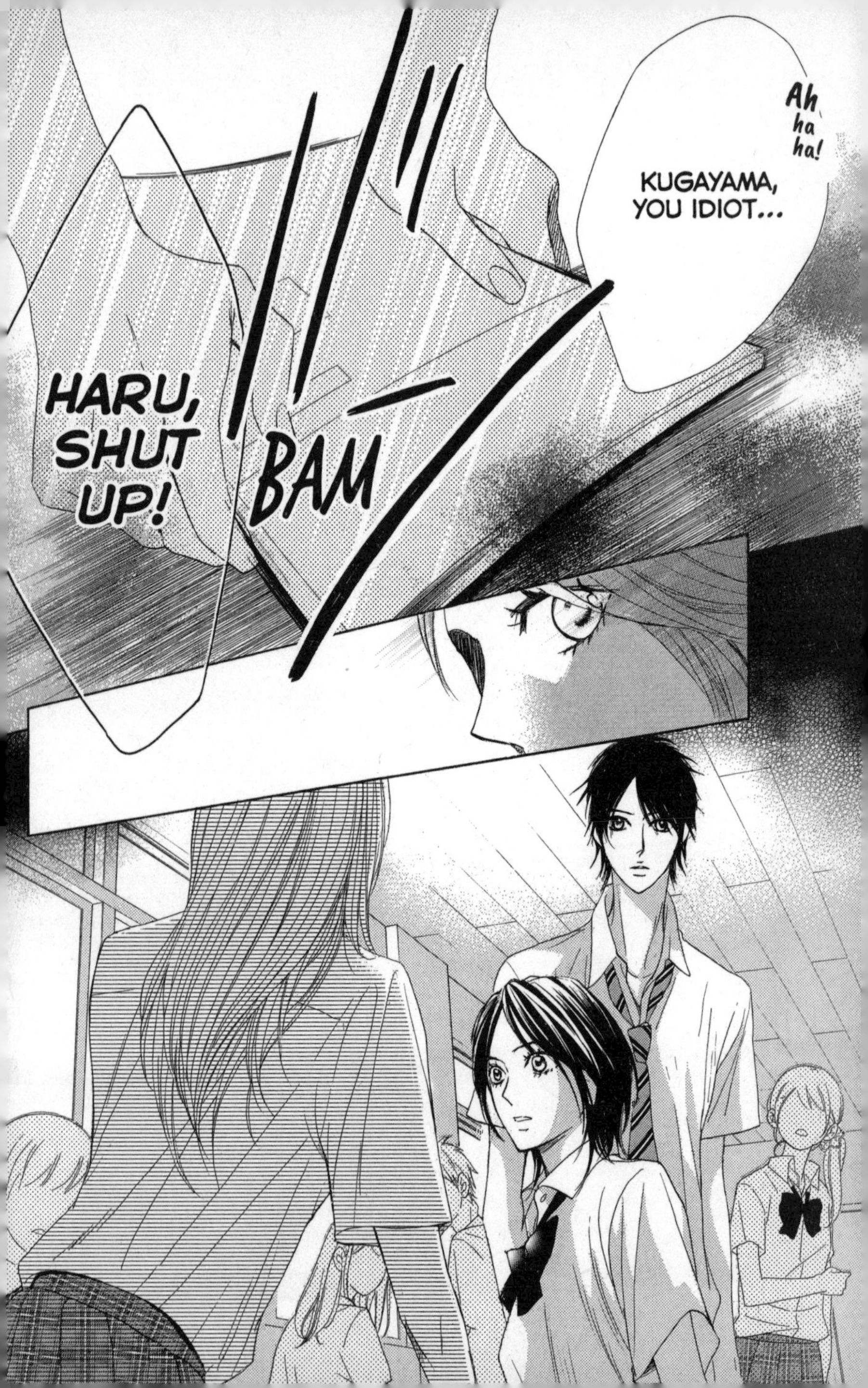
Ah ha ha!
KUGAYAMA, YOU IDIOT...
BAM
HARU, SHUT UP!

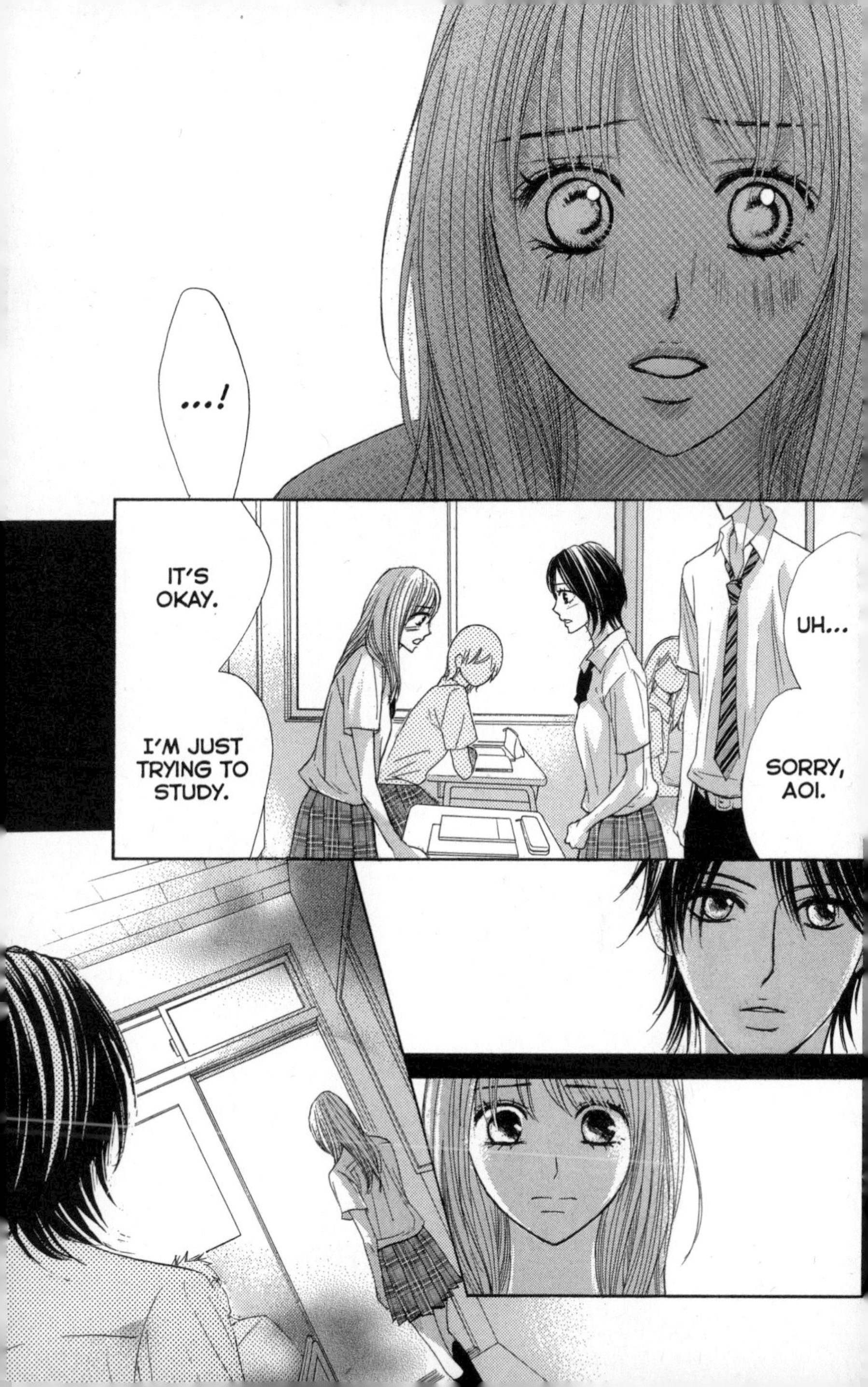
...!
UH...
SORRY, AOI.
IT'S OKAY.
I'M JUST TRYING TO STUDY.

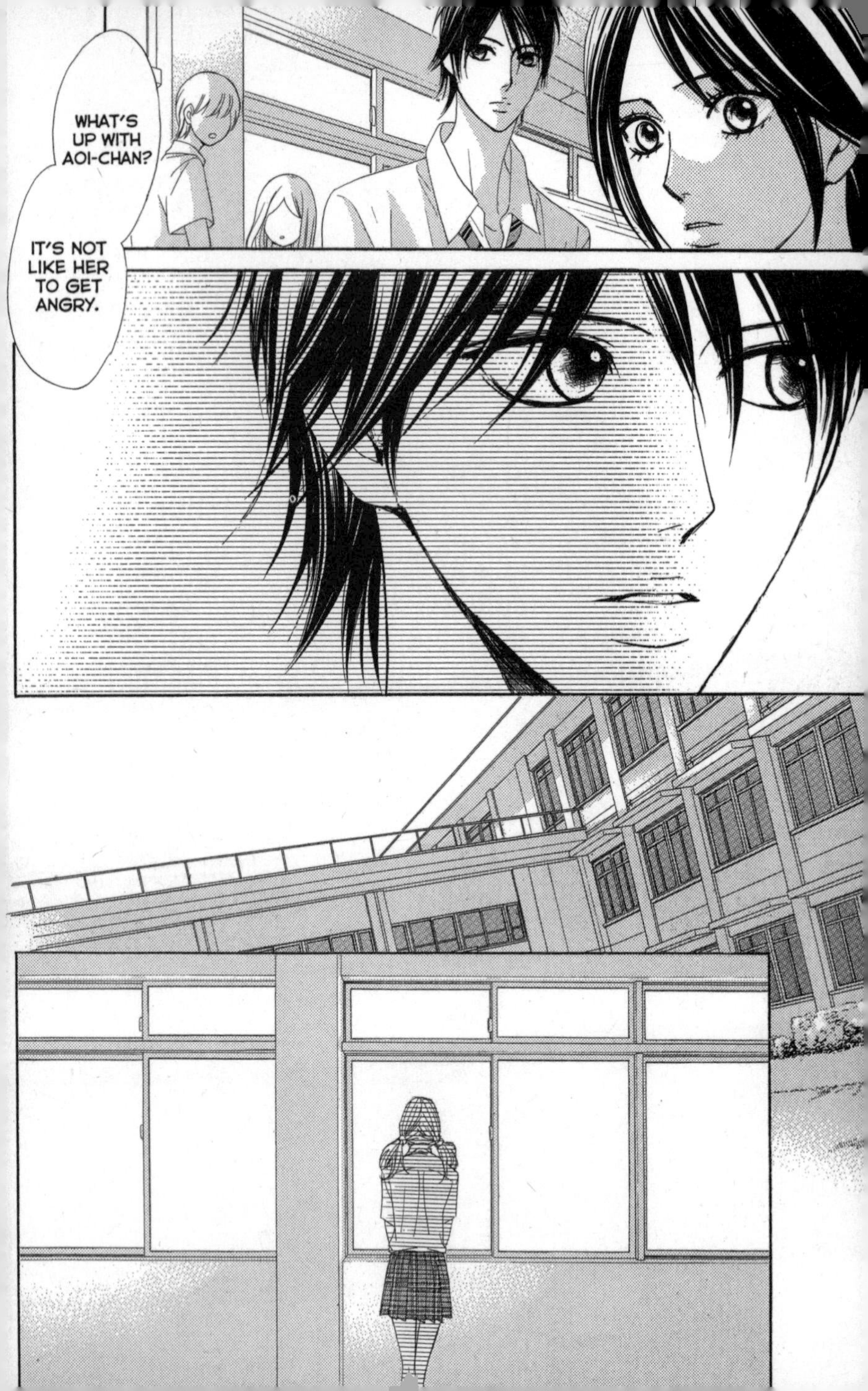
WHAT'S UP WITH AOI-CHAN?
IT'S NOT LIKE HER TO GET ANGRY.

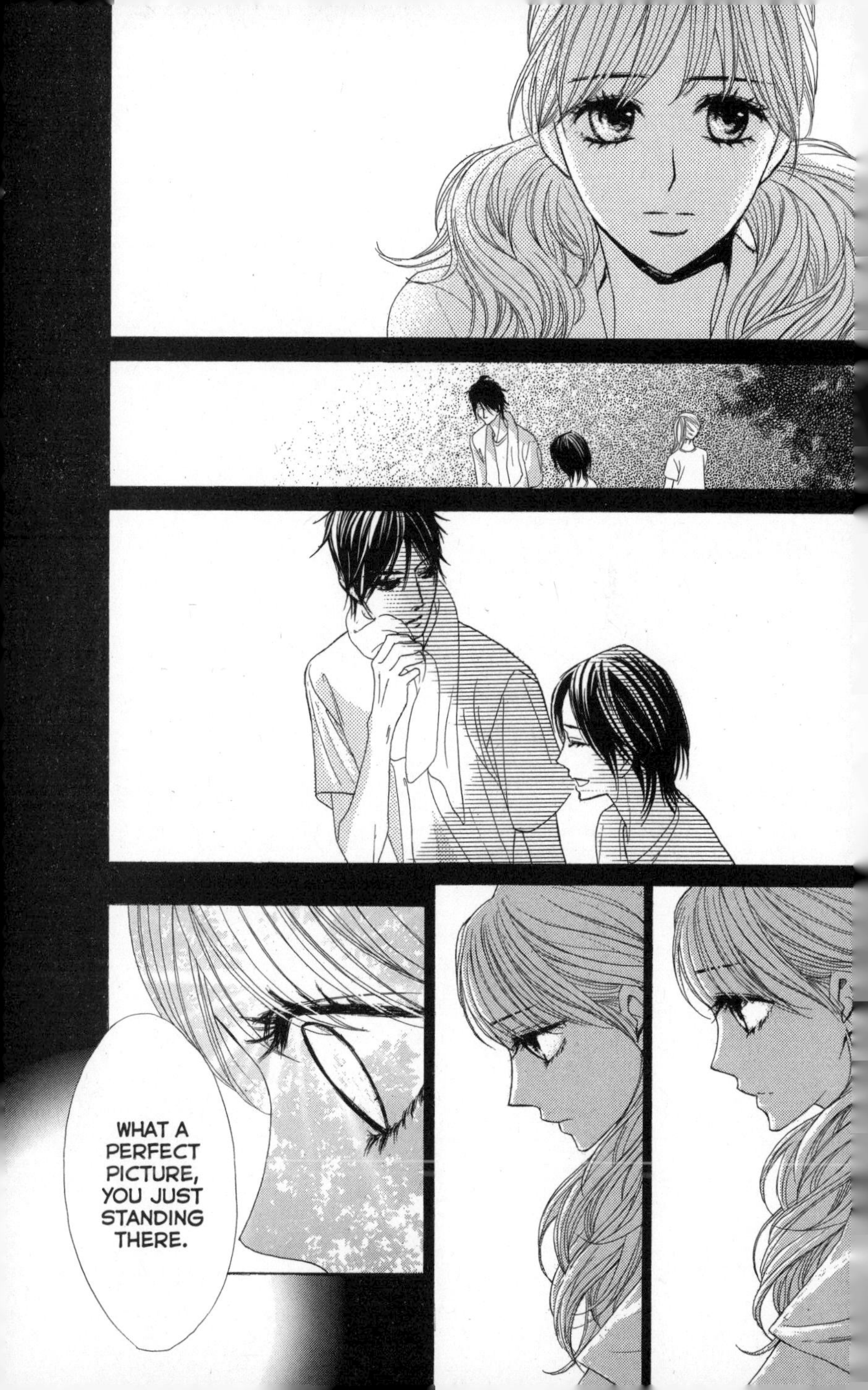
WHAT A PERFECT PICTURE, YOU JUST STANDING THERE.

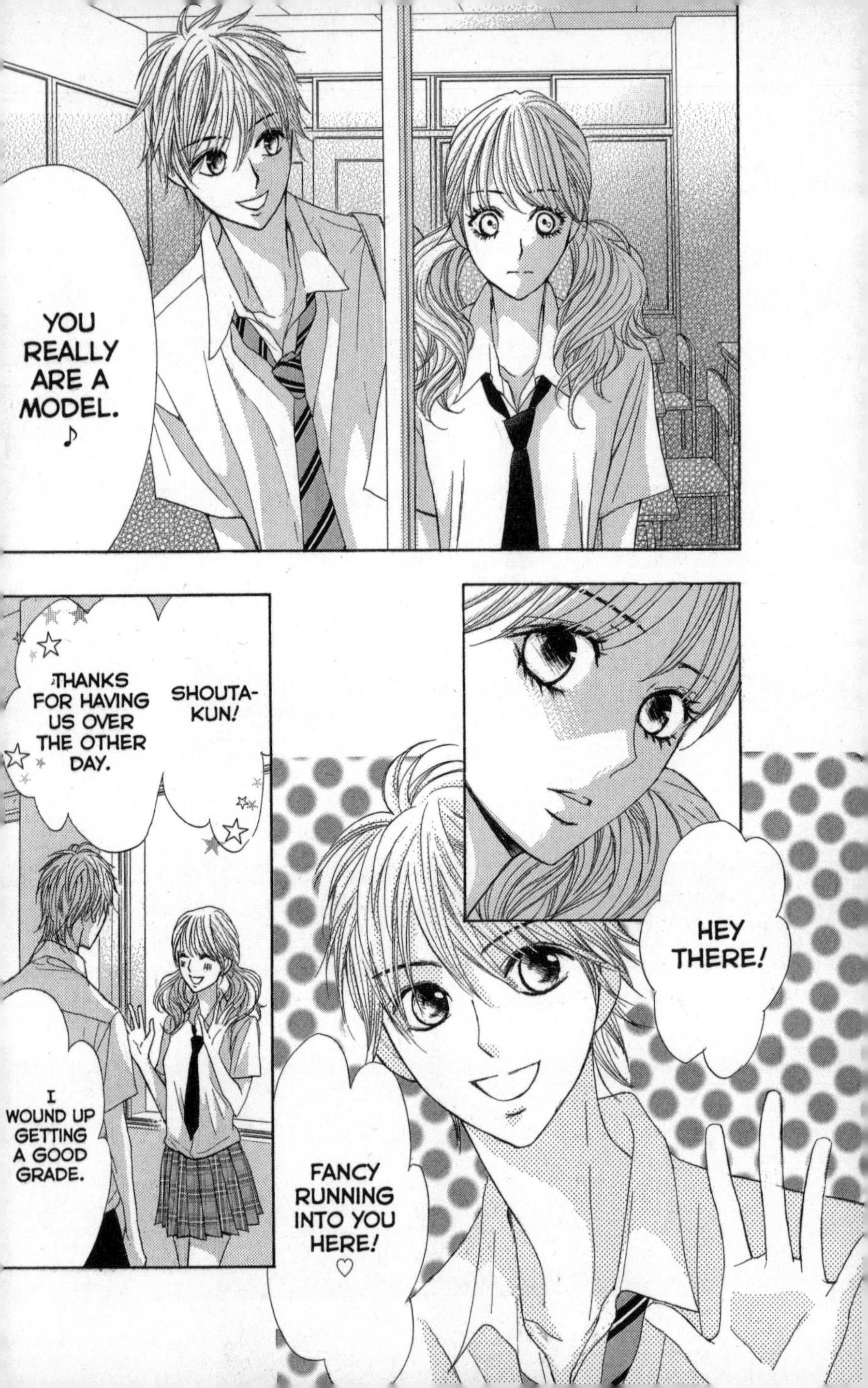
YOU REALLY ARE A MODEL. ♪
HEY THERE!
FANCY RUNNING INTO YOU HERE! ♡
SHOUTA-KUN!
THANKS FOR HAVING US OVER THE OTHER DAY.
I WOUND UP GETTING A GOOD GRADE.

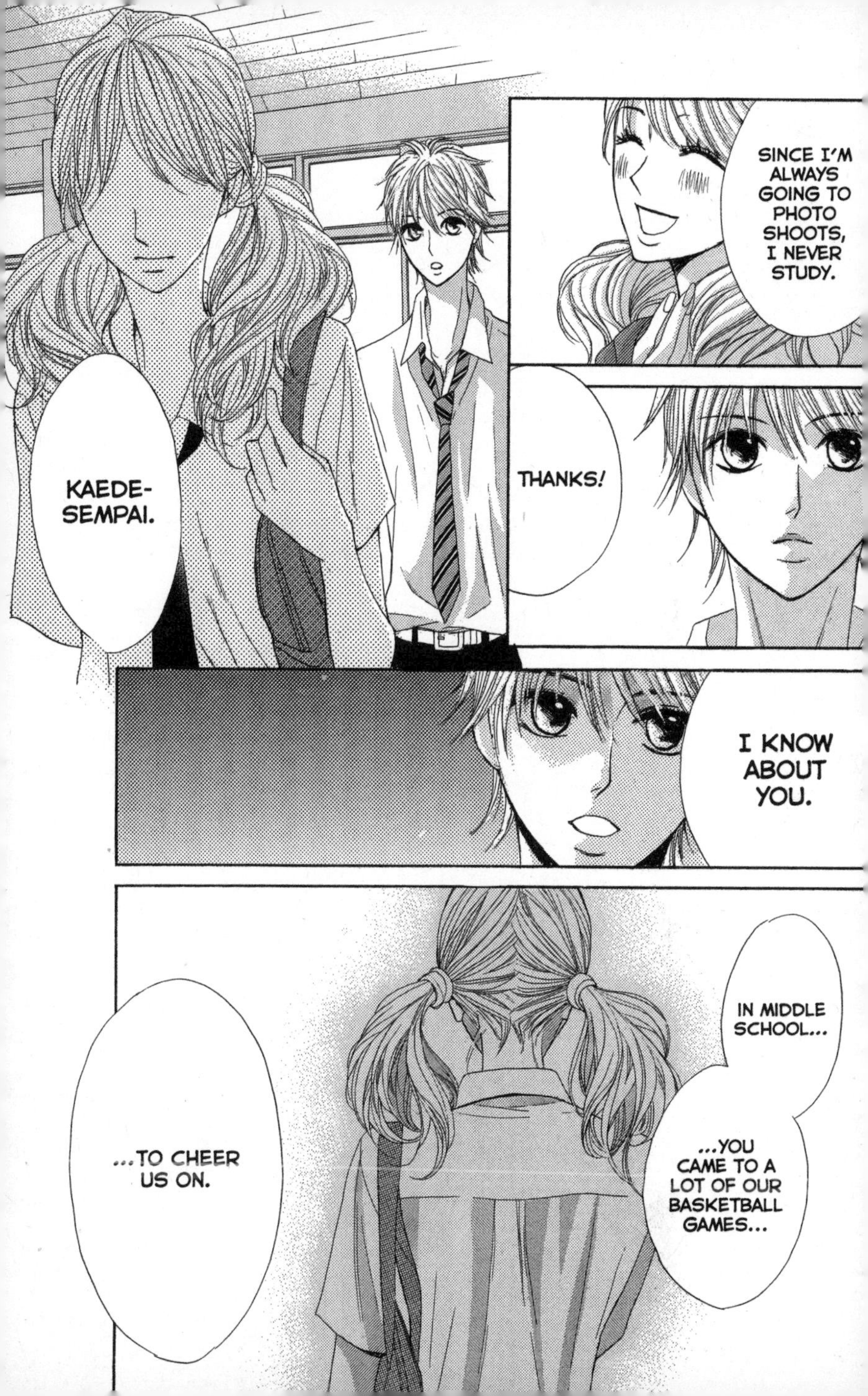
SINCE I'M ALWAYS GOING TO PHOTO SHOOTS, I NEVER STUDY.
THANKS!
KAEDE-SEMPAI.
I KNOW ABOUT YOU.
IN MIDDLE SCHOOL...
...YOU CAME TO A LOT OF OUR BASKETBALL GAMES...
...TO CHEER US ON.

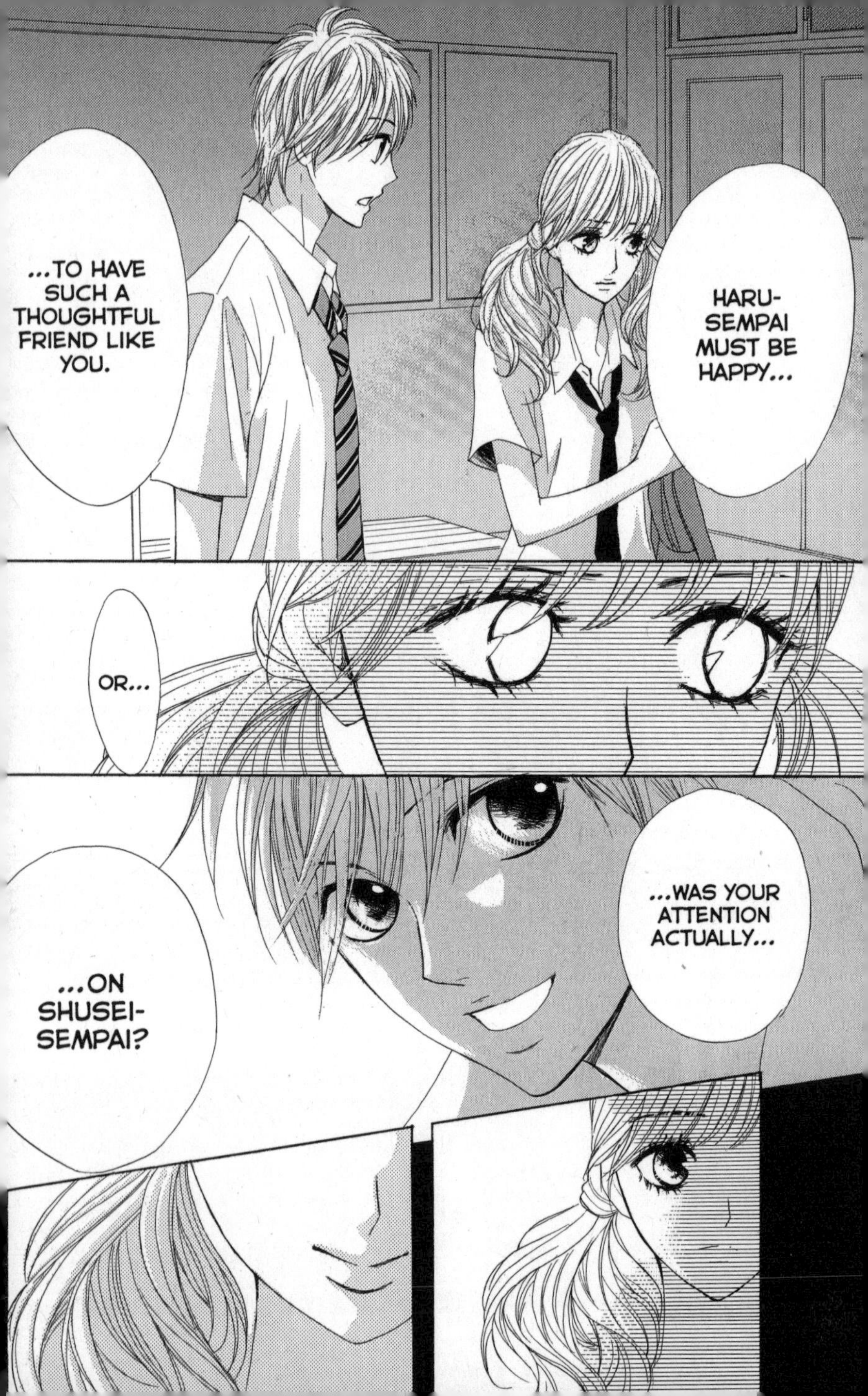
HARU-SEMPAI MUST BE HAPPY...
...TO HAVE SUCH A THOUGHTFUL FRIEND LIKE YOU.
OR...
...WAS YOUR ATTENTION ACTUALLY...
...ON SHUSEI-SEMPAI?

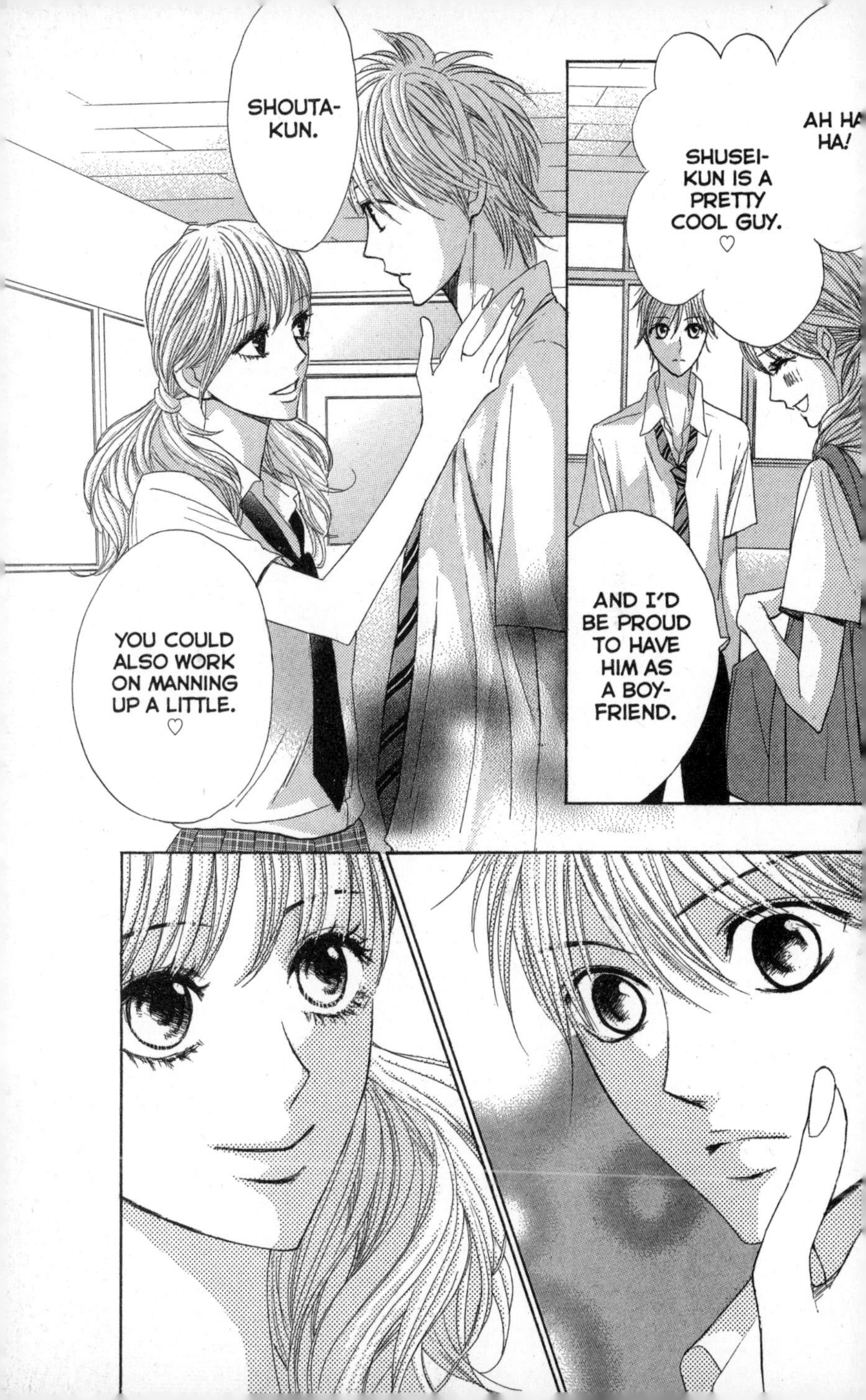
AH HA HA!
SHUSEI-KUN IS A PRETTY COOL GUY. ♡
AND I'D BE PROUD TO HAVE HIM AS A BOY-FRIEND.
SHOUTA-KUN.
YOU COULD ALSO WORK ON MANNING UP A LITTLE. ♡

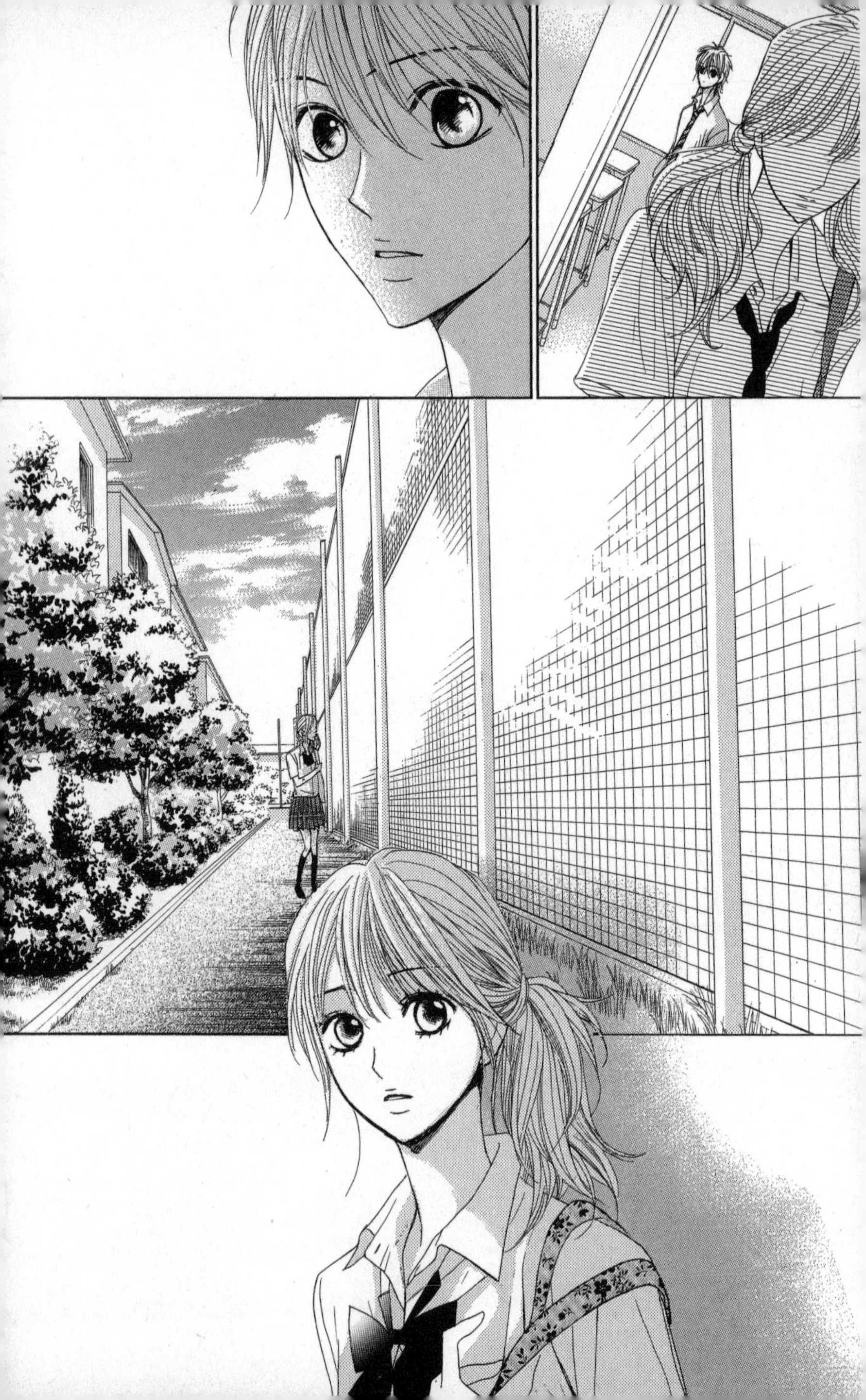

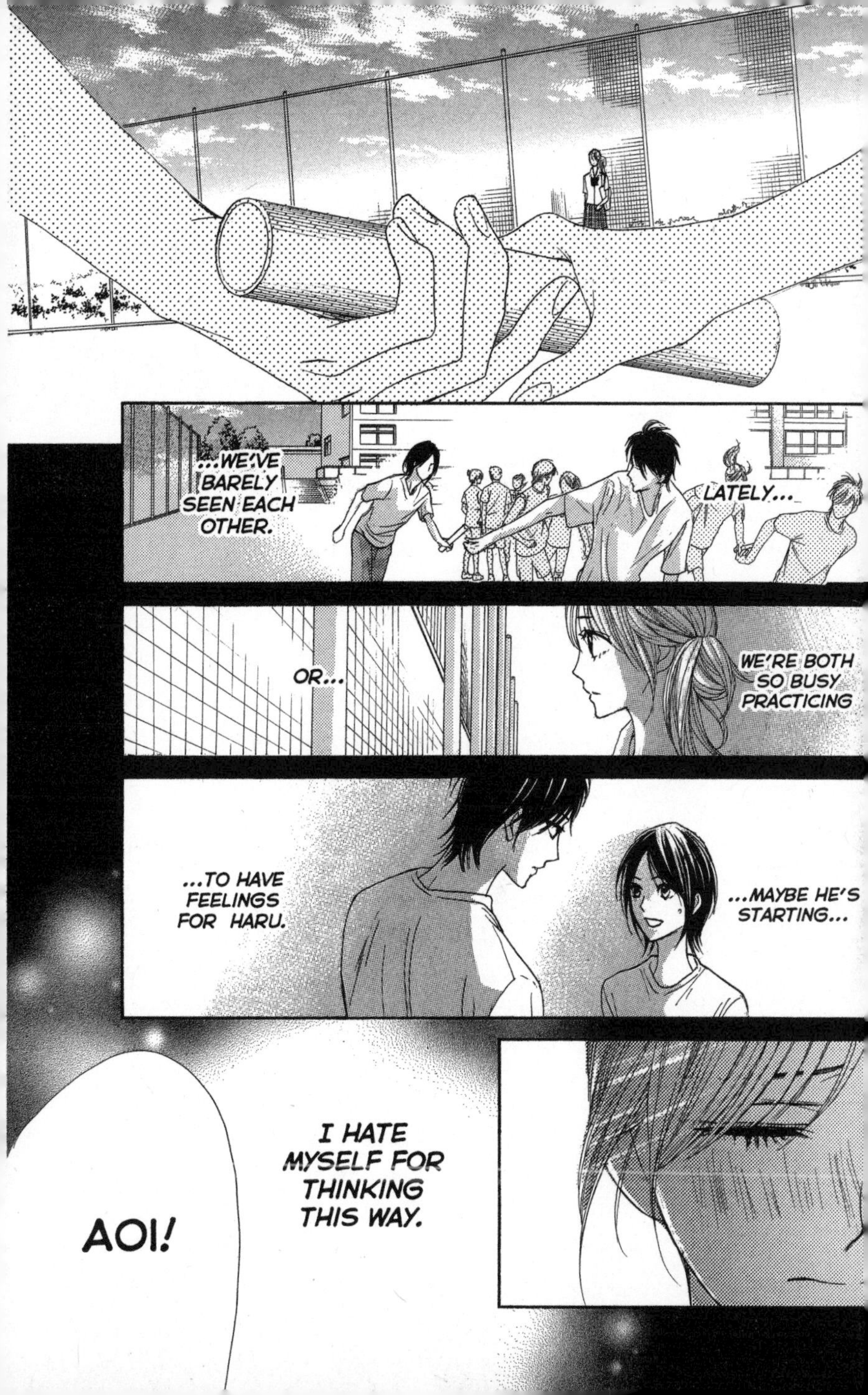
LATELY...
...WE'VE BARELY SEEN EACH OTHER.
WE'RE BOTH SO BUSY PRACTICING
OR...
...MAYBE HE'S STARTING...
...TO HAVE FEELINGS FOR HARU.
I HATE MYSELF FOR THINKING THIS WAY.
AOI!

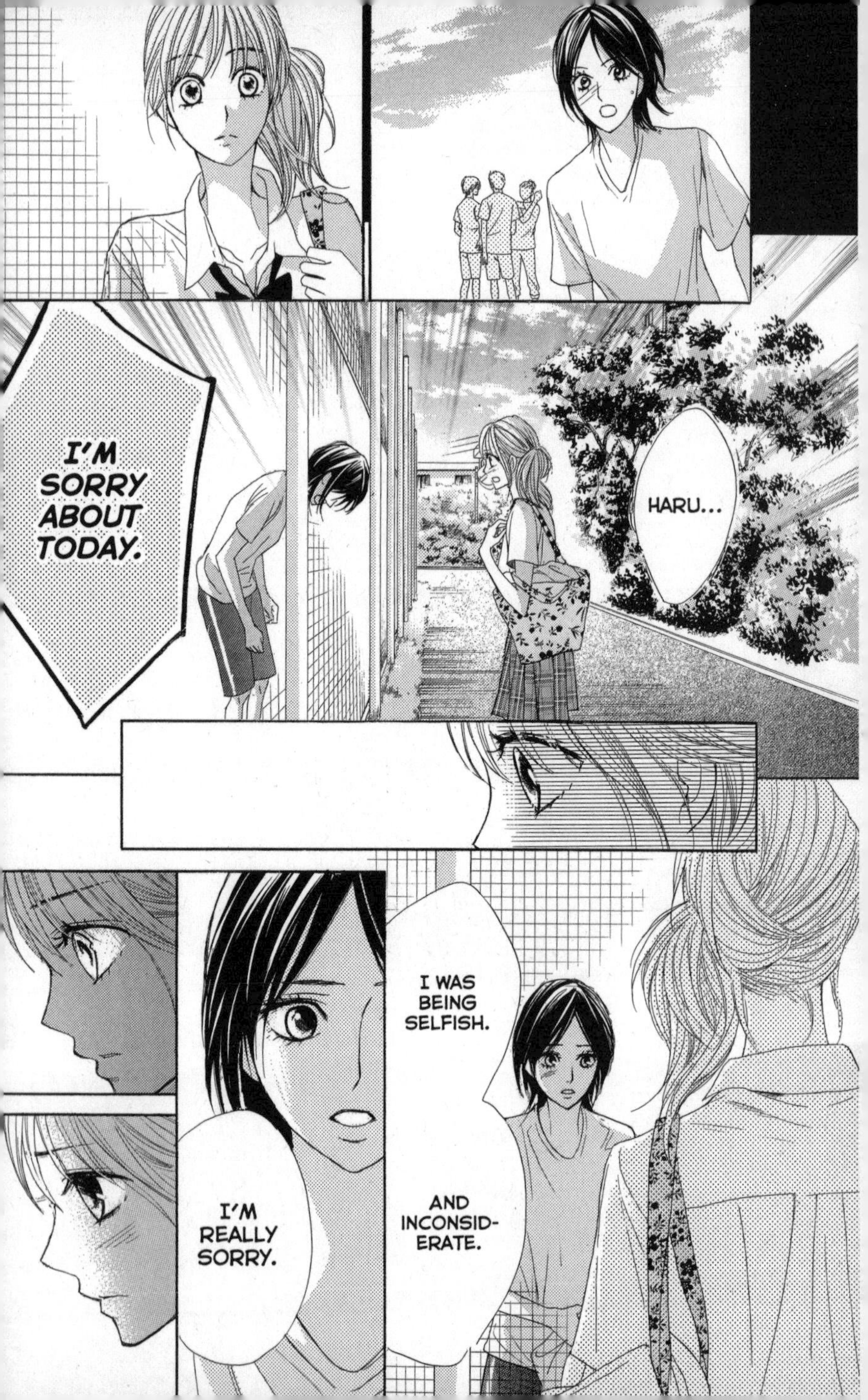
HARU...
I'M SORRY ABOUT TODAY.
I WAS BEING SELFISH.
AND INCONSID-ERATE.
I'M REALLY SORRY.

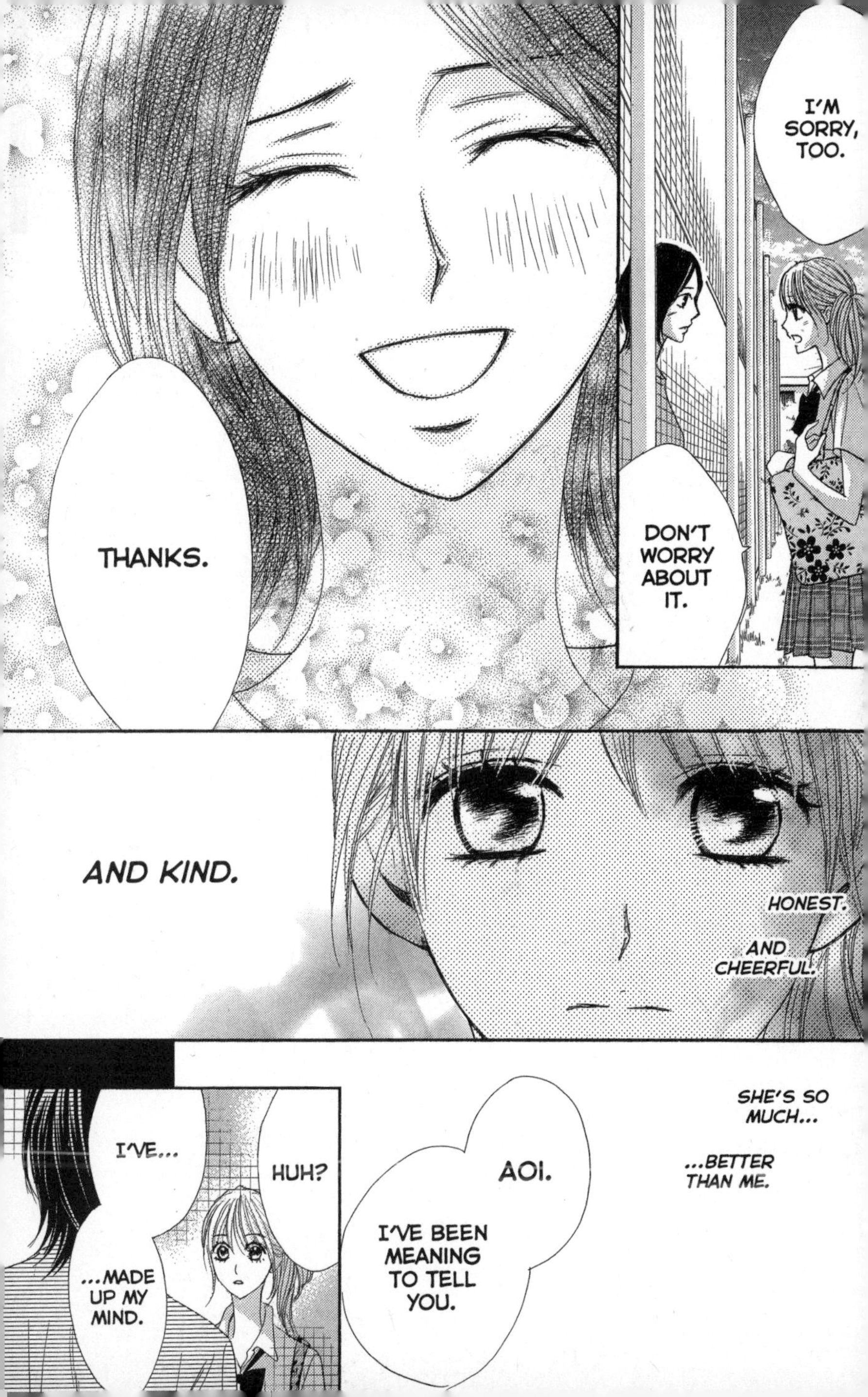
I'M SORRY, TOO.
DON'T WORRY ABOUT IT.
THANKS.
HONEST.
AND CHEERFUL.
AND KIND.
SHE'S SO MUCH...
...BETTER THAN ME.
AOI.
I'VE BEEN MEANING TO TELL YOU.
HUH?
I'VE...
...MADE UP MY MIND.

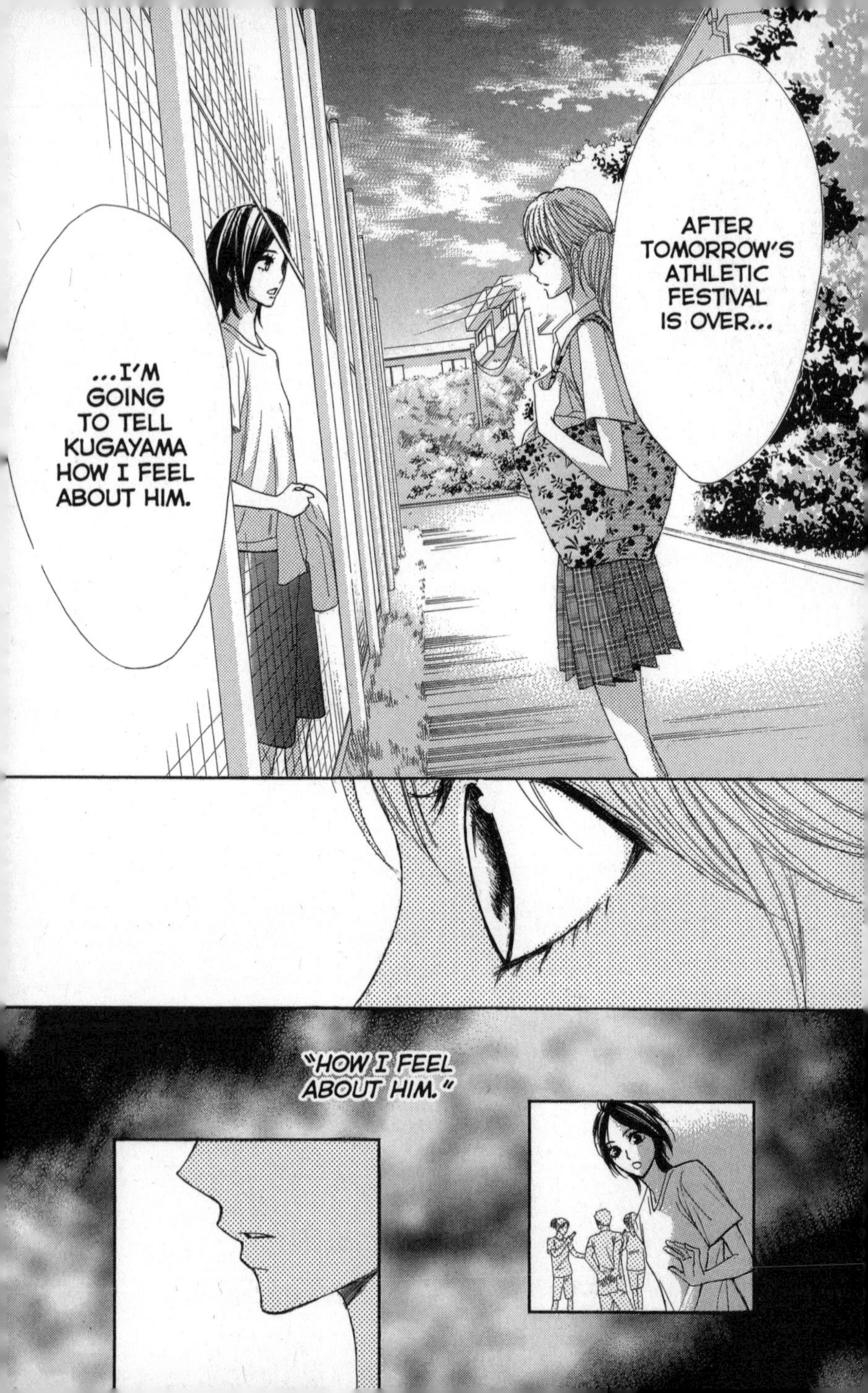
AFTER TOMORROW'S ATHLETIC FESTIVAL IS OVER...
...I'M GOING TO TELL KUGAYAMA HOW I FEEL ABOUT HIM.
"HOW I FEEL ABOUT HIM."

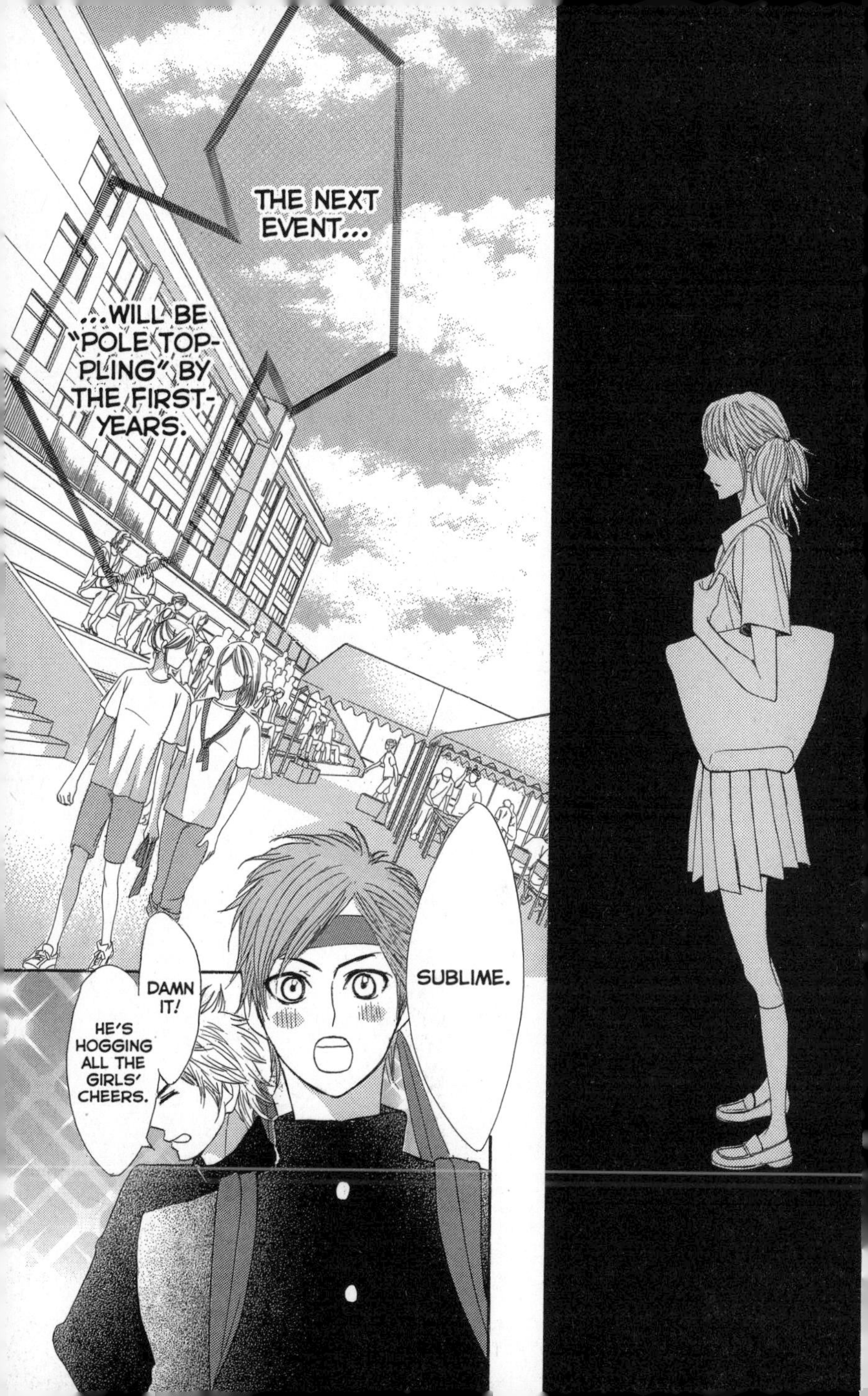
THE NEXT EVENT...
...WILL BE "POLE TOP-PLING" BY THE FIRST-YEARS.
SUBLIME.
DAMN IT!
HE'S HOGGING ALL THE GIRLS' CHEERS.

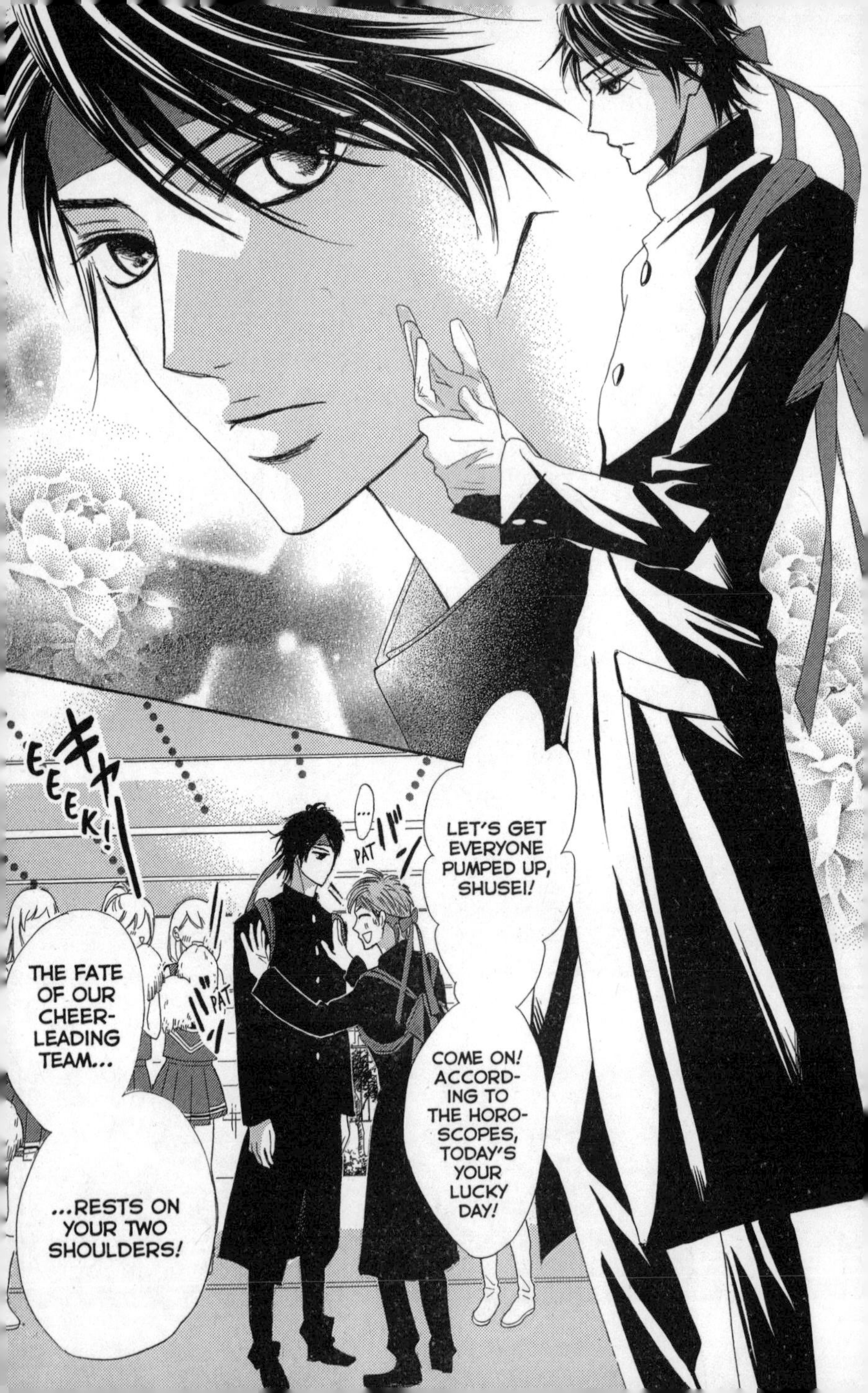
LET'S GET EVERYONE PUMPED UP, SHUSEI!
PAT
...
キャー
EEEEK!
COME ON! ACCORDING TO THE HOROSCOPES, TODAY'S YOUR LUCKY DAY!
PAT
THE FATE OF OUR CHEERLEADING TEAM...
...RESTS ON YOUR TWO SHOULDERS!

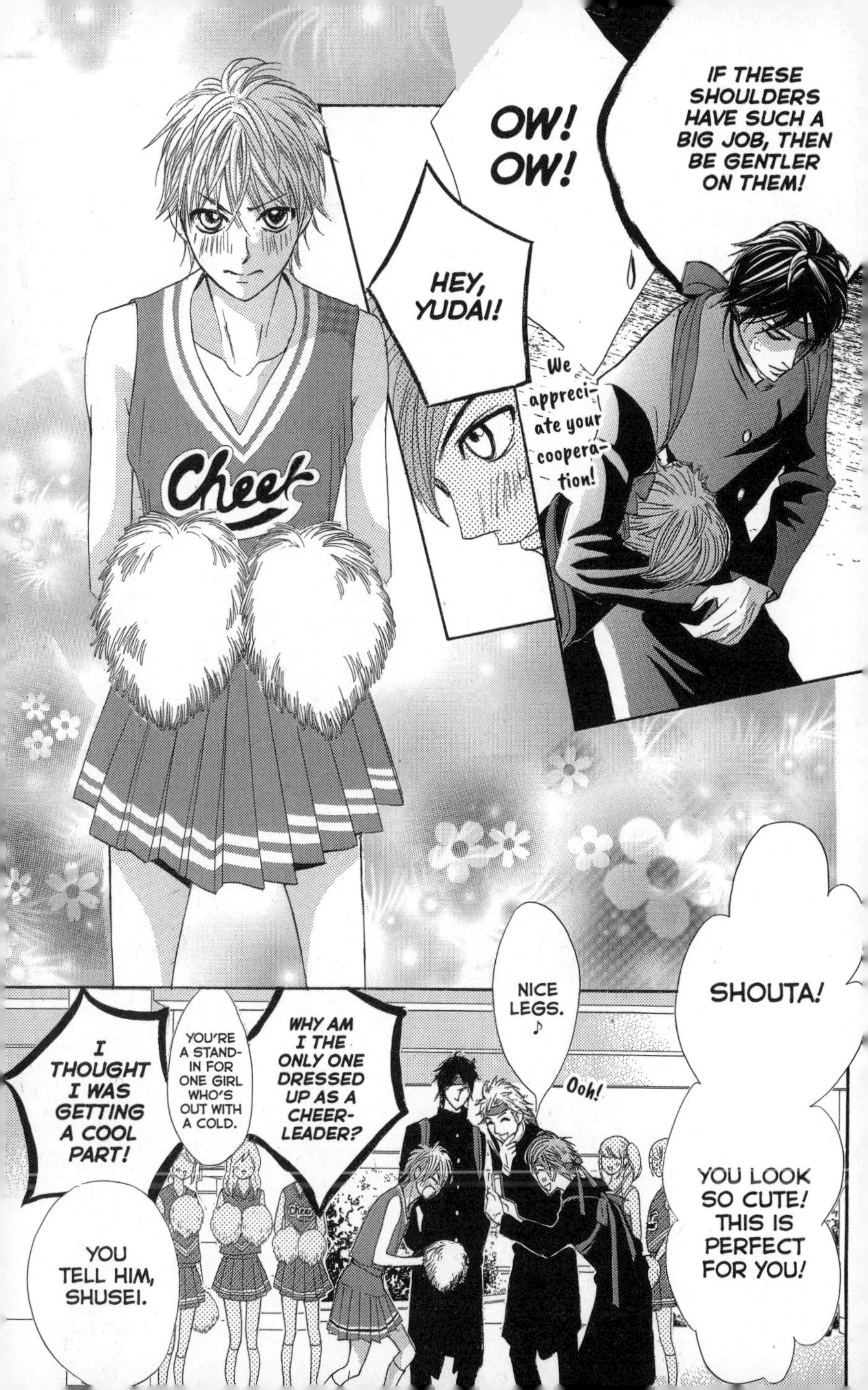
IF THESE SHOULDERS HAVE SUCH A BIG JOB, THEN BE GENTLER ON THEM!
OW! OW!
We appreciate your cooperation!
HEY, YUDAI!
SHOUTA!
YOU LOOK SO CUTE! THIS IS PERFECT FOR YOU!
NICE LEGS. ♪
Ooh!
WHY AM I THE ONLY ONE DRESSED UP AS A CHEER-LEADER?
YOU'RE A STAND-IN FOR ONE GIRL WHO'S OUT WITH A COLD.
I THOUGHT I WAS GETTING A COOL PART!
YOU TELL HIM, SHUSEI.

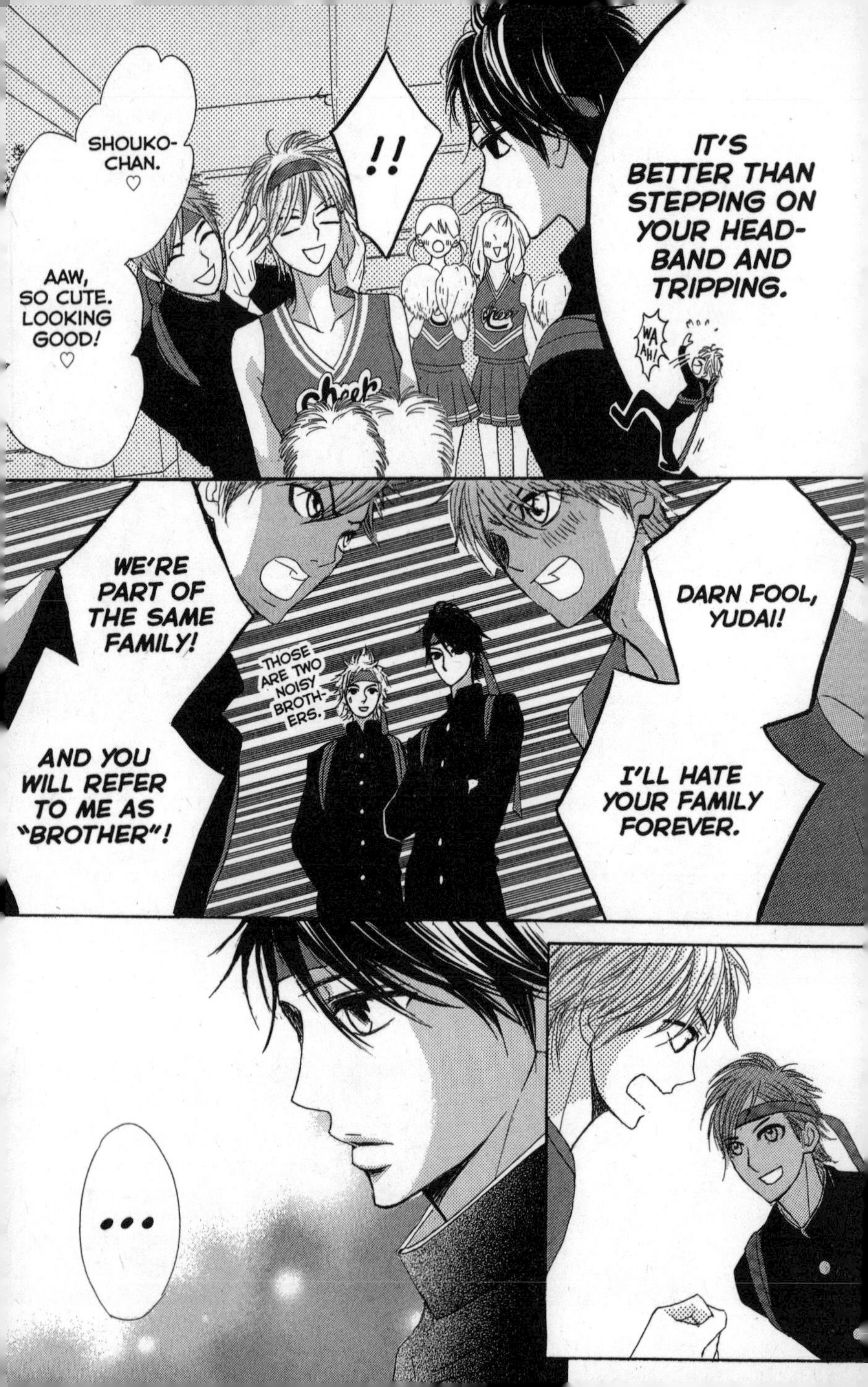
IT'S BETTER THAN STEPPING ON YOUR HEAD-BAND AND TRIPPING.
WA AH!
!!
SHOUKO-CHAN. ♡
AAW, SO CUTE. LOOKING GOOD! ♡
DARN FOOL, YUDAI!
WE'RE PART OF THE SAME FAMILY!
I'LL HATE YOUR FAMILY FOREVER.
AND YOU WILL REFER TO ME AS "BROTHER"!
THOSE ARE TWO NOISY BROTH-ERS.
...

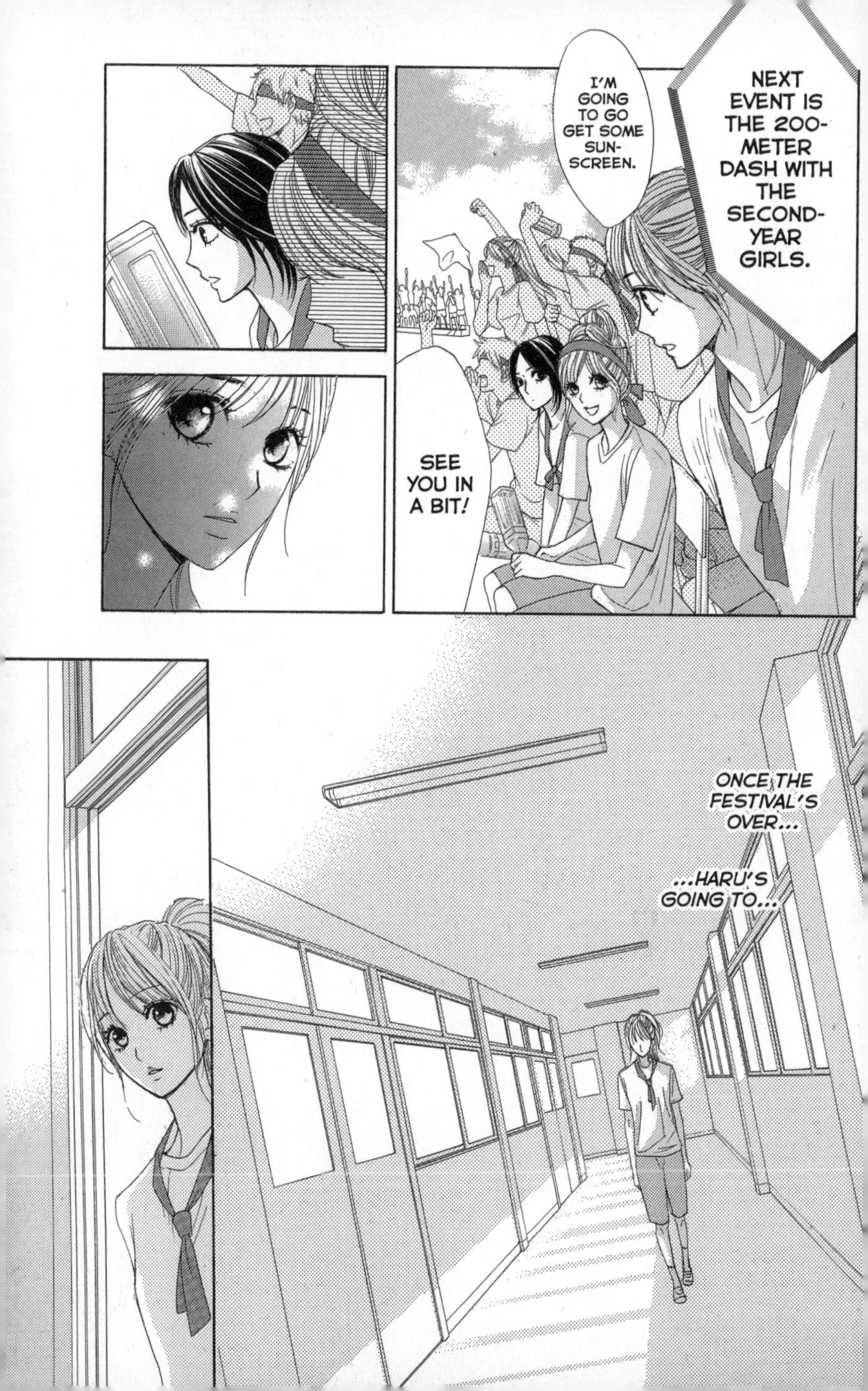
NEXT EVENT IS THE 200-METER DASH WITH THE SECOND-YEAR GIRLS.
I'M GOING TO GO GET SOME SUN-SCREEN.
SEE YOU IN A BIT!
ONCE THE FESTIVAL'S OVER...
...HARU'S GOING TO...

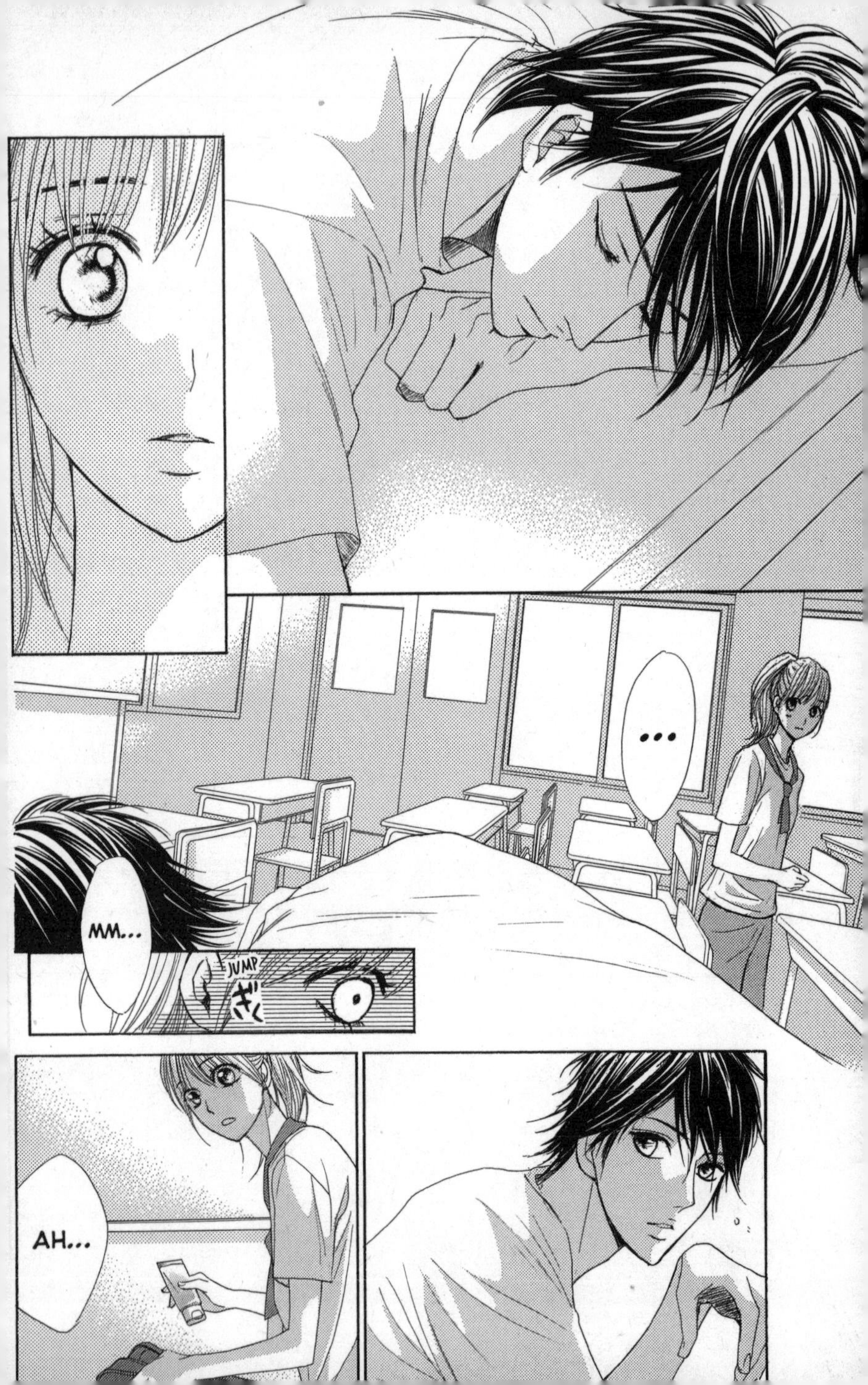
...
MM...
JUMP
ぎく
AH...

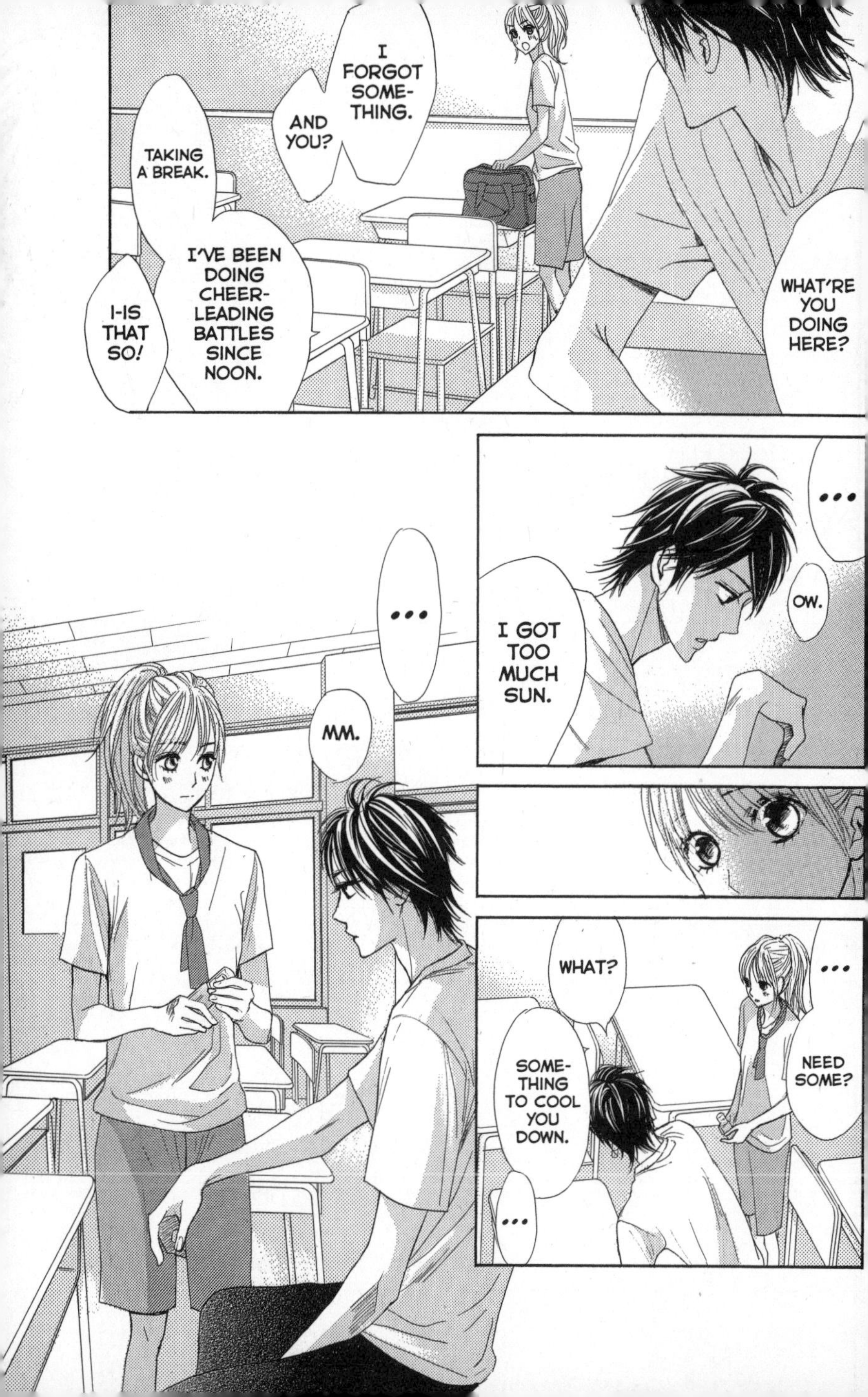
WHAT'RE YOU DOING HERE?
I FORGOT SOME-THING.
AND YOU?
TAKING A BREAK.
I'VE BEEN DOING CHEER-LEADING BATTLES SINCE NOON.
I-IS THAT SO!
...
OW.
I GOT TOO MUCH SUN.
...
NEED SOME?
WHAT?
SOME-THING TO COOL YOU DOWN.
...
...
MM.

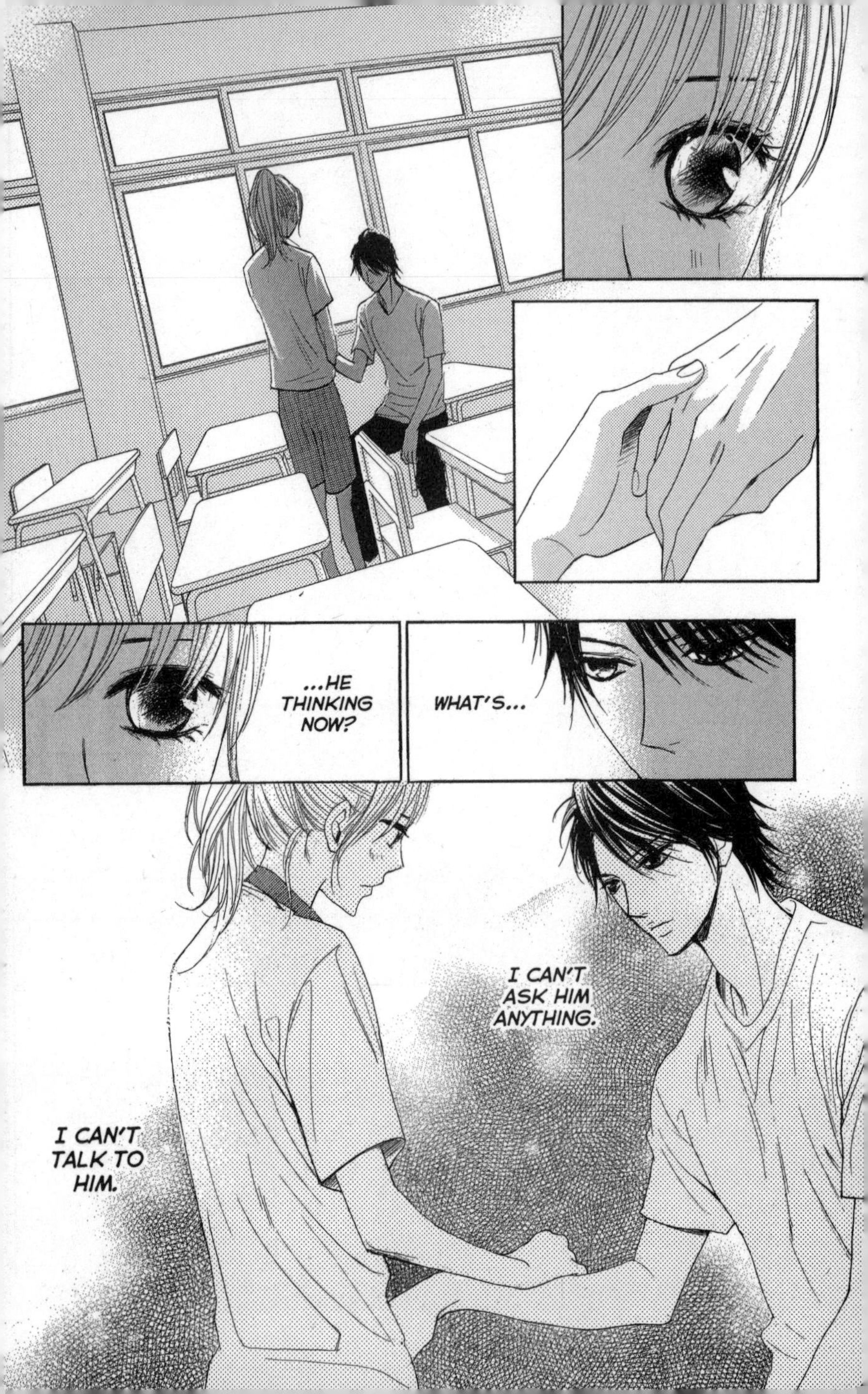
WHAT'S...
...HE THINKING NOW?
I CAN'T ASK HIM ANYTHING.
I CAN'T TALK TO HIM.

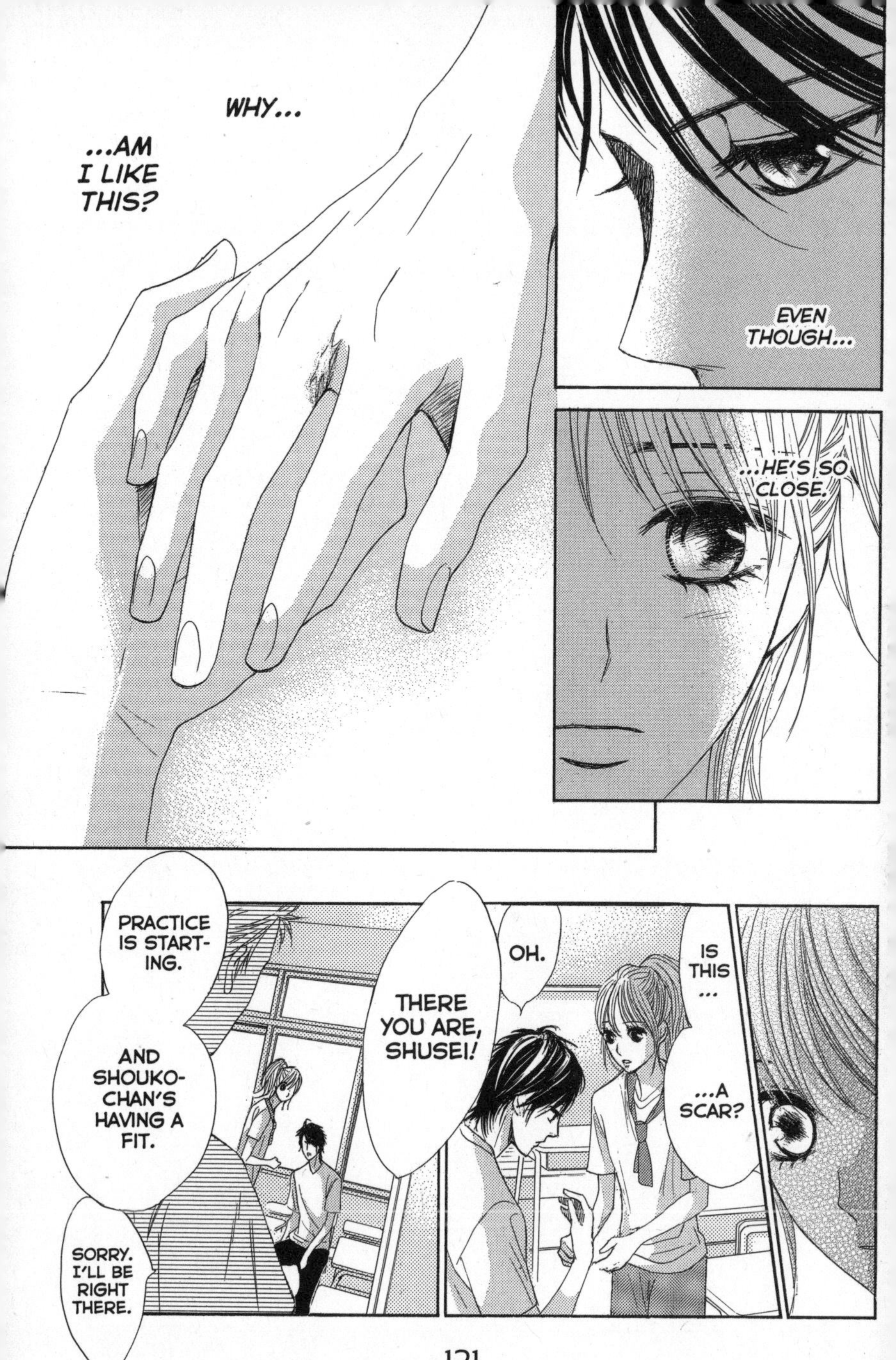
EVEN THOUGH...
...HE'S SO CLOSE.
WHY...
...AM I LIKE THIS?
IS THIS...
...A SCAR?
OH.
THERE YOU ARE, SHUSEI!
PRACTICE IS START-ING.
AND SHOUKO-CHAN'S HAVING A FIT.
SORRY. I'LL BE RIGHT THERE.

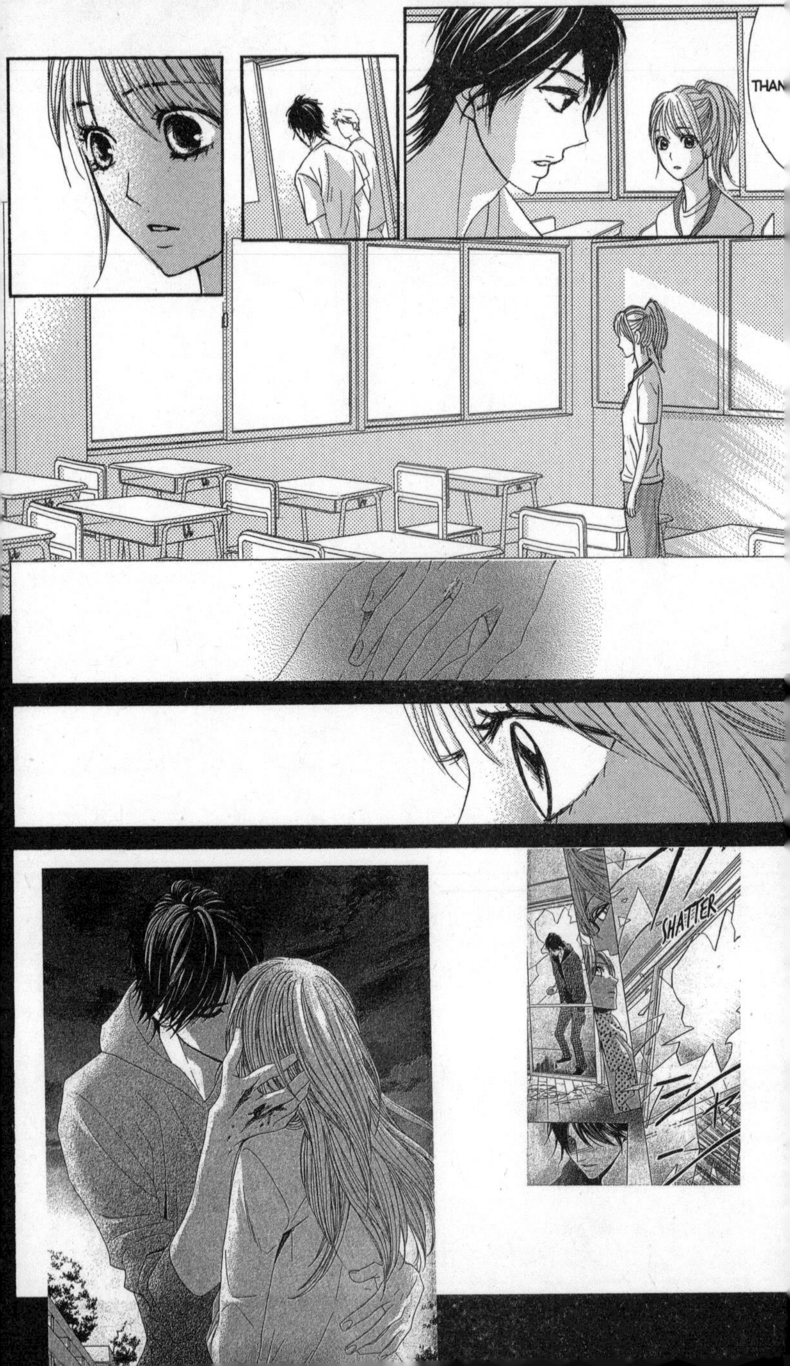
THAN
SHATTER

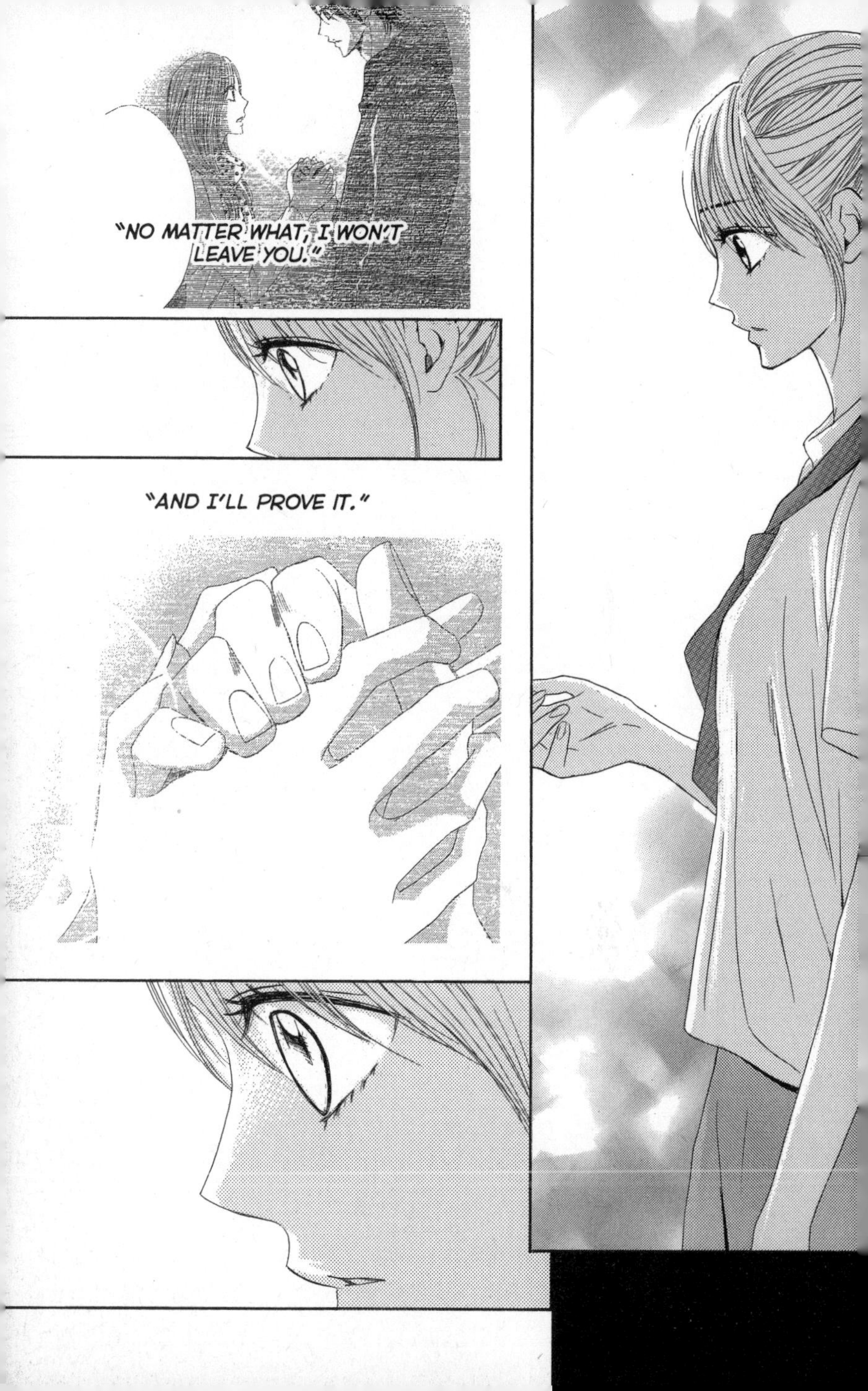
"NO MATTER WHAT, I WON'T LEAVE YOU."
"AND I'LL PROVE IT."

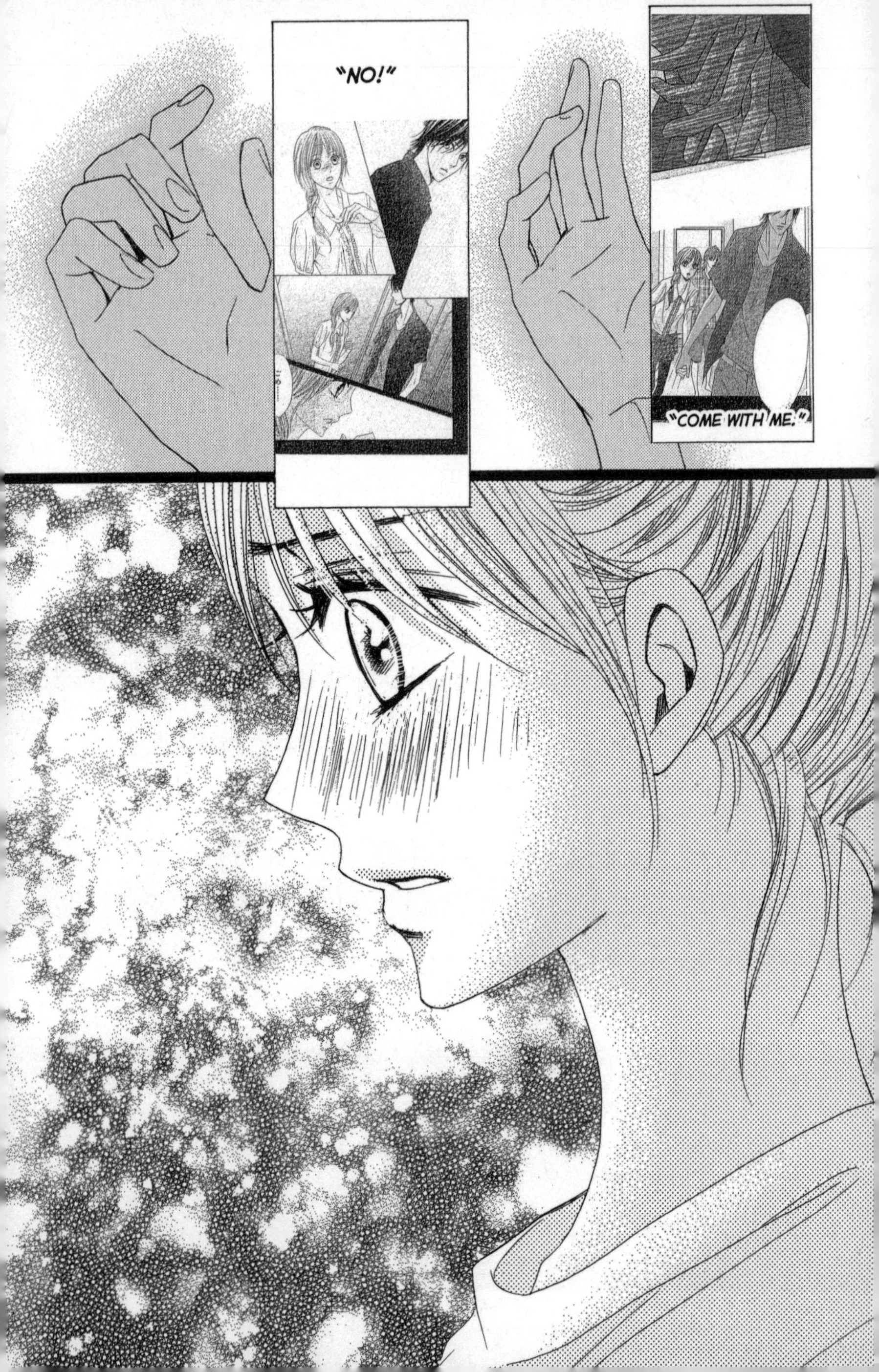
"COME WITH ME."
"NO!"

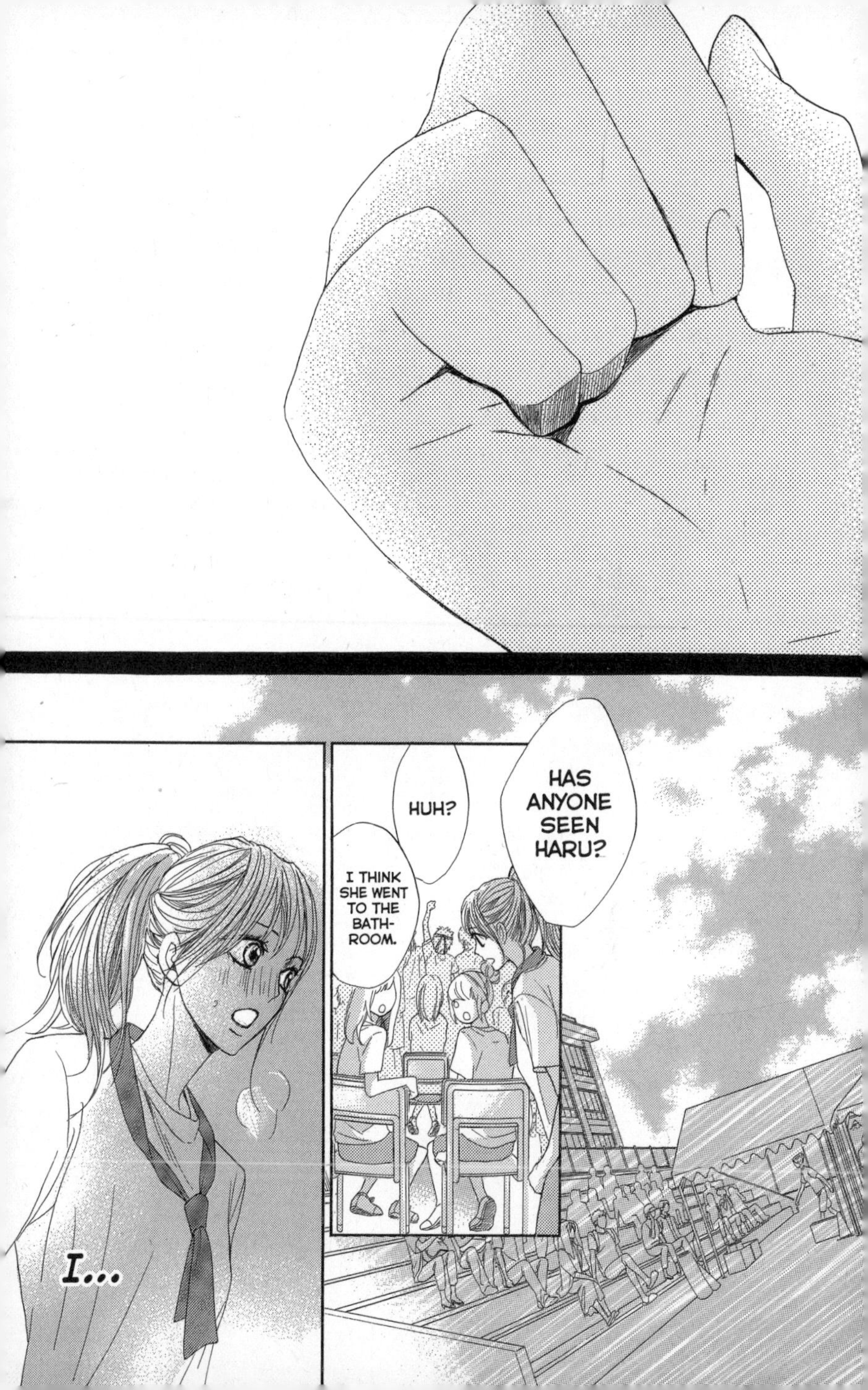
HAS ANYONE SEEN HARU?
HUH?
I THINK SHE WENT TO THE BATH-ROOM.
I...

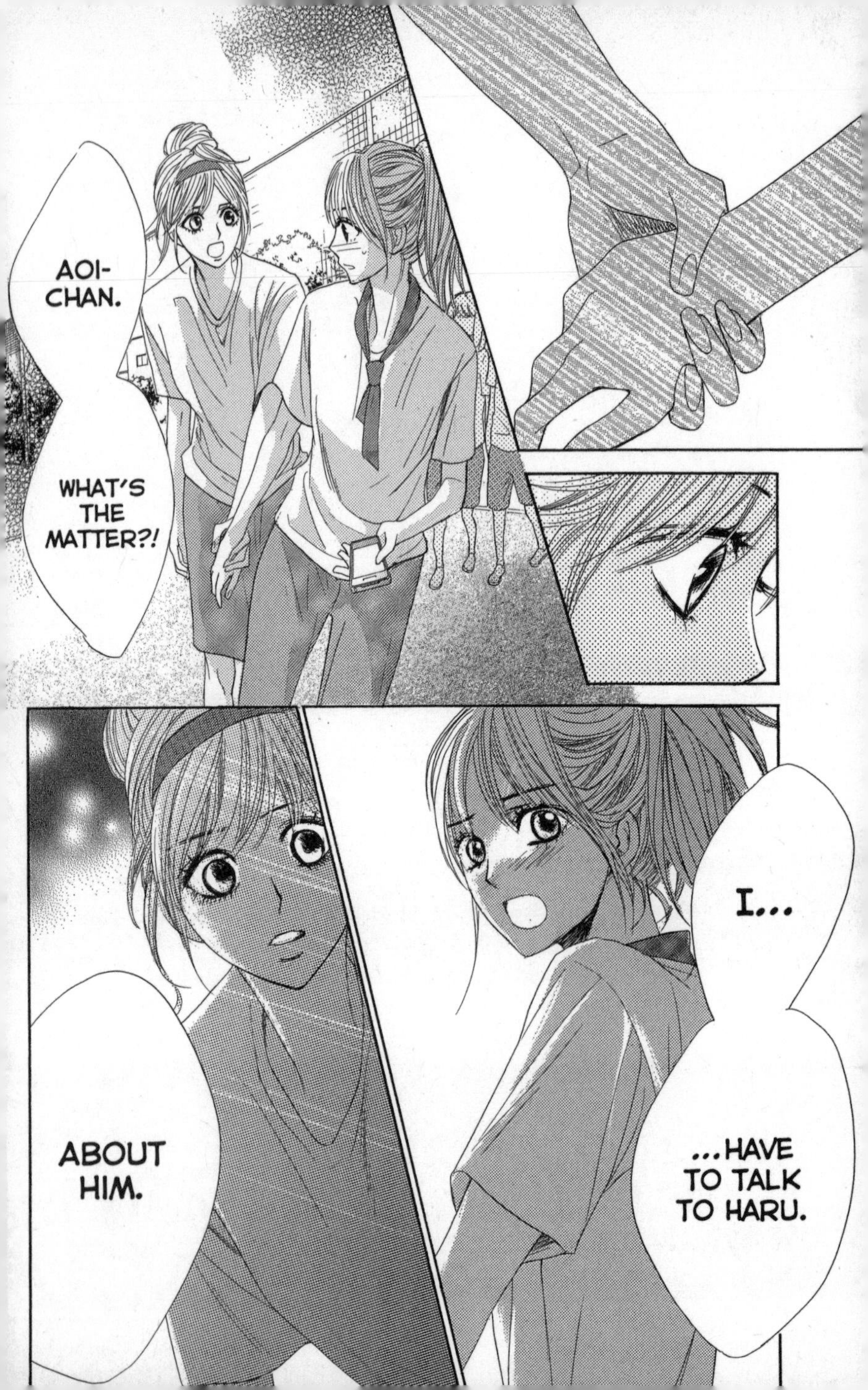
AOI-CHAN.
WHAT'S THE MATTER?!
I...
...HAVE TO TALK TO HARU.
ABOUT HIM.

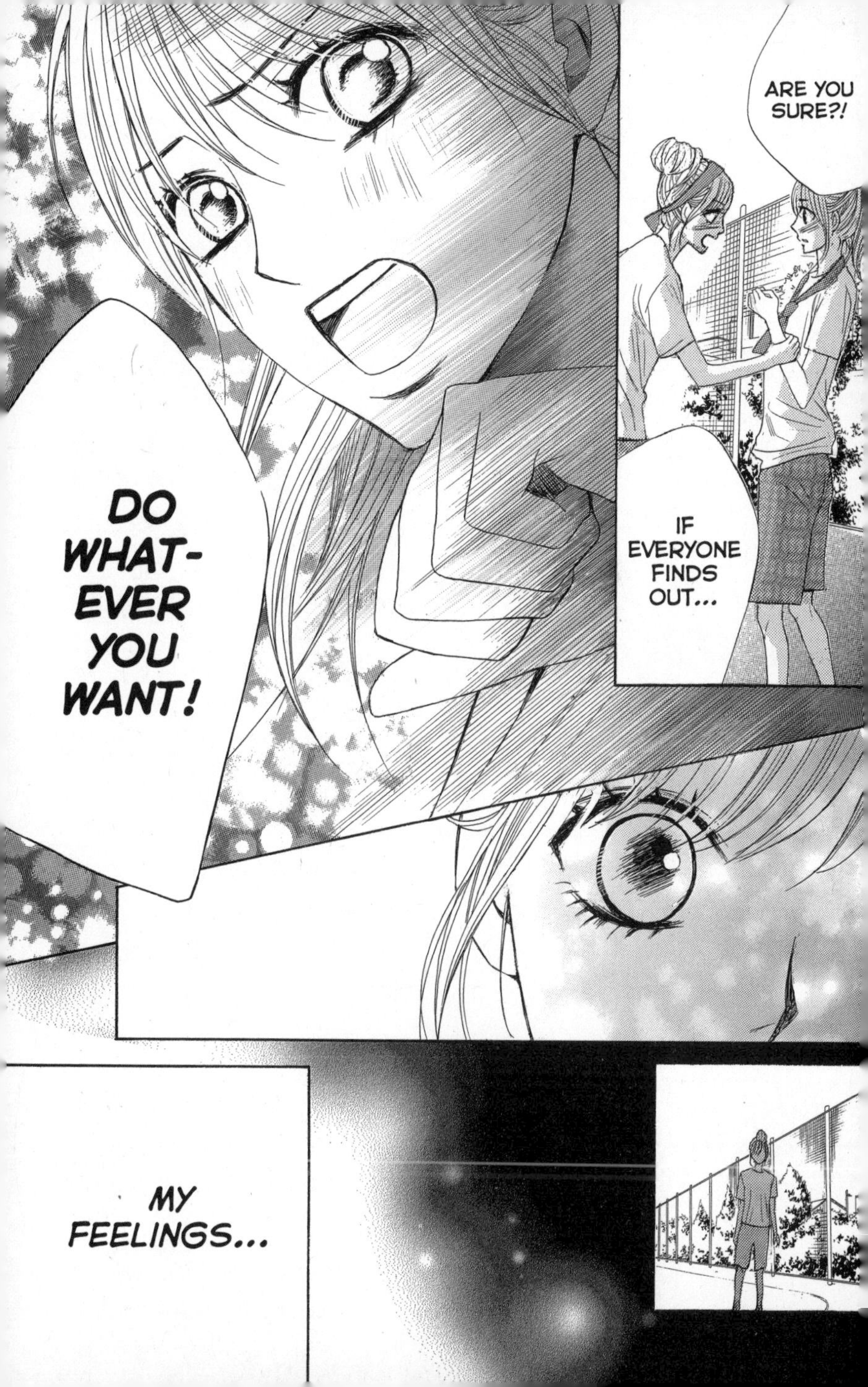
ARE YOU SURE?!
IF EVERYONE FINDS OUT...
DO WHAT-EVER YOU WANT!
MY FEELINGS...

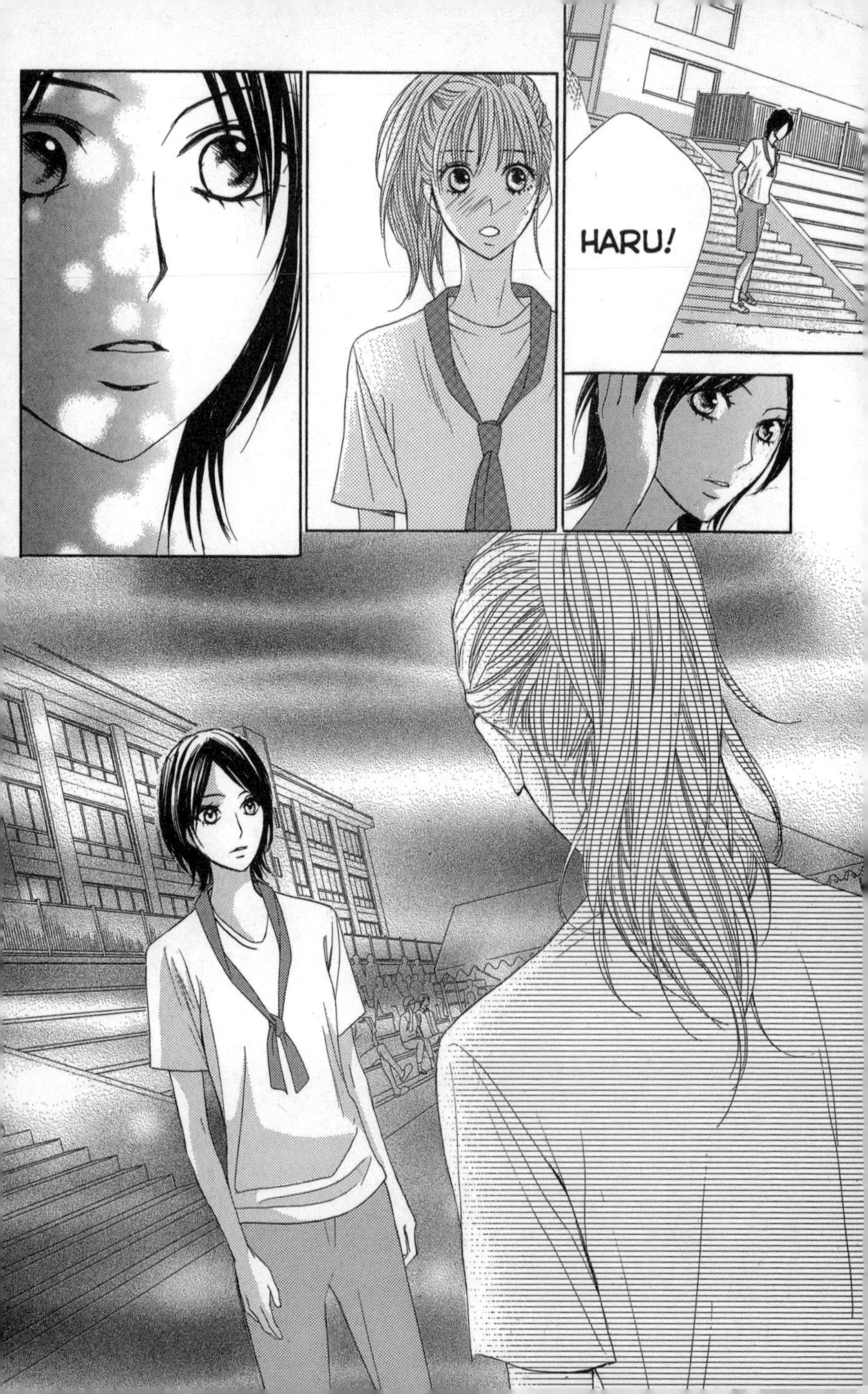
HARU!

L♥DK

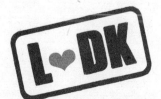

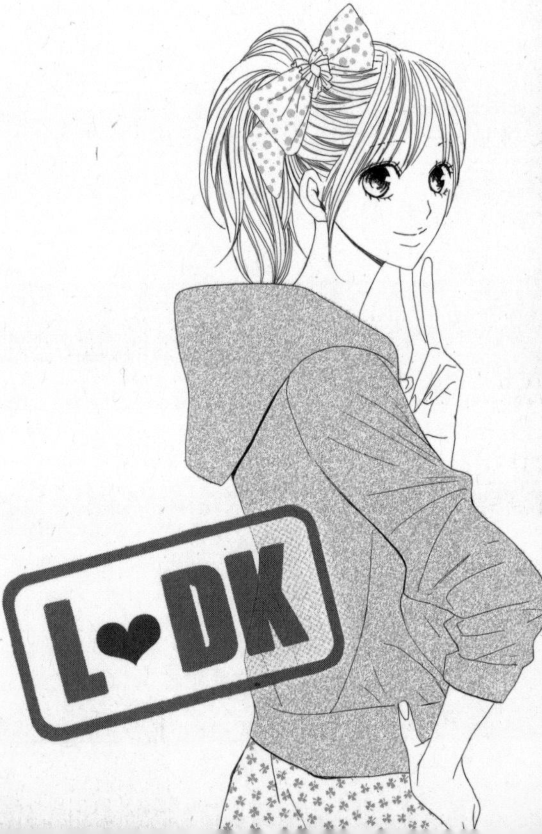
L♥DK

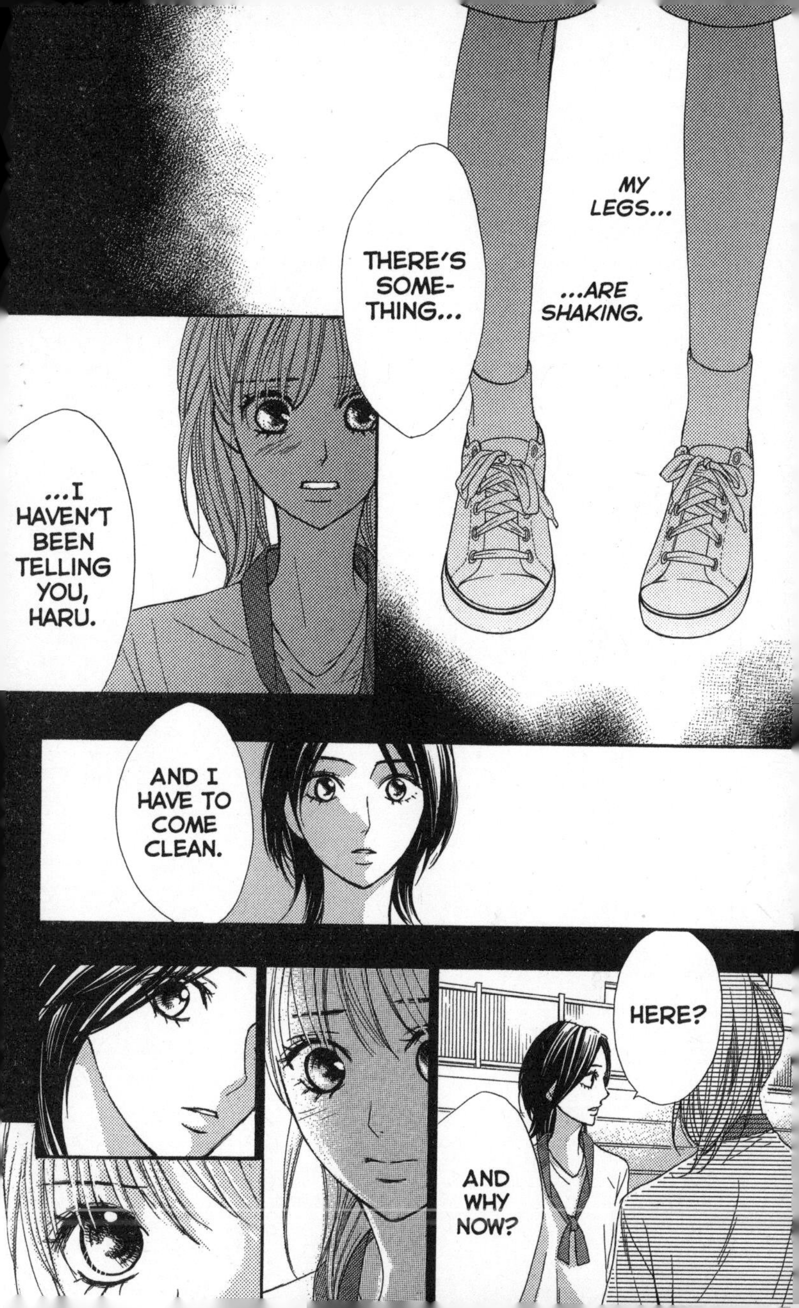
MY LEGS...
...ARE SHAKING.
THERE'S SOME-THING...
...I HAVEN'T BEEN TELLING YOU, HARU.
AND I HAVE TO COME CLEAN.
HERE?
AND WHY NOW?

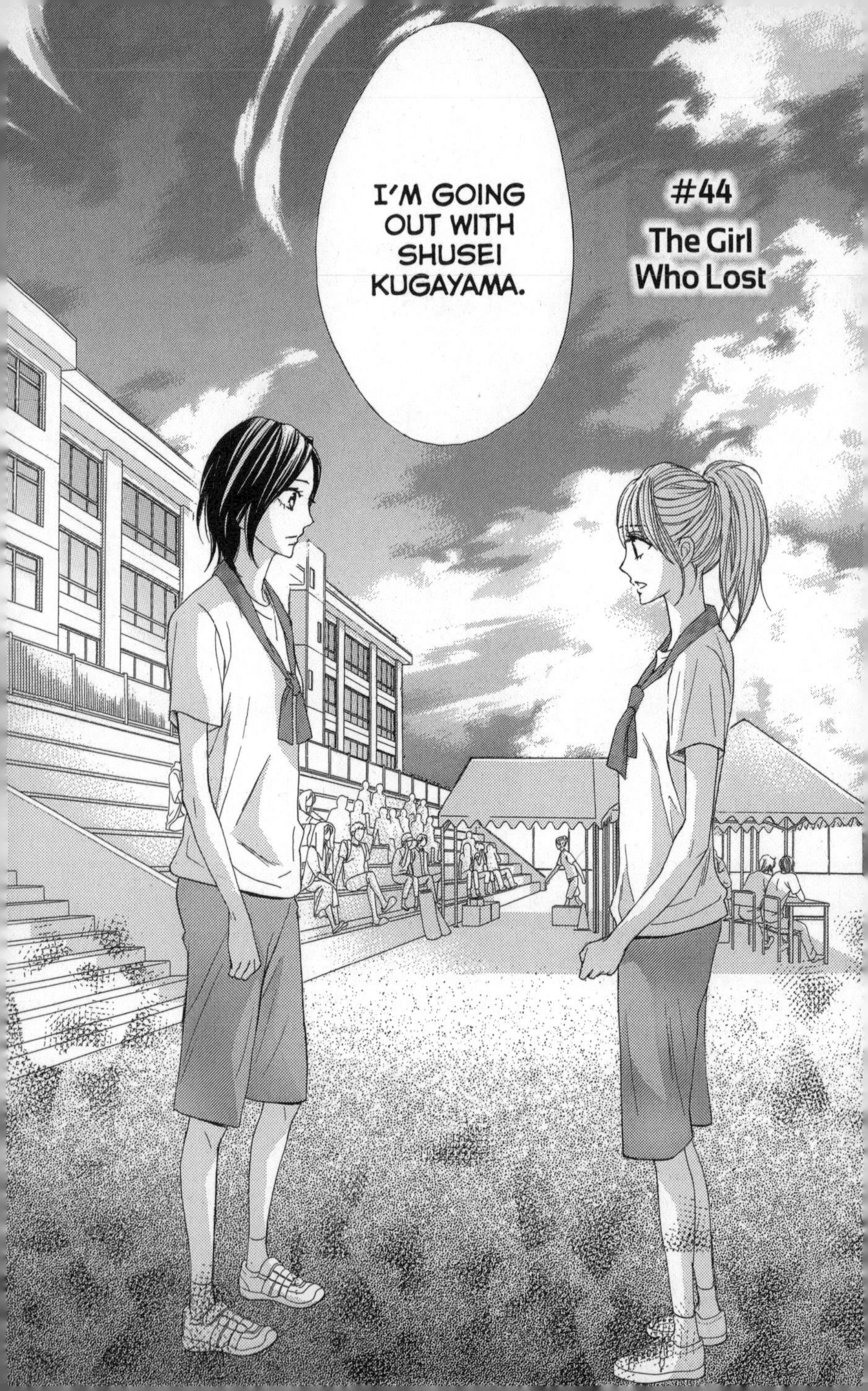
I'M GOING OUT WITH SHUSEI KUGAYAMA.
#44
The Girl Who Lost

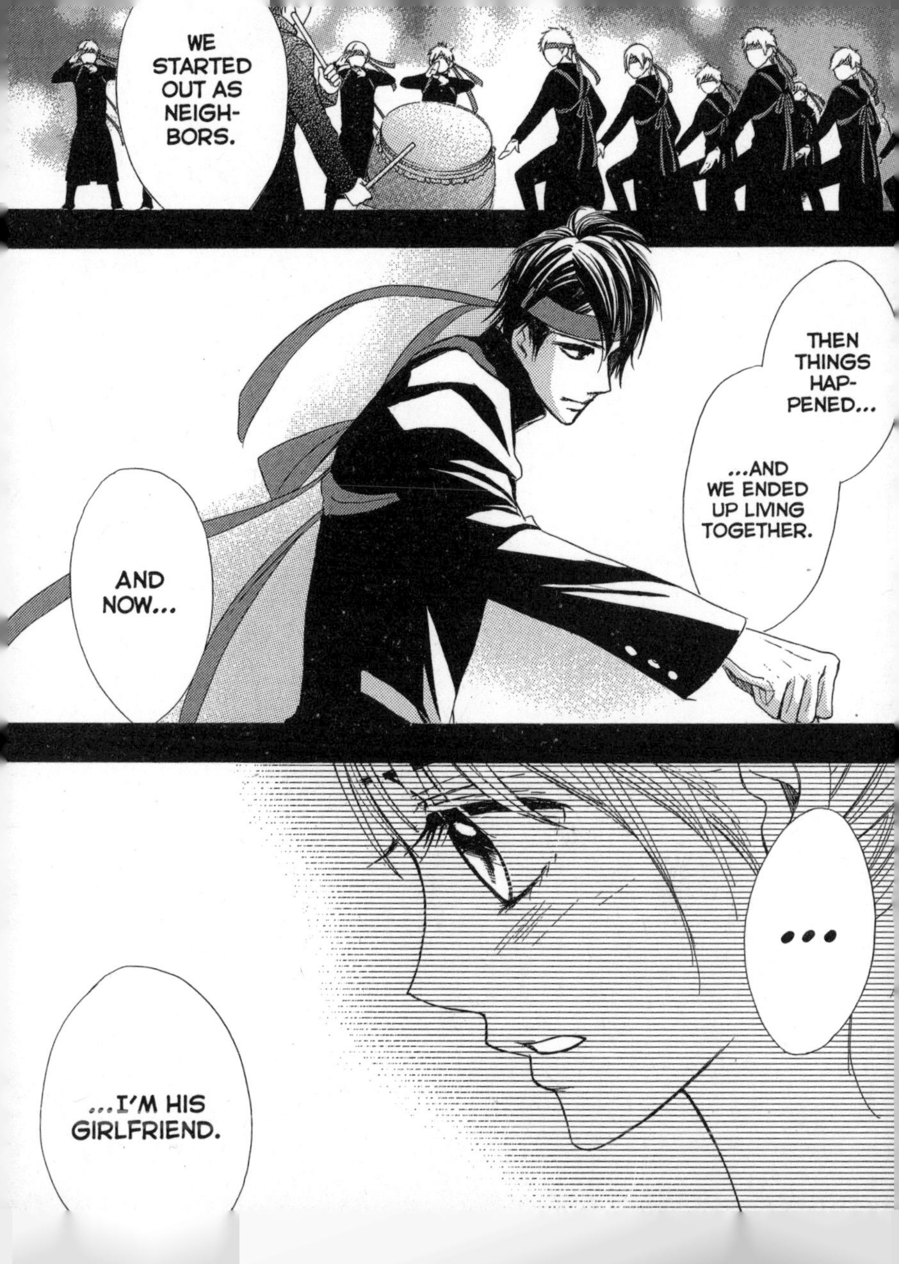
WE STARTED OUT AS NEIGHBORS.
THEN THINGS HAPPENED...
...AND WE ENDED UP LIVING TOGETHER.
AND NOW...
...
...I'M HIS GIRLFRIEND.

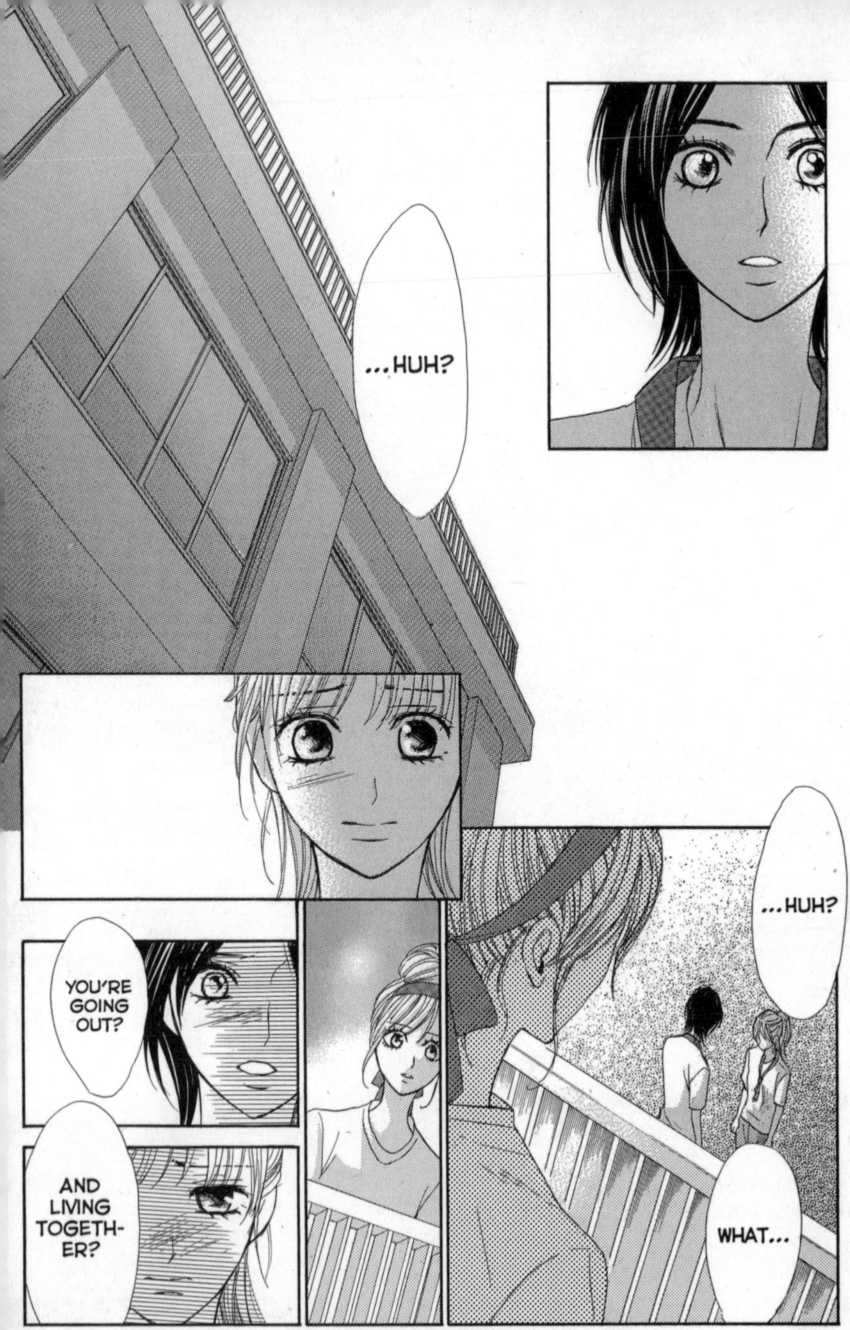
...HUH?
...HUH?
WHAT...
YOU'RE GOING OUT?
AND LIVING TOGETHER?

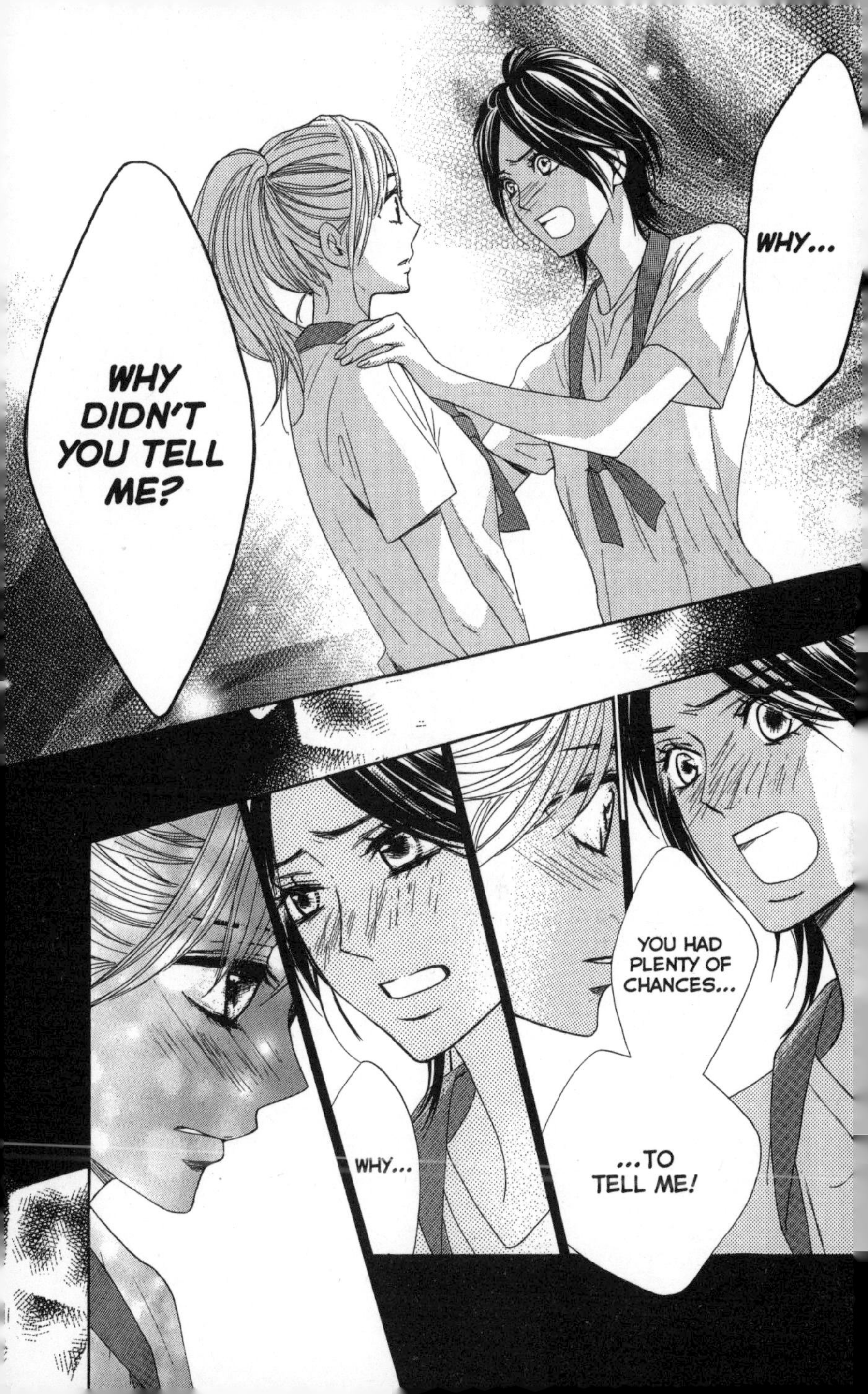
WHY...
WHY DIDN'T YOU TELL ME?
YOU HAD PLENTY OF CHANCES...
...TO TELL ME!
WHY...

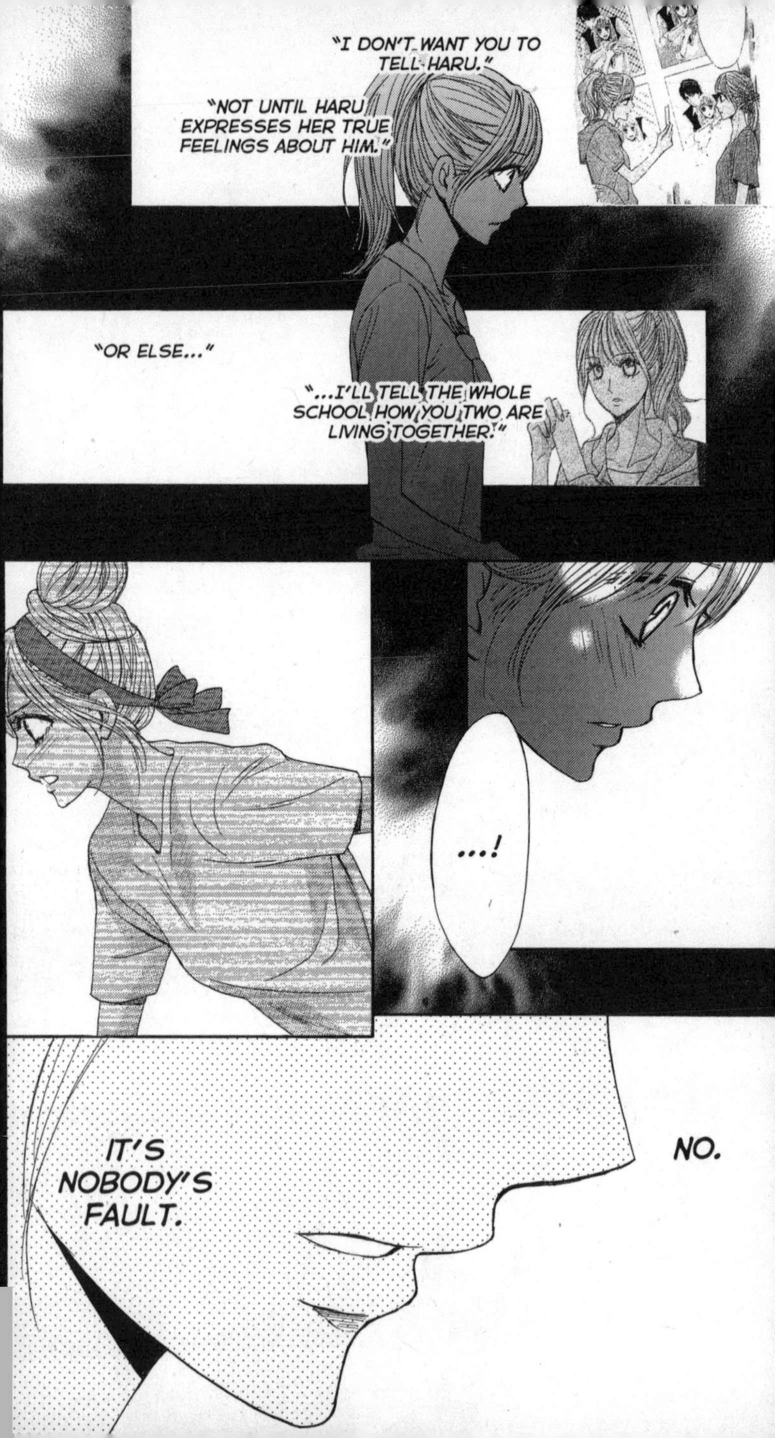
"I DON'T WANT YOU TO TELL HARU."
"NOT UNTIL HARU EXPRESSES HER TRUE FEELINGS ABOUT HIM."
"OR ELSE..."
"...I'LL TELL THE WHOLE SCHOOL HOW YOU TWO ARE LIVING TOGETHER."
...!
NO.
IT'S NOBODY'S FAULT.

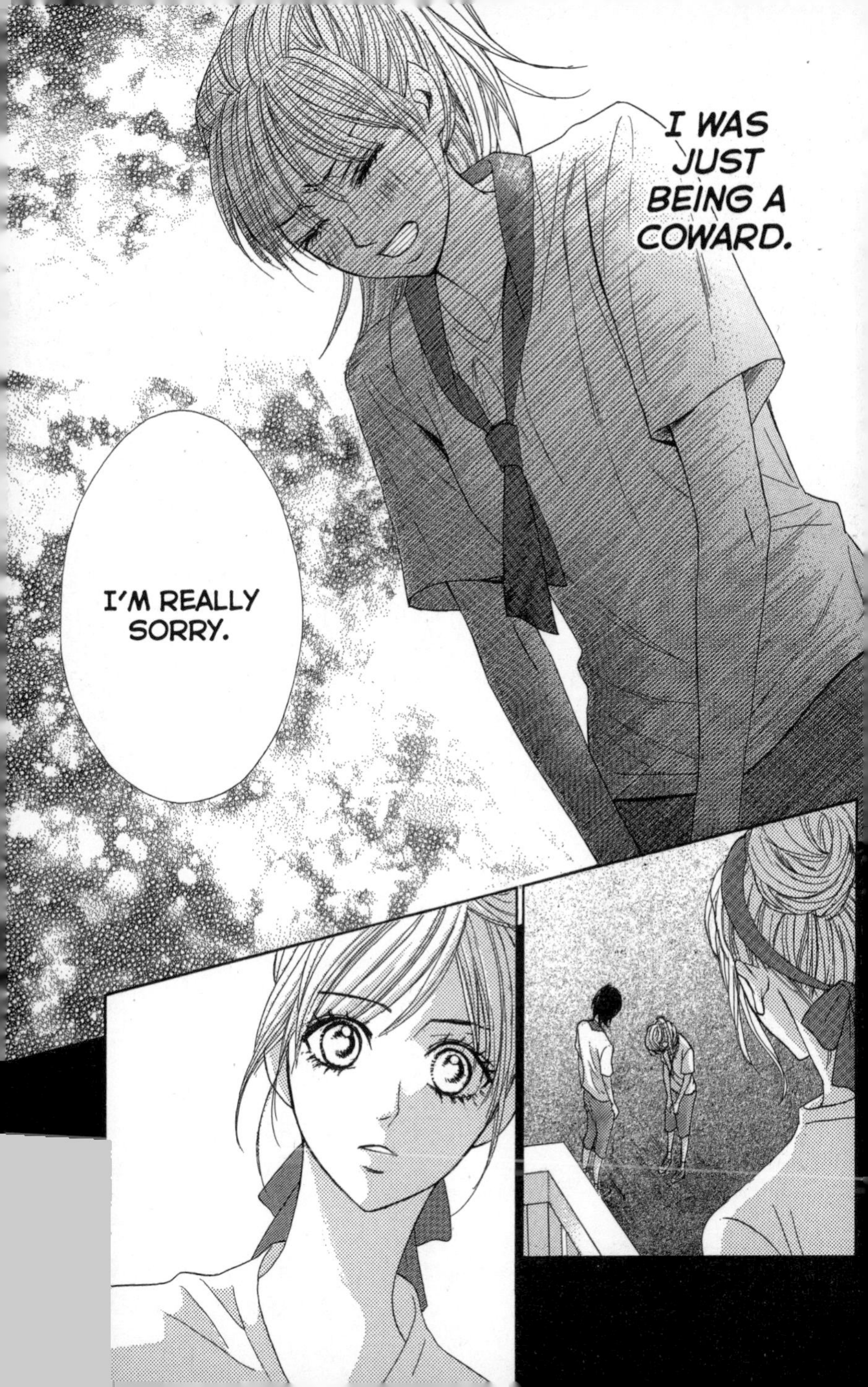
I WAS JUST BEING A COWARD.
I'M REALLY SORRY.

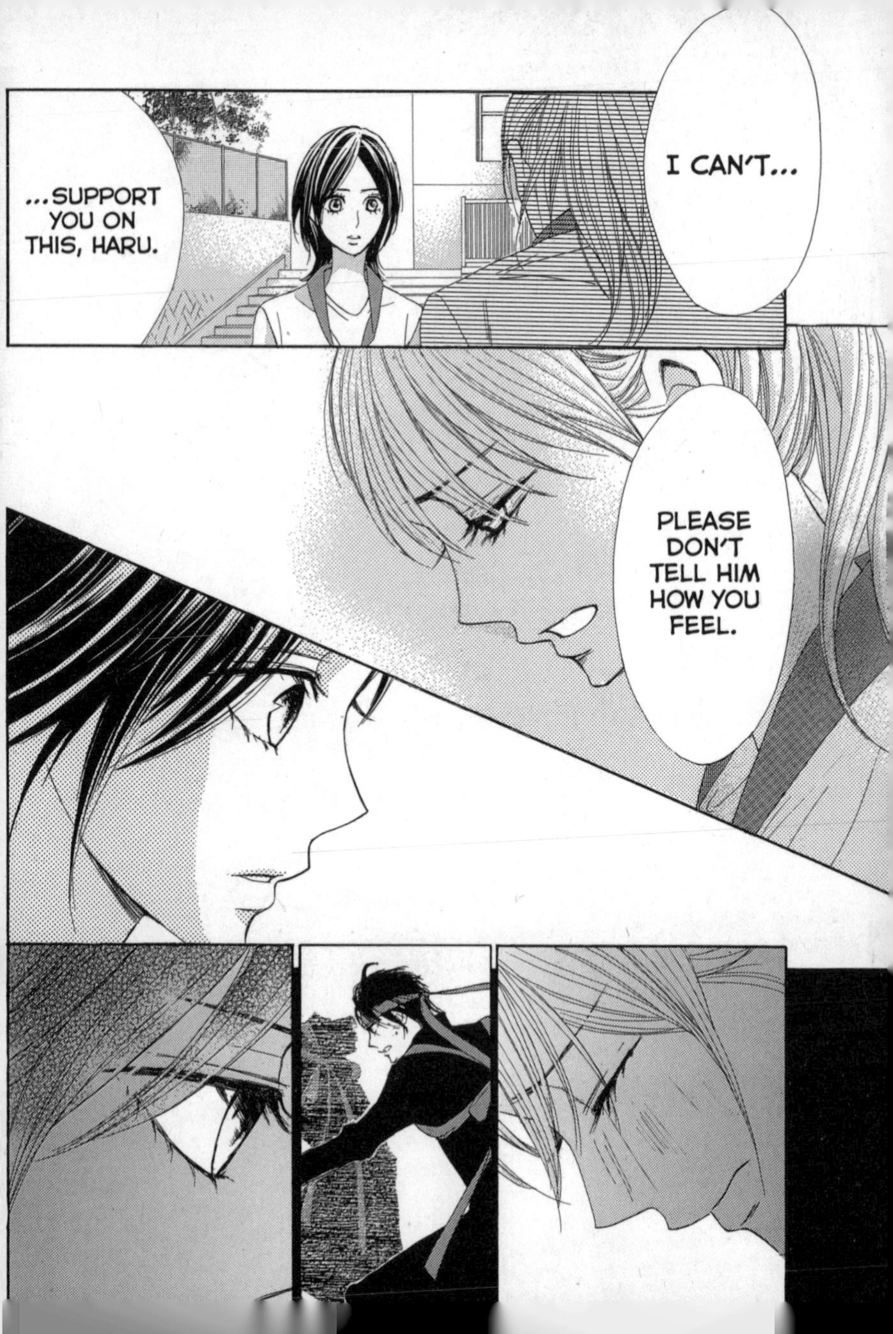
I CAN'T...
...SUPPORT YOU ON THIS, HARU.
PLEASE DON'T TELL HIM HOW YOU FEEL.

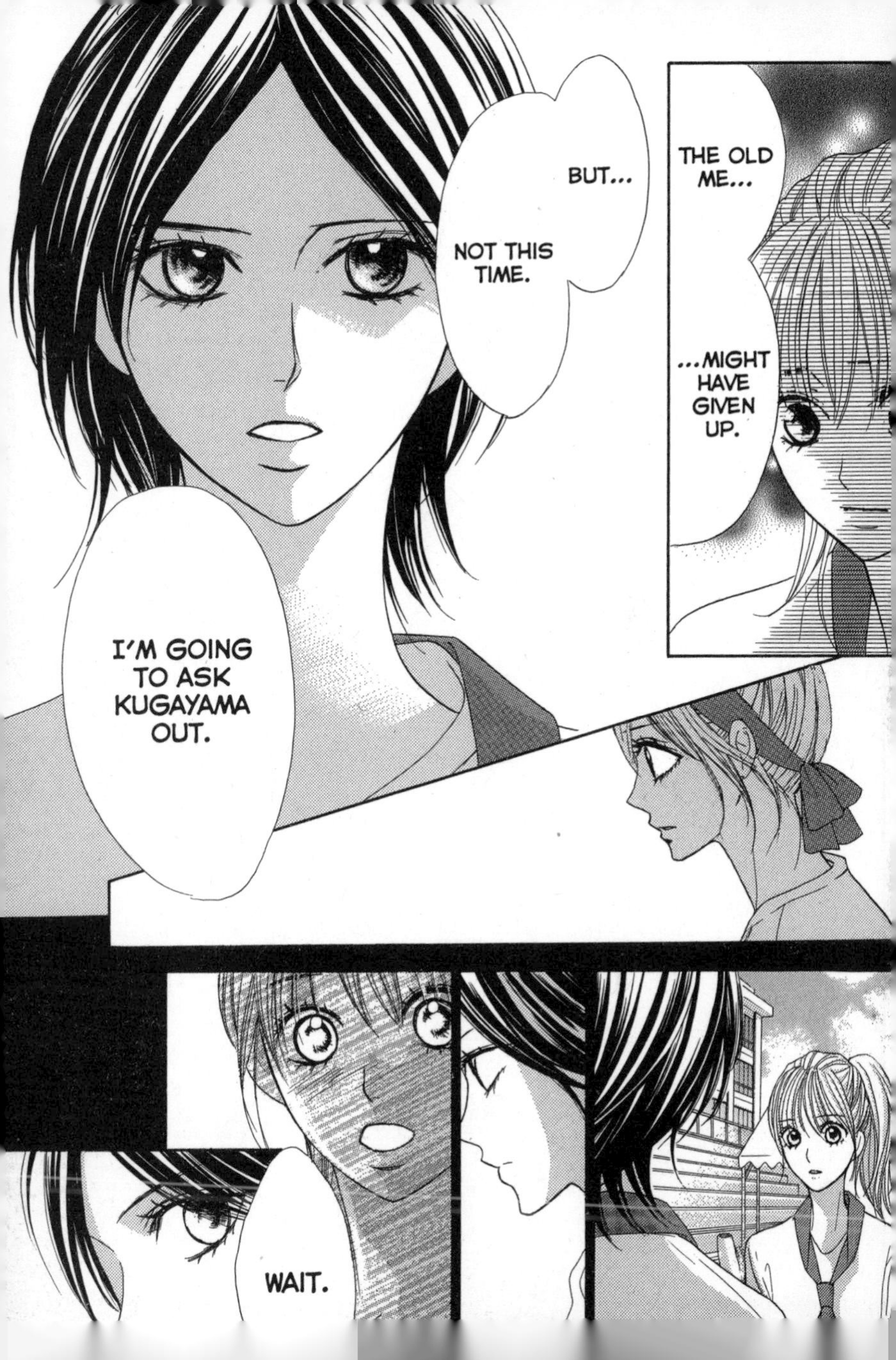
THE OLD ME...
...MIGHT HAVE GIVEN UP.
BUT...
NOT THIS TIME.
I'M GOING TO ASK KUGAYAMA OUT.
WAIT.

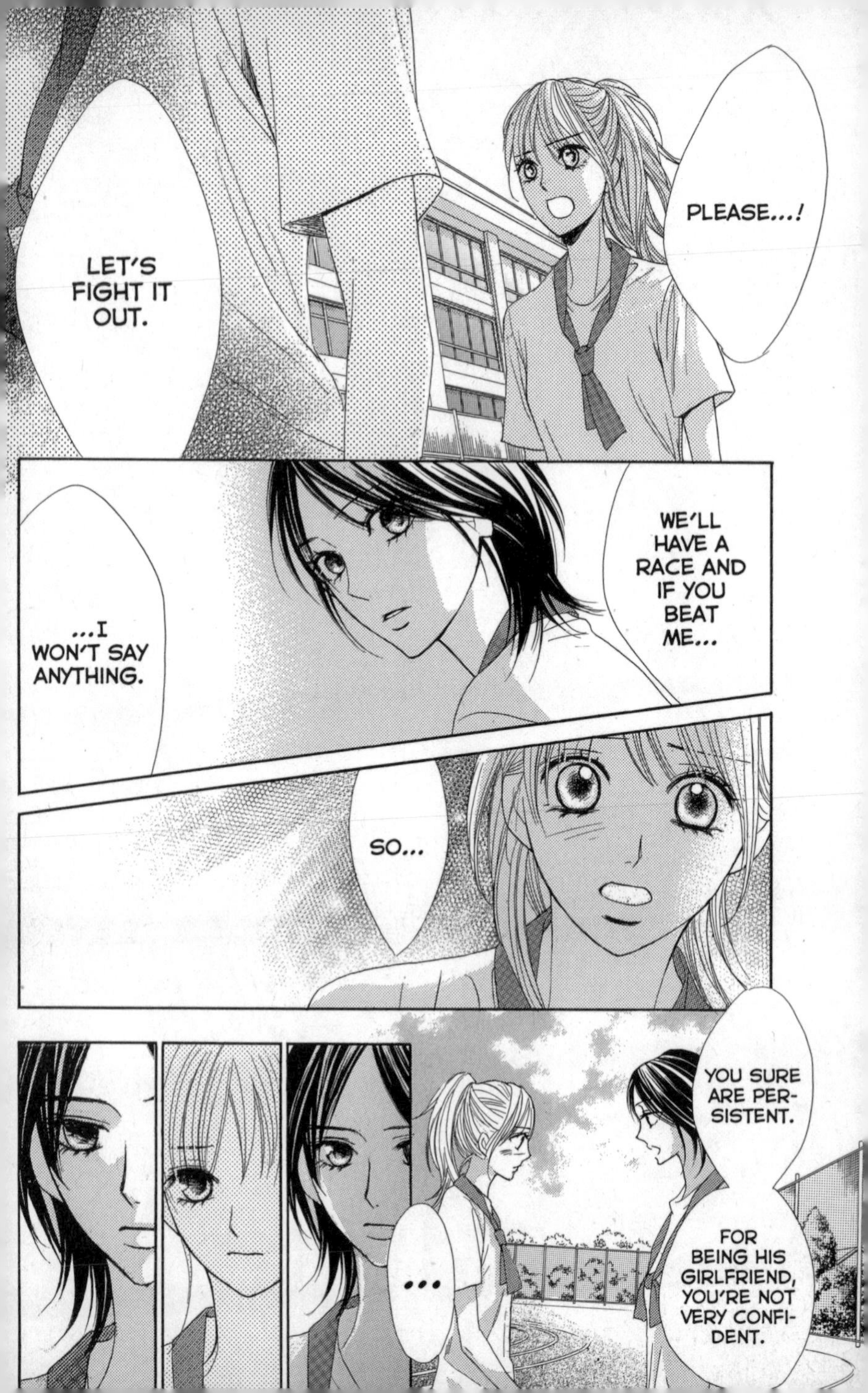
PLEASE...!
LET'S FIGHT IT OUT.
WE'LL HAVE A RACE AND IF YOU BEAT ME...
...I WON'T SAY ANYTHING.
SO...
YOU SURE ARE PERSISTENT.
FOR BEING HIS GIRLFRIEND, YOU'RE NOT VERY CONFIDENT.
...

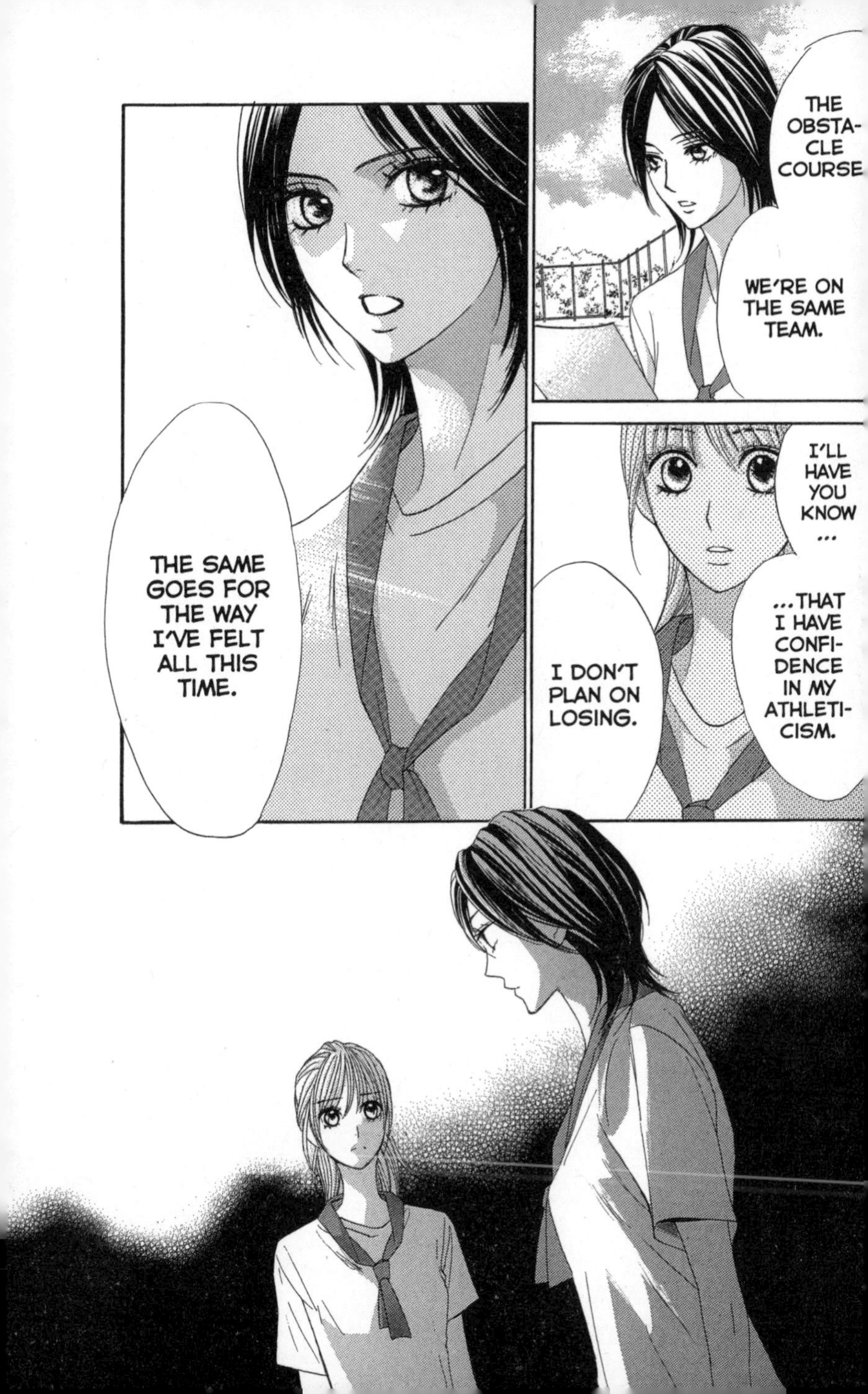
THE OBSTACLE COURSE
WE'RE ON THE SAME TEAM.
I'LL HAVE YOU KNOW...
...THAT I HAVE CONFIDENCE IN MY ATHLETICISM.
I DON'T PLAN ON LOSING.
THE SAME GOES FOR THE WAY I'VE FELT ALL THIS TIME.

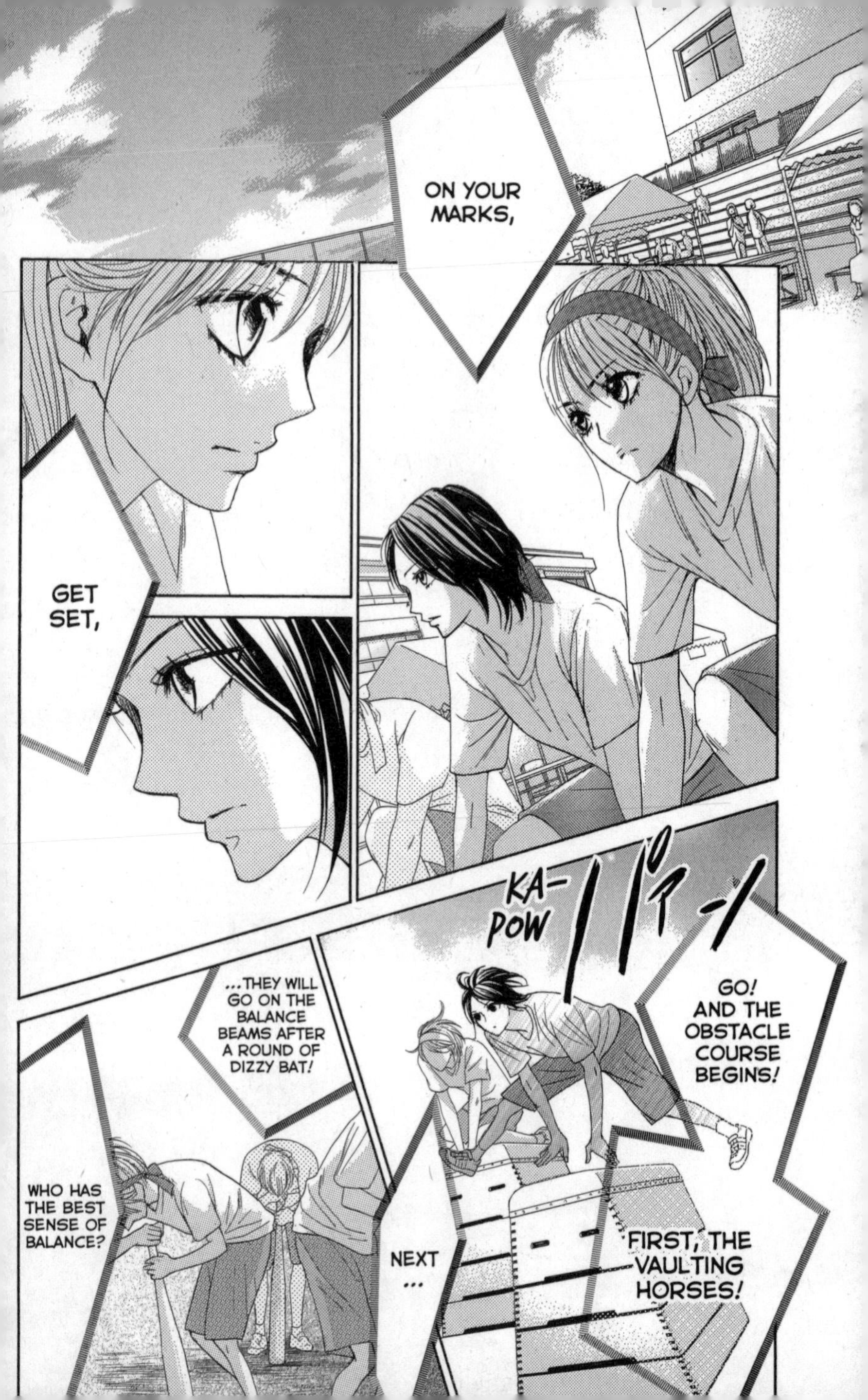
ON YOUR MARKS,
GET SET,
KA-POW
GO! AND THE OBSTACLE COURSE BEGINS!
FIRST, THE VAULTING HORSES!
NEXT ...
...THEY WILL GO ON THE BALANCE BEAMS AFTER A ROUND OF DIZZY BAT!
WHO HAS THE BEST SENSE OF BALANCE?

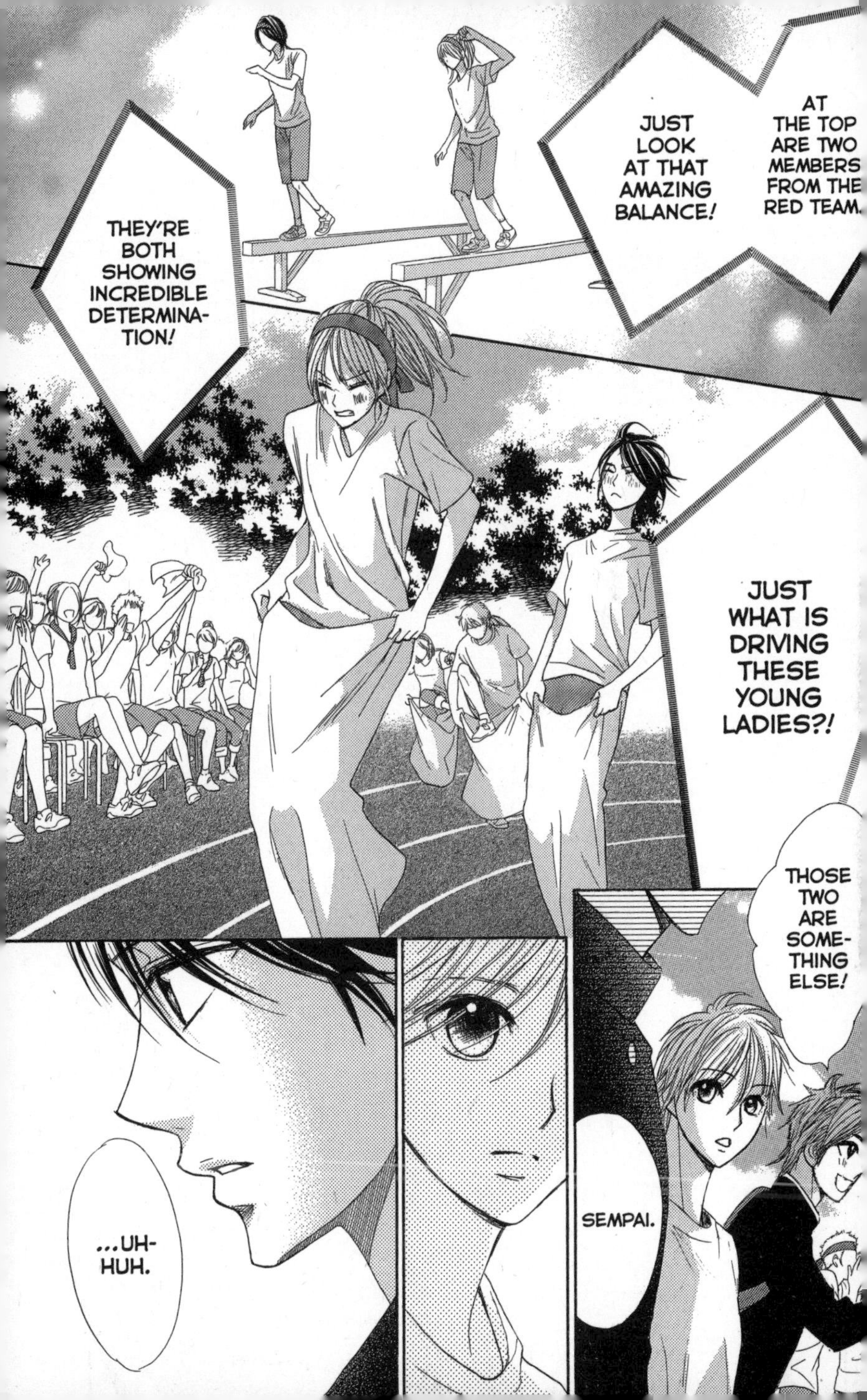
AT THE TOP ARE TWO MEMBERS FROM THE RED TEAM.
JUST LOOK AT THAT AMAZING BALANCE!
THEY'RE BOTH SHOWING INCREDIBLE DETERMINA-TION!
JUST WHAT IS DRIVING THESE YOUNG LADIES?!
THOSE TWO ARE SOME-THING ELSE!
SEMPAI.
...UH-HUH.

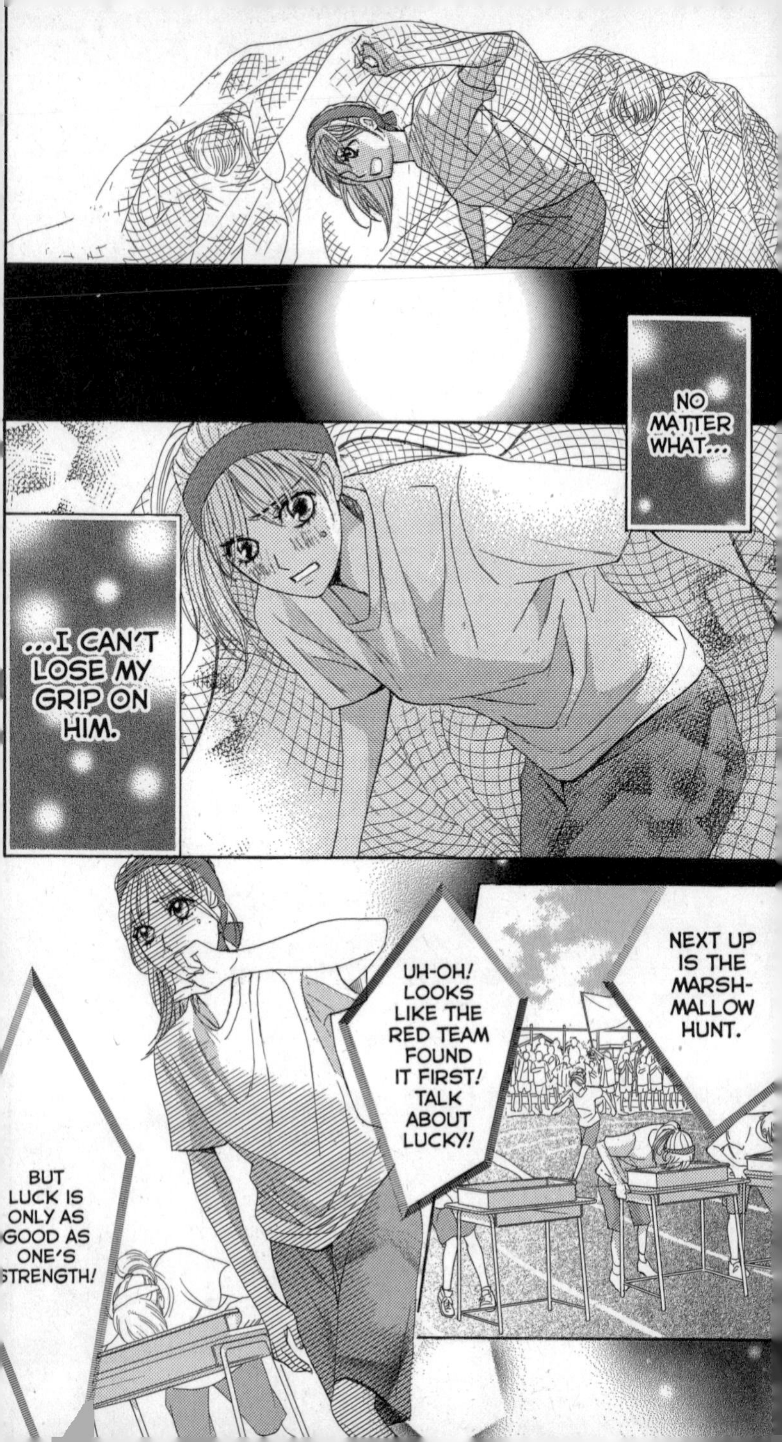
NO MATTER WHAT...
...I CAN'T LOSE MY GRIP ON HIM.
NEXT UP IS THE MARSH-MALLOW HUNT.
UH-OH! LOOKS LIKE THE RED TEAM FOUND IT FIRST! TALK ABOUT LUCKY!
BUT LUCK IS ONLY AS GOOD AS ONE'S STRENGTH!

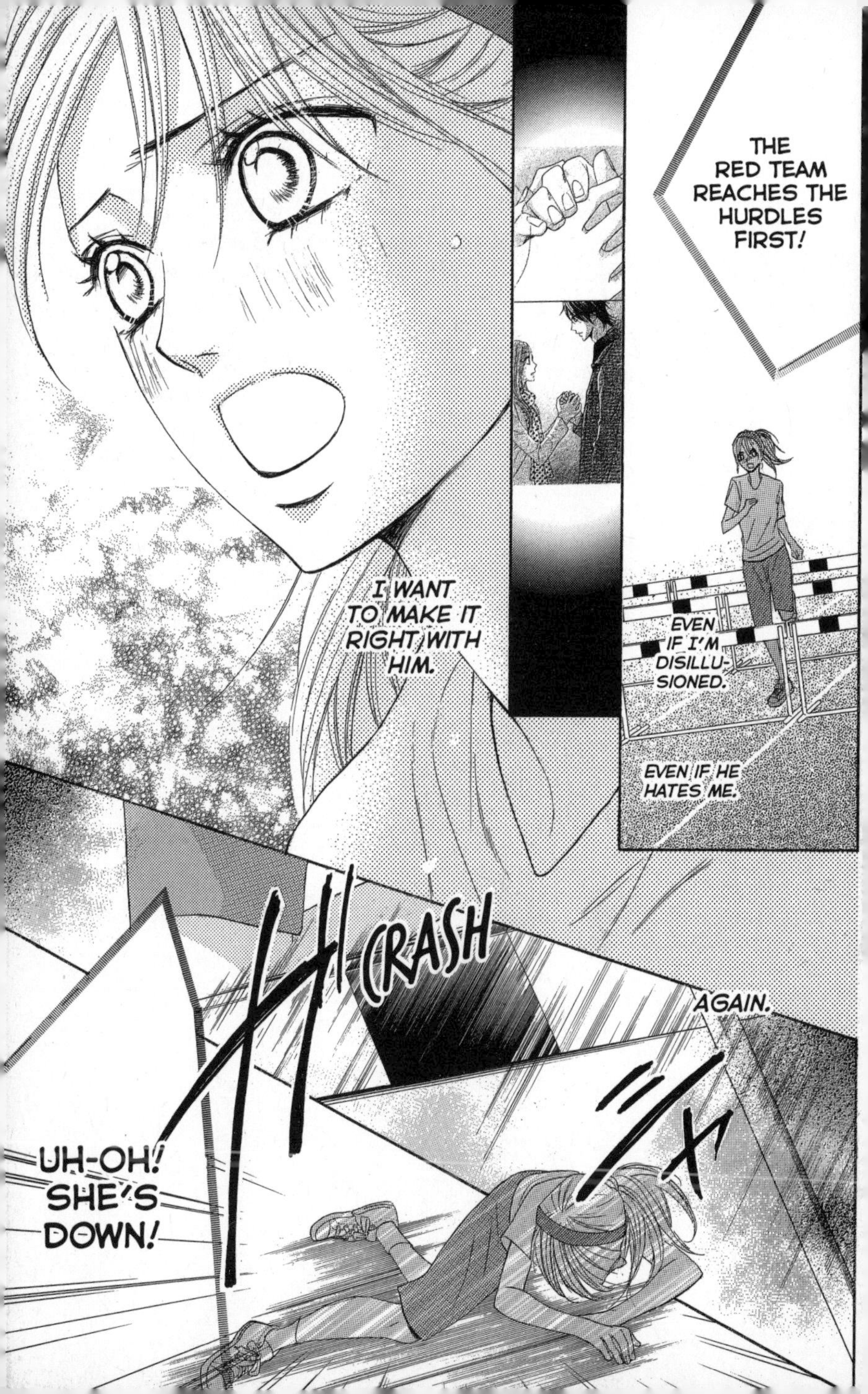
THE RED TEAM REACHES THE HURDLES FIRST!
EVEN IF I'M DISILLUSIONED.
EVEN IF HE HATES ME.
I WANT TO MAKE IT RIGHT WITH HIM.
AGAIN.
CRASH
UH-OH! SHE'S DOWN!

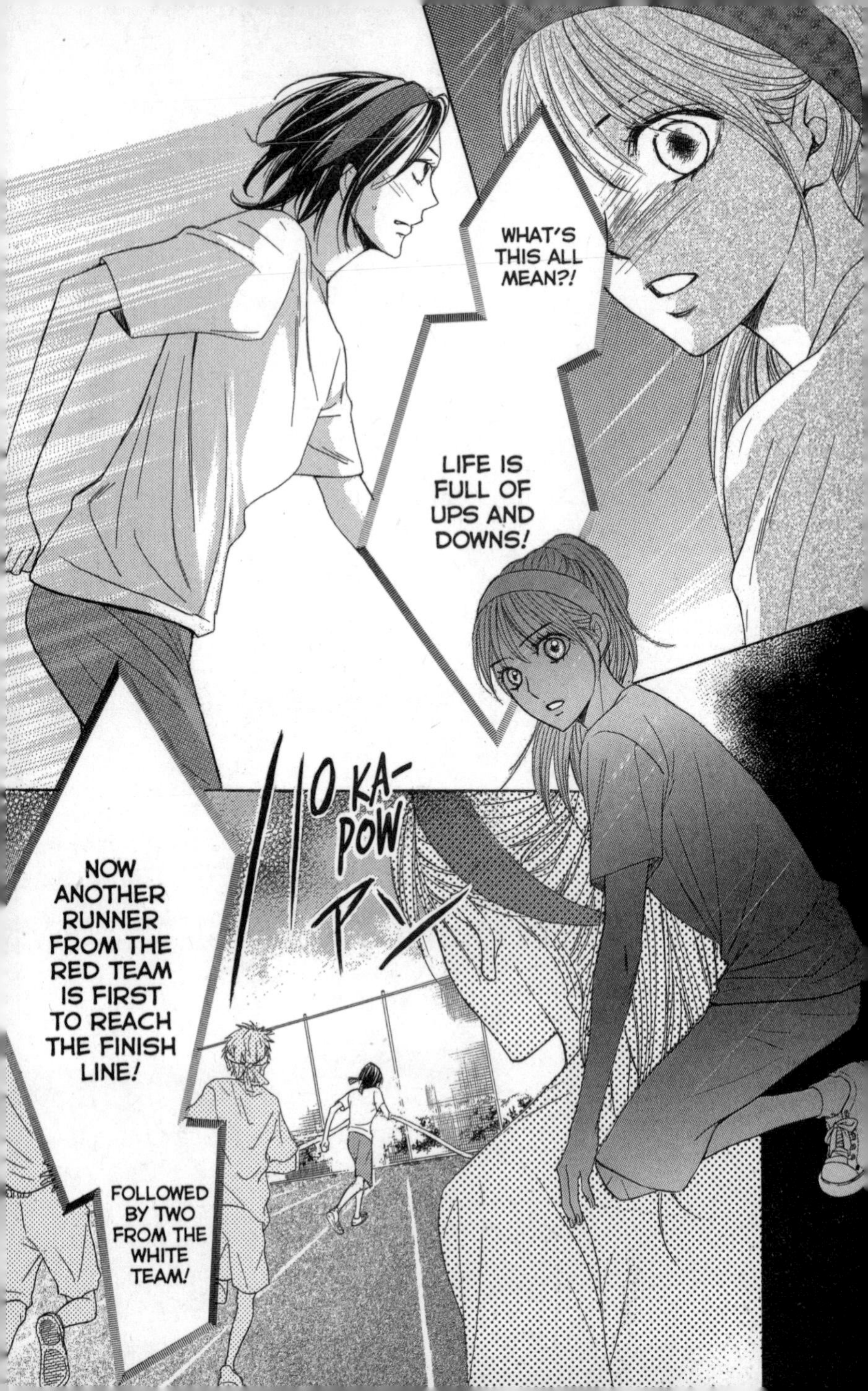
WHAT'S THIS ALL MEAN?!
LIFE IS FULL OF UPS AND DOWNS!
KA-POW
NOW ANOTHER RUNNER FROM THE RED TEAM IS FIRST TO REACH THE FINISH LINE!
FOLLOWED BY TWO FROM THE WHITE TEAM!

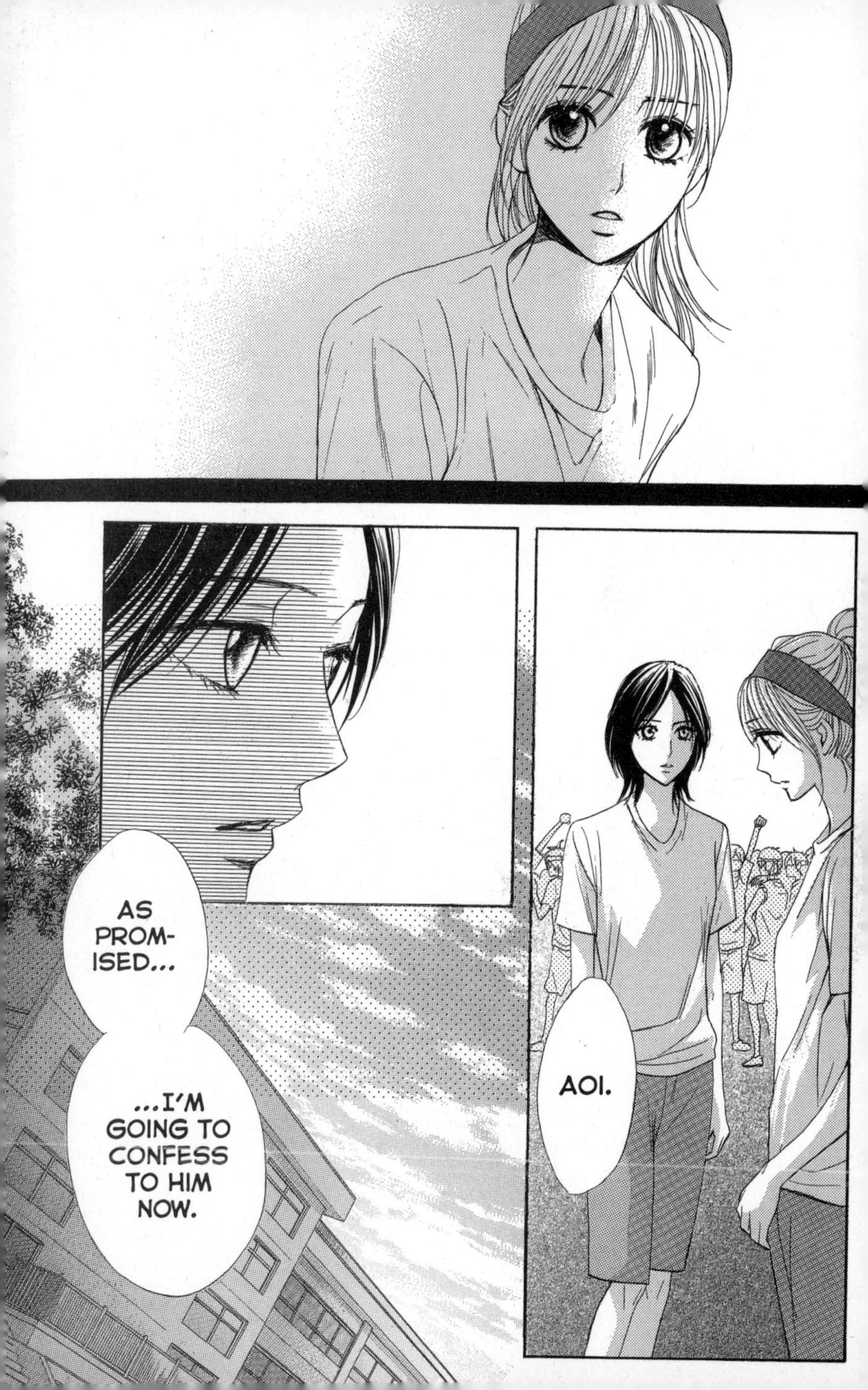
AOI.
AS PROMISED...
...I'M GOING TO CONFESS TO HIM NOW.

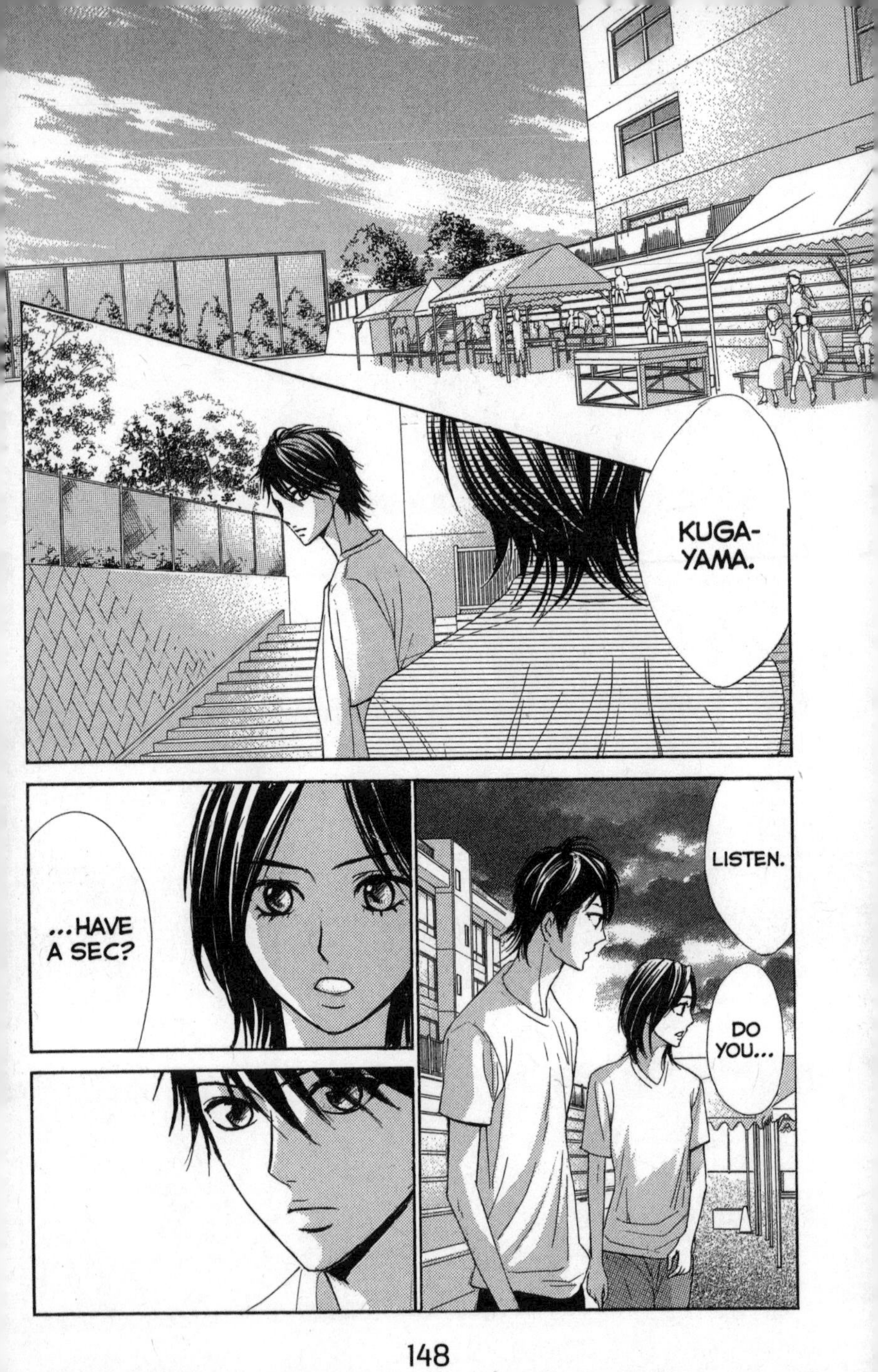
KUGA-
YAMA.
LISTEN.
DO
YOU...
...HAVE
A SEC?

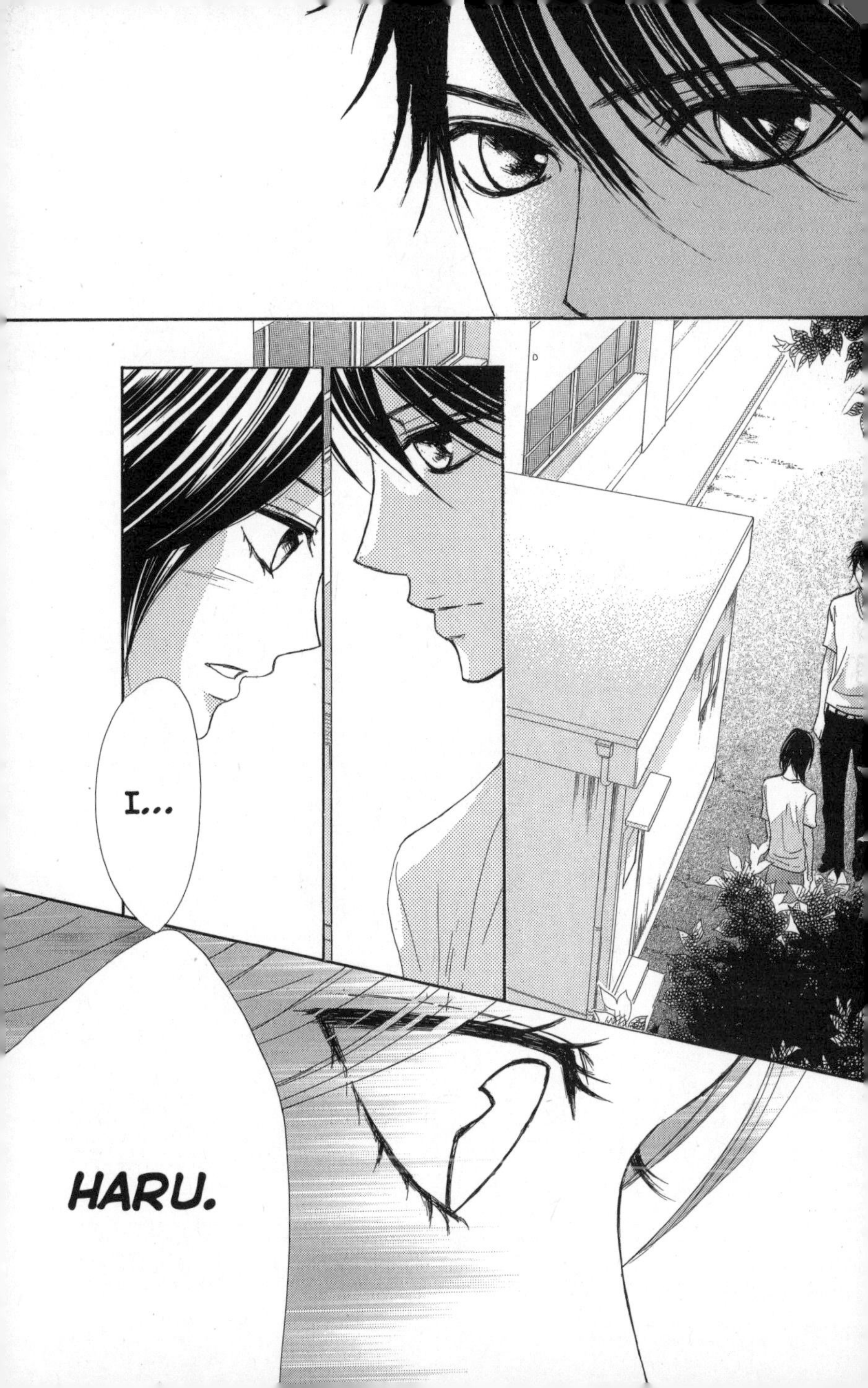
I...
HARU.

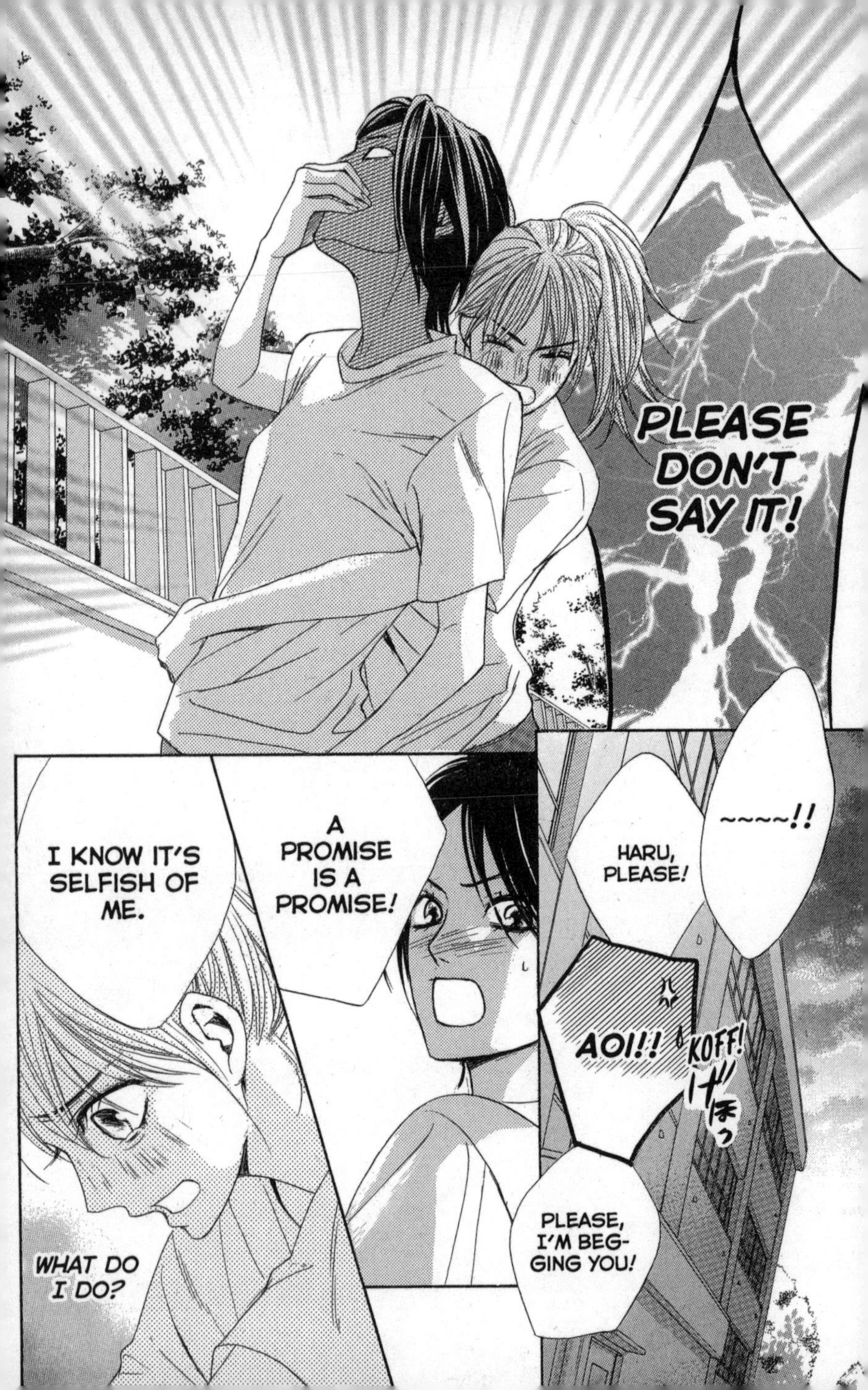
PLEASE DON'T SAY IT!
~~~~!!
HARU, PLEASE!
KOFF!
げほっ
AOI!!
PLEASE, I'M BEG-GING YOU!
A PROMISE IS A PROMISE!
I KNOW IT'S SELFISH OF ME.
WHAT DO I DO?
~~~~

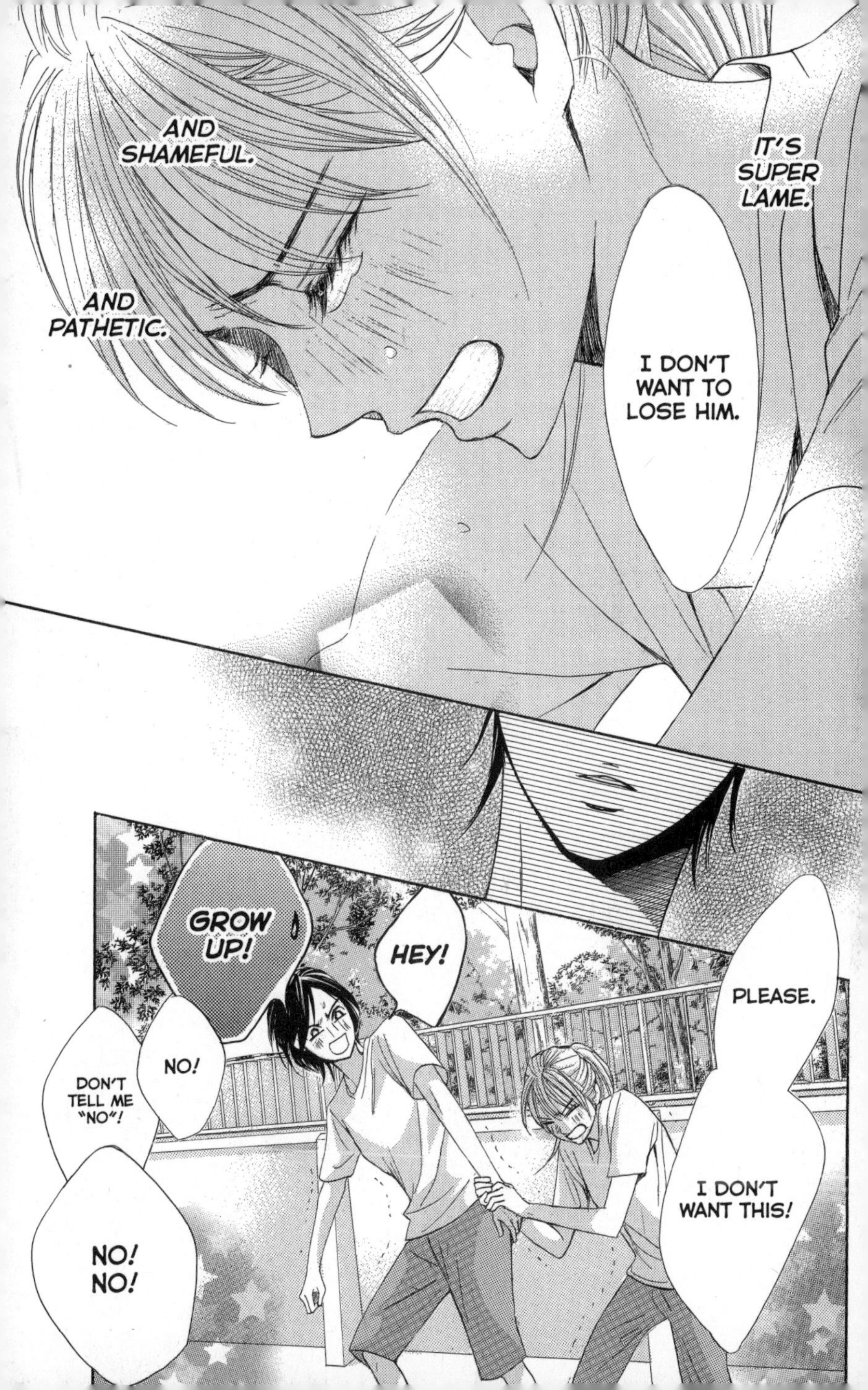
IT'S SUPER LAME.
I DON'T WANT TO LOSE HIM.
AND SHAMEFUL.
AND PATHETIC.
PLEASE.
I DON'T WANT THIS!
HEY!
GROW UP!
NO!
DON'T TELL ME "NO"!
NO! NO!

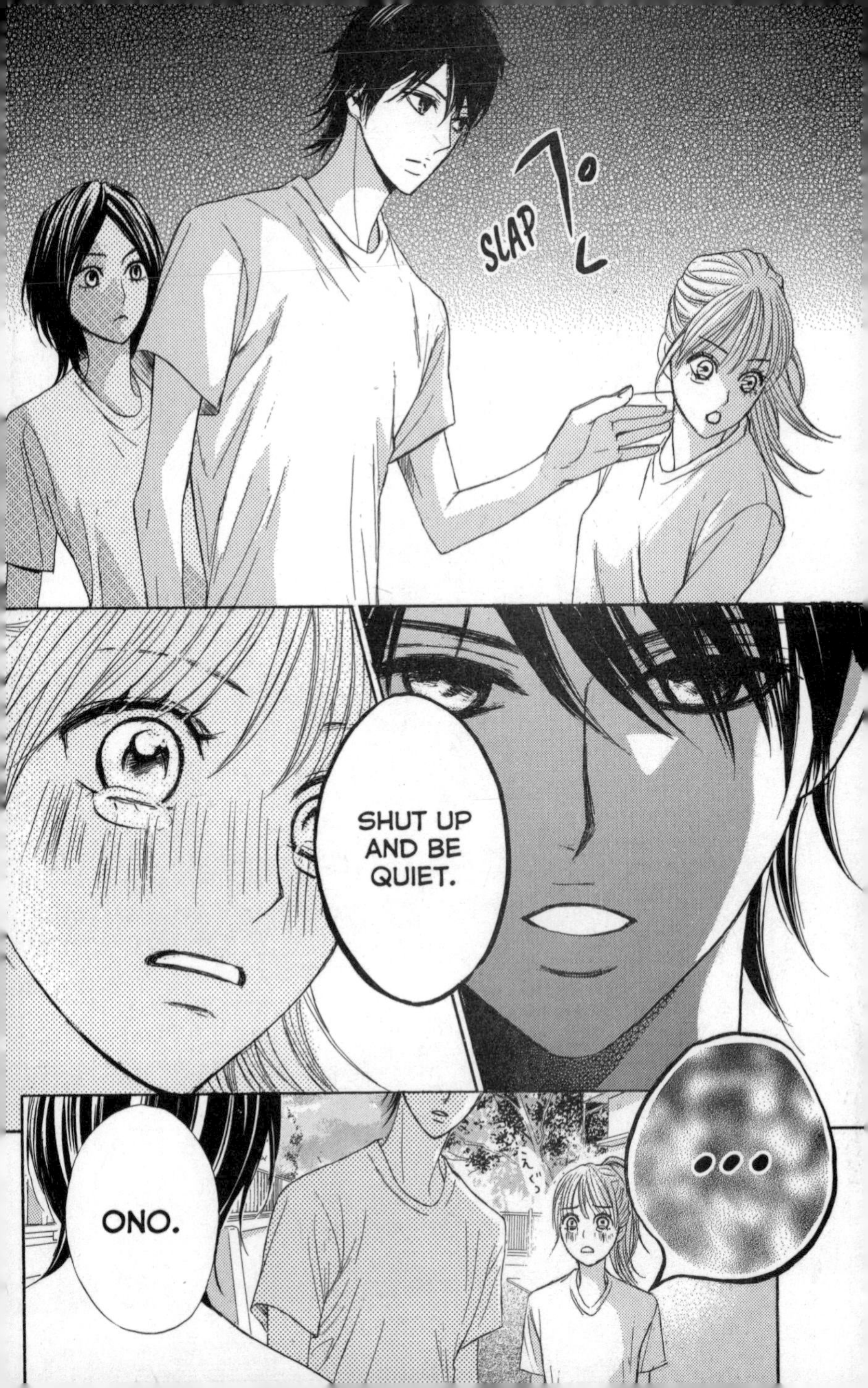
SLAP
SHUT UP AND BE QUIET.
...
ONO.

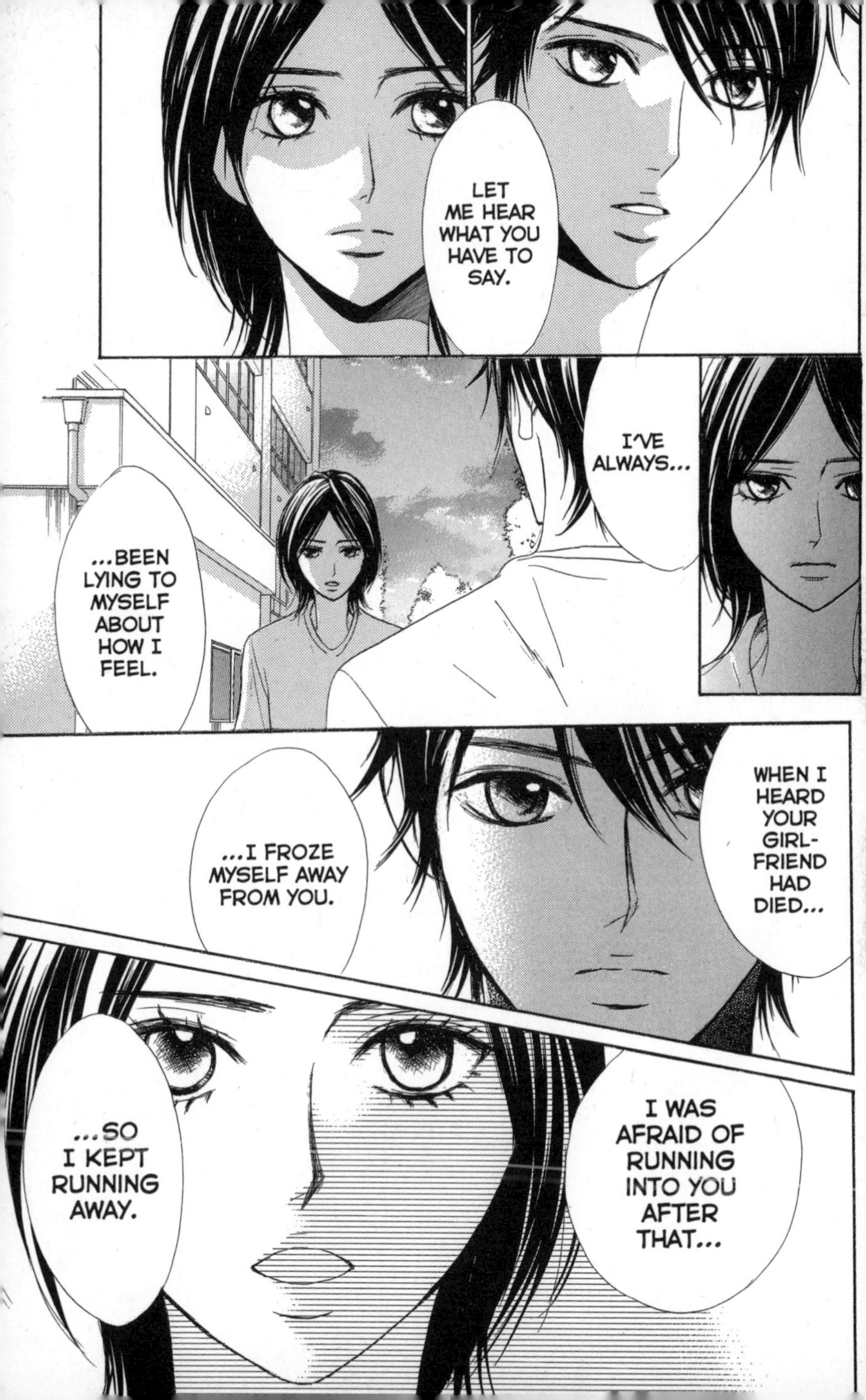
LET ME HEAR WHAT YOU HAVE TO SAY.
I'VE ALWAYS...
...BEEN LYING TO MYSELF ABOUT HOW I FEEL.
WHEN I HEARD YOUR GIRL-FRIEND HAD DIED...
...I FROZE MYSELF AWAY FROM YOU.
I WAS AFRAID OF RUNNING INTO YOU AFTER THAT...
...SO I KEPT RUNNING AWAY.

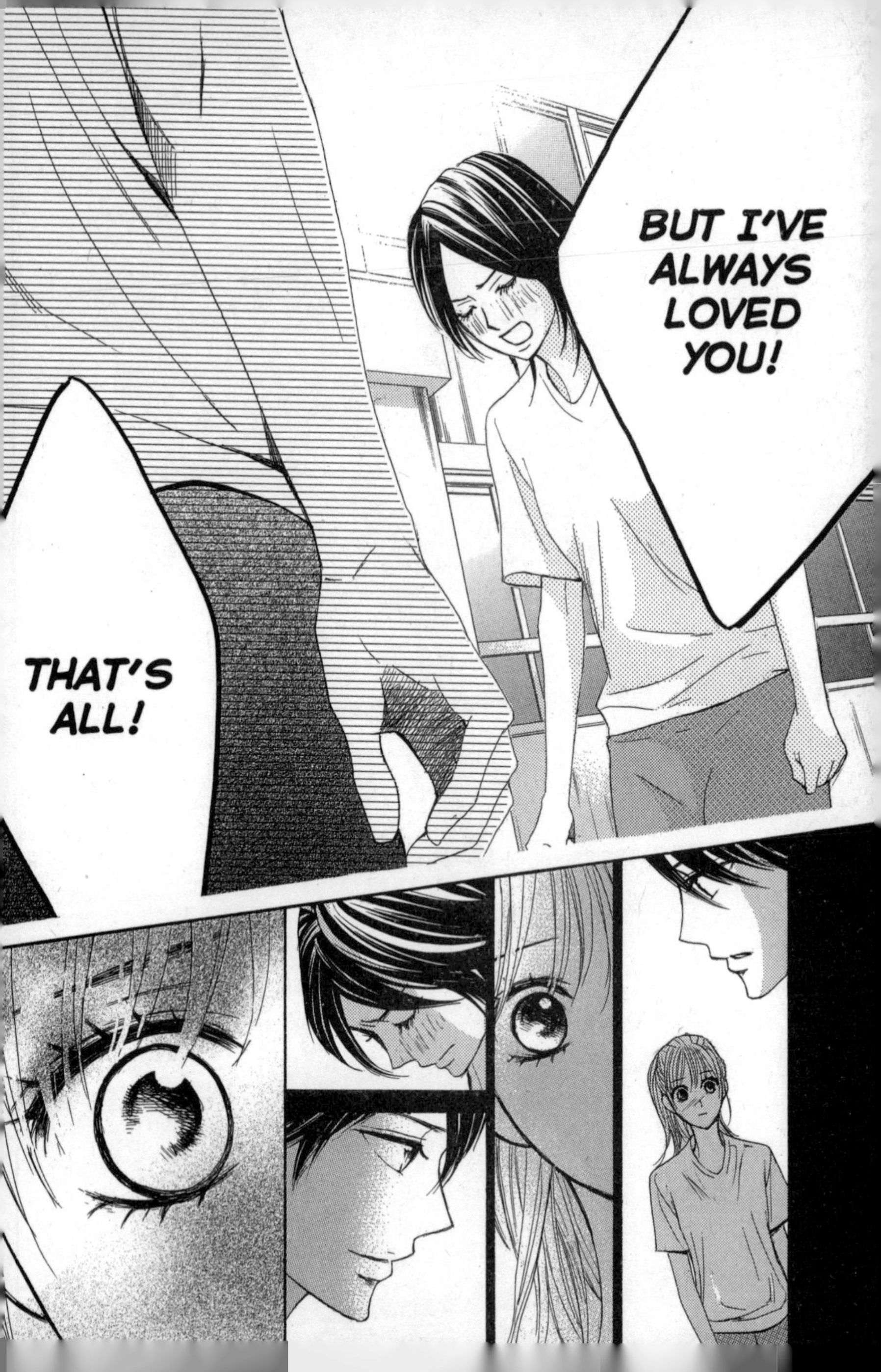
BUT I'VE ALWAYS LOVED YOU!
THAT'S ALL!

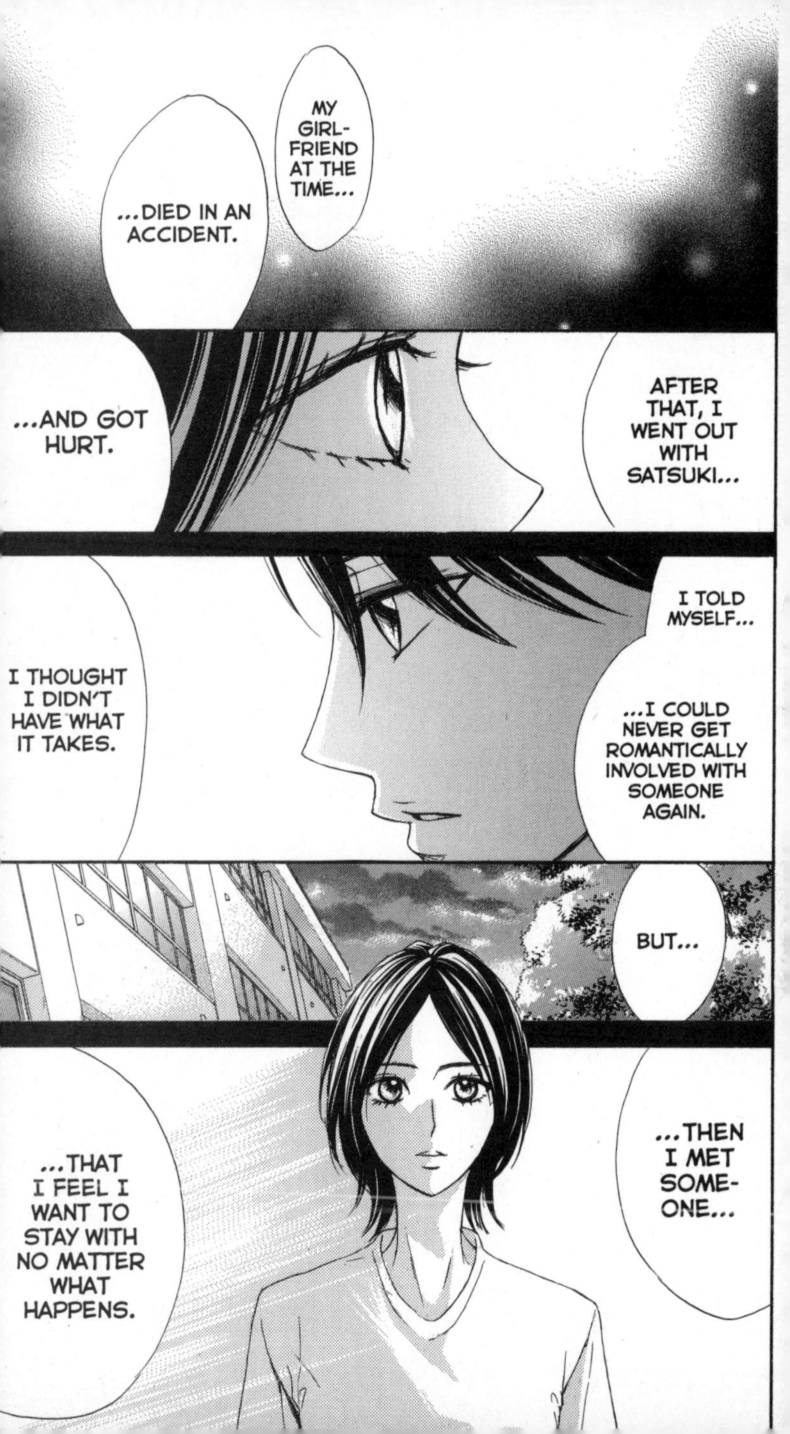
MY GIRL-FRIEND AT THE TIME...
...DIED IN AN ACCIDENT.
AFTER THAT, I WENT OUT WITH SATSUKI...
...AND GOT HURT.
I TOLD MYSELF...
...I COULD NEVER GET ROMANTICALLY INVOLVED WITH SOMEONE AGAIN.
I THOUGHT I DIDN'T HAVE WHAT IT TAKES.
BUT...
...THEN I MET SOME-ONE...
...THAT I FEEL I WANT TO STAY WITH NO MATTER WHAT HAPPENS.

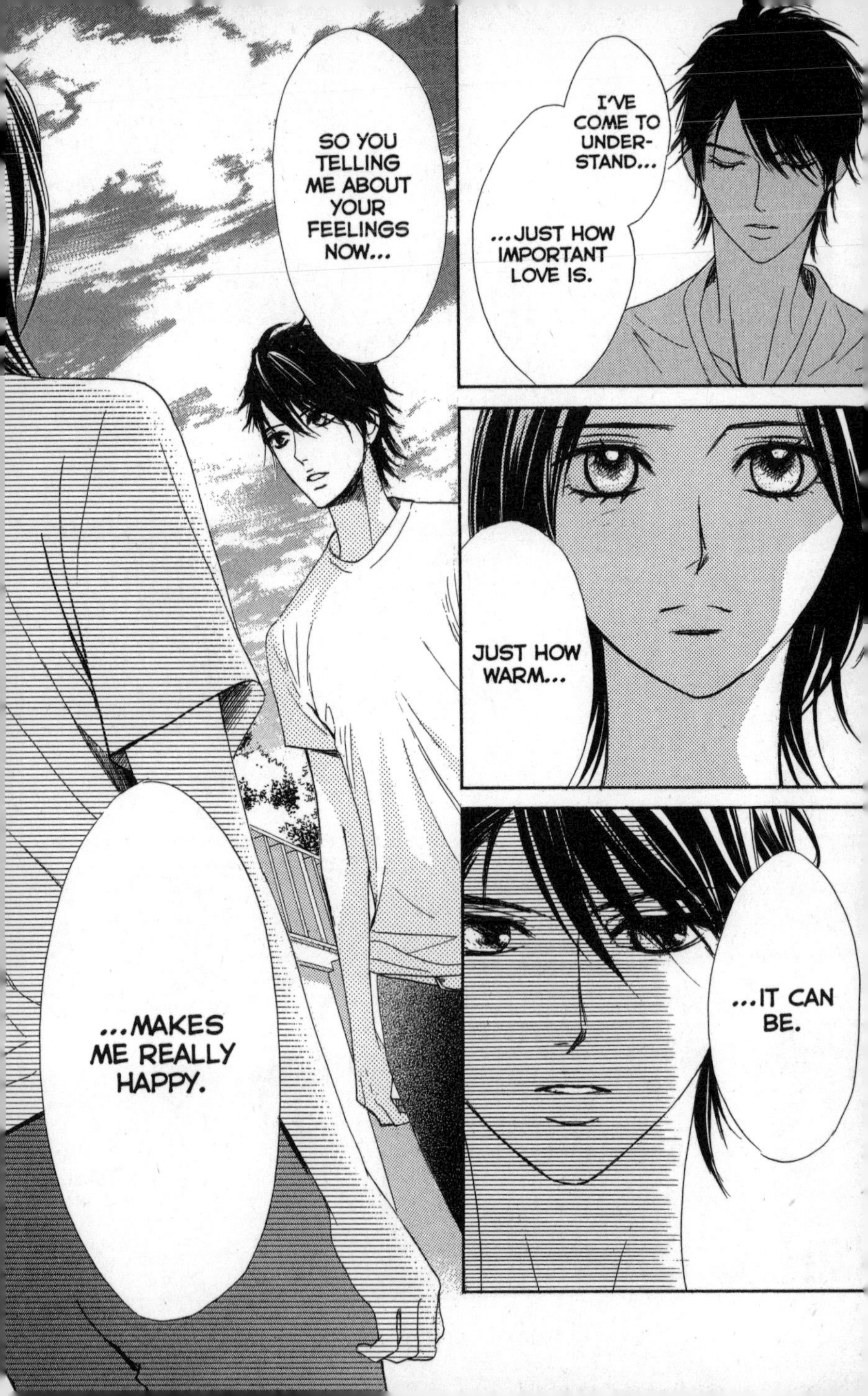
I'VE COME TO UNDER-STAND...
...JUST HOW IMPORTANT LOVE IS.
JUST HOW WARM...
...IT CAN BE.
SO YOU TELLING ME ABOUT YOUR FEELINGS NOW...
...MAKES ME REALLY HAPPY.

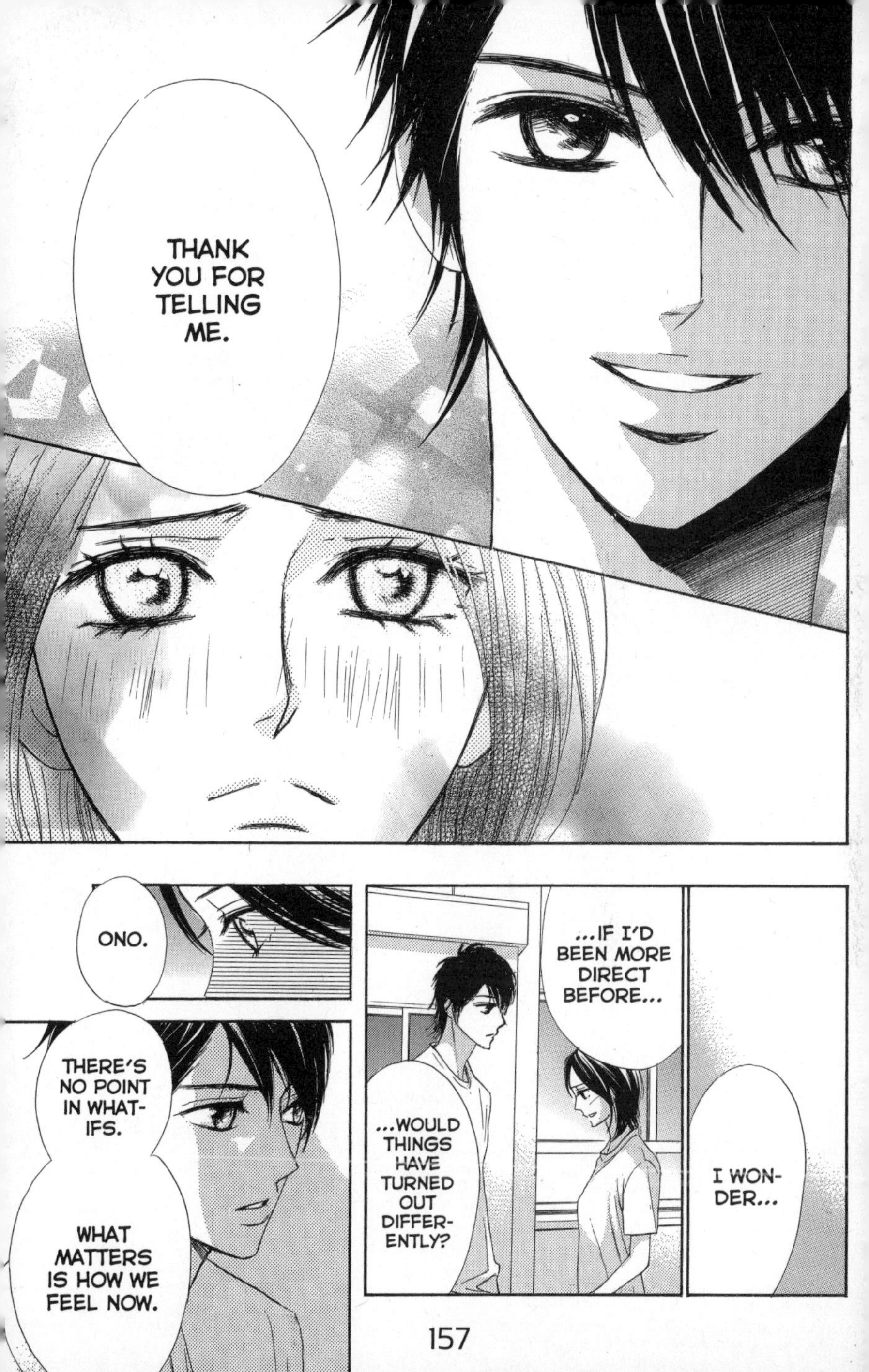
THANK YOU FOR TELLING ME.
I WON-DER...
...IF I'D BEEN MORE DIRECT BEFORE...
...WOULD THINGS HAVE TURNED OUT DIFFER-ENTLY?
ONO.
THERE'S NO POINT IN WHAT-IFS.
WHAT MATTERS IS HOW WE FEEL NOW.

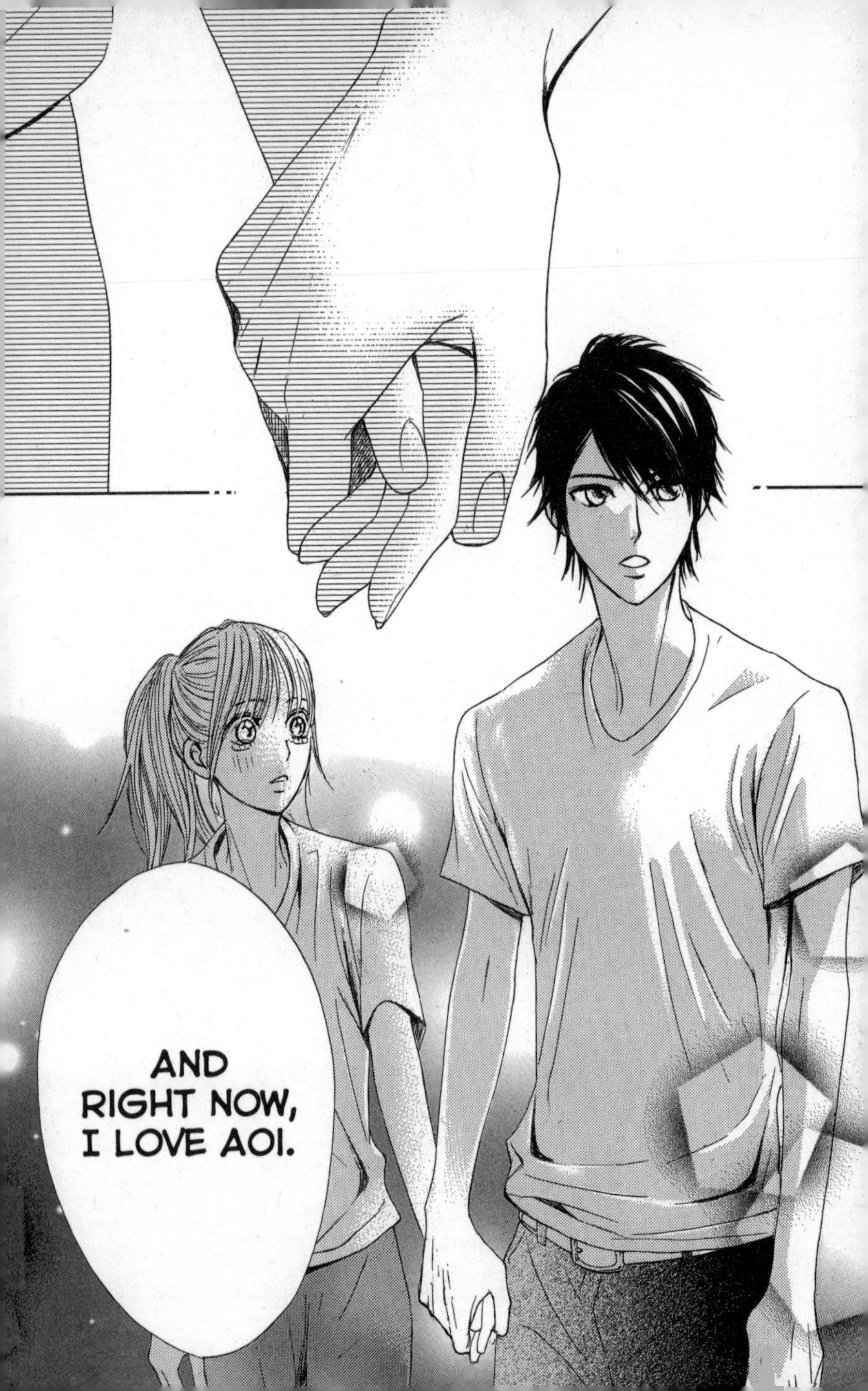
AND RIGHT NOW, I LOVE AOI.

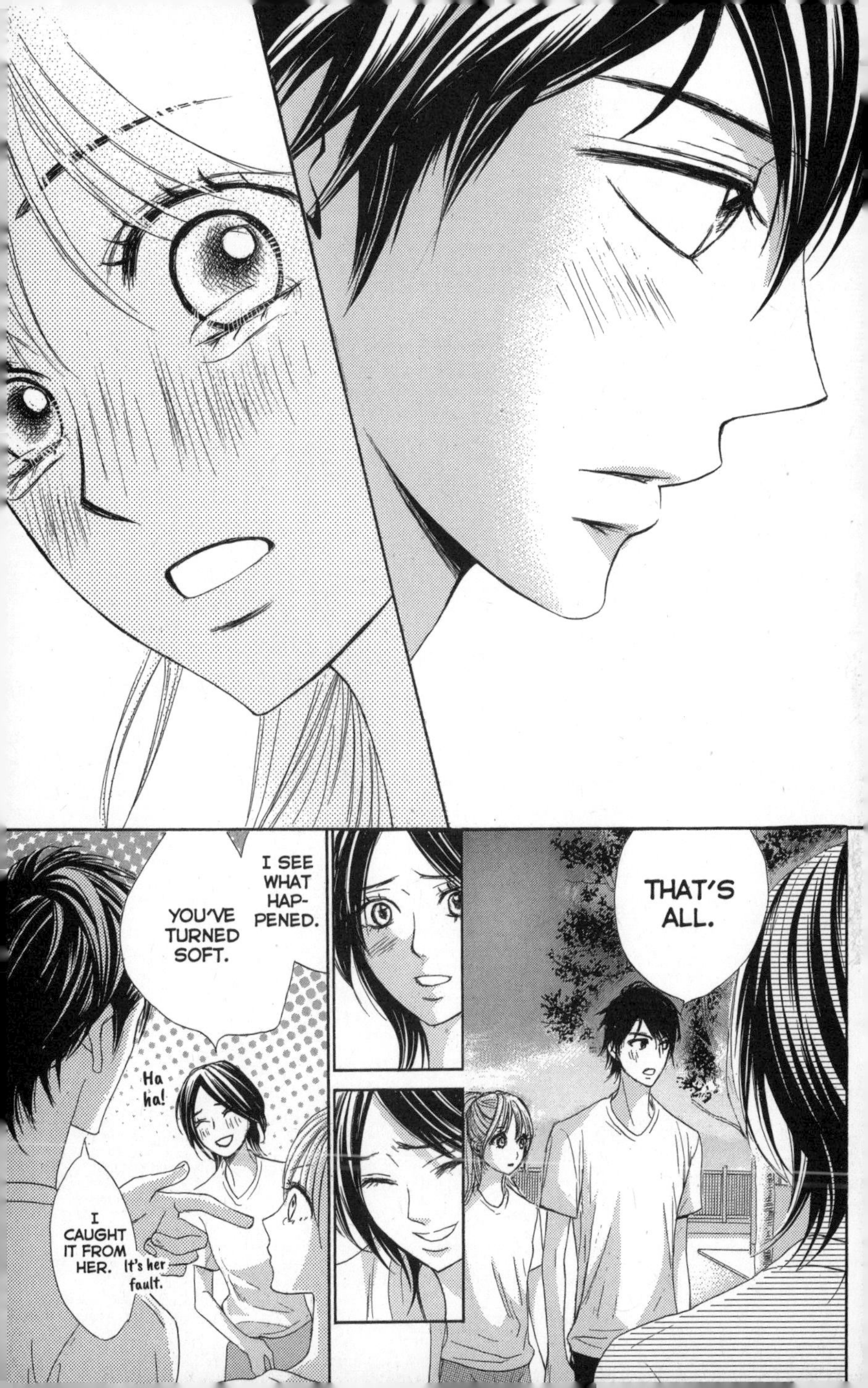
THAT'S ALL.
I SEE WHAT HAPPENED.
YOU'VE TURNED SOFT.
Ha ha!
I CAUGHT IT FROM HER.
It's her fault.

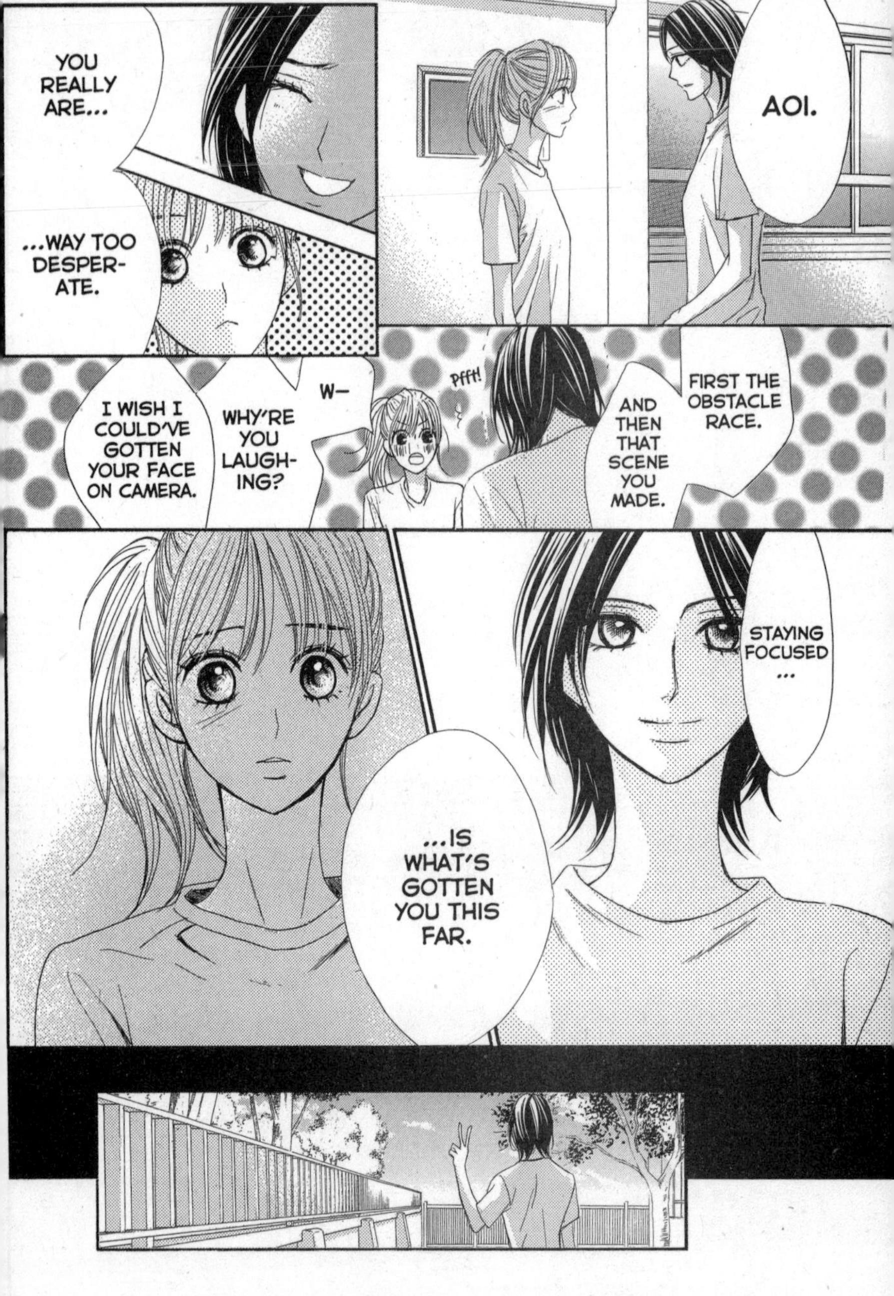
AOI.
YOU REALLY ARE...
...WAY TOO DESPER-ATE.
FIRST THE OBSTACLE RACE.
AND THEN THAT SCENE YOU MADE.
Pfft!
W—
WHY'RE YOU LAUGH-ING?
I WISH I COULD'VE GOTTEN YOUR FACE ON CAMERA.
STAYING FOCUSED...
...IS WHAT'S GOTTEN YOU THIS FAR.

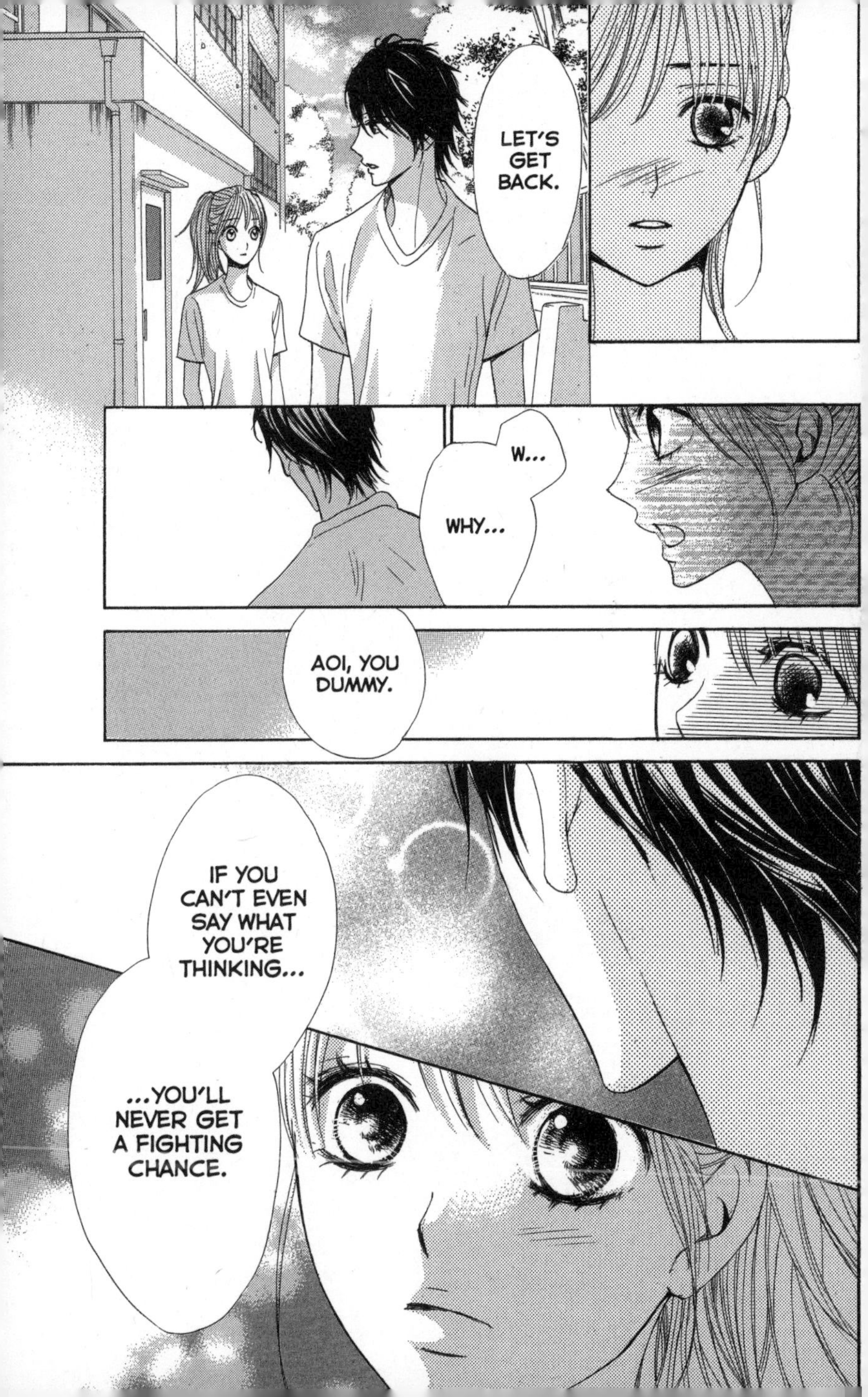
LET'S GET BACK.
W...
WHY...
AOI, YOU DUMMY.
IF YOU CAN'T EVEN SAY WHAT YOU'RE THINKING...
...YOU'LL NEVER GET A FIGHTING CHANCE.

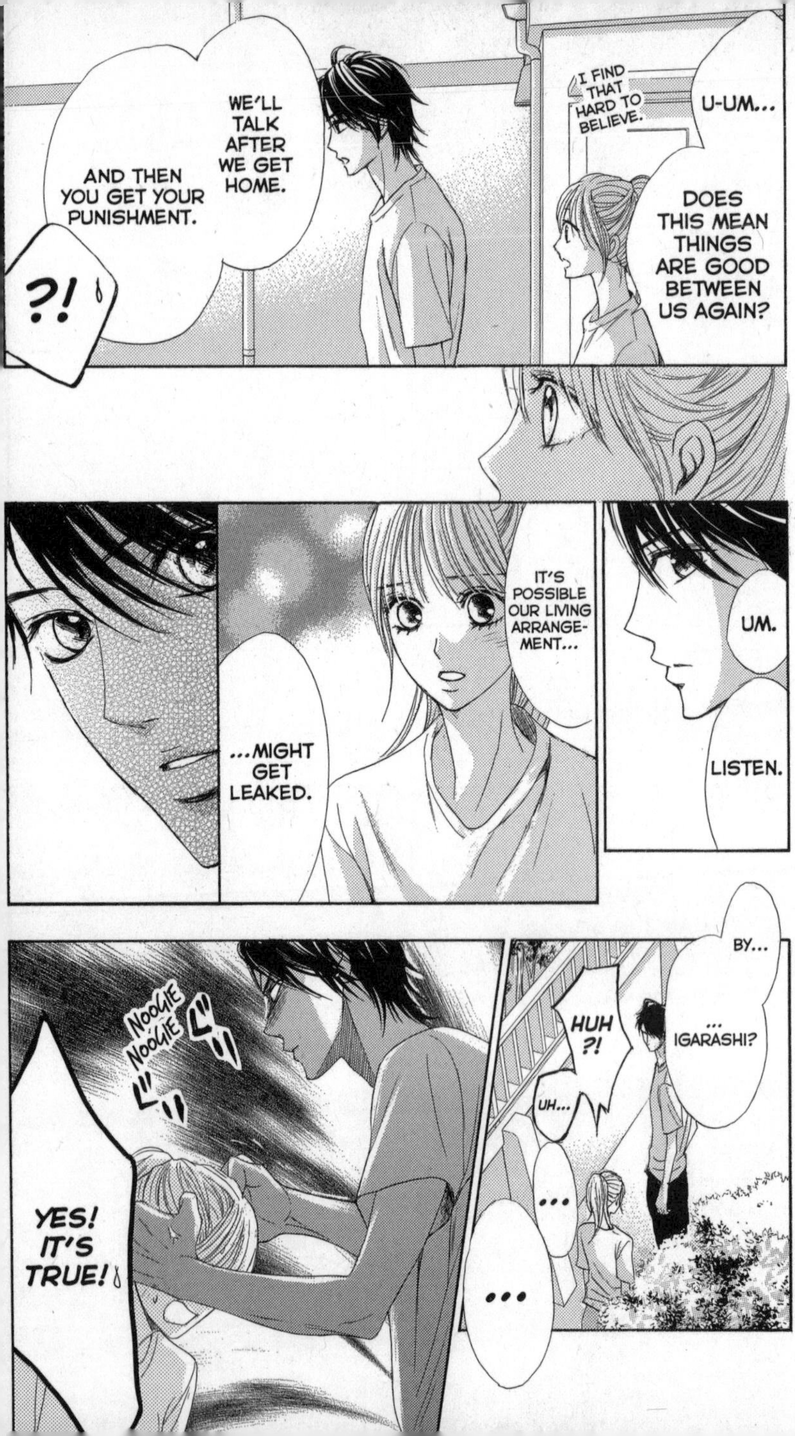
U-UM...
DOES THIS MEAN THINGS ARE GOOD BETWEEN US AGAIN?
I FIND THAT HARD TO BELIEVE.
WE'LL TALK AFTER WE GET HOME.
AND THEN YOU GET YOUR PUNISHMENT.
?!
UM.
LISTEN.
IT'S POSSIBLE OUR LIVING ARRANGEMENT...
...MIGHT GET LEAKED.
BY...
...IGARASHI?
HUH ?!
UH...
...
...
NOOGIE NOOGIE
YES! IT'S TRUE!

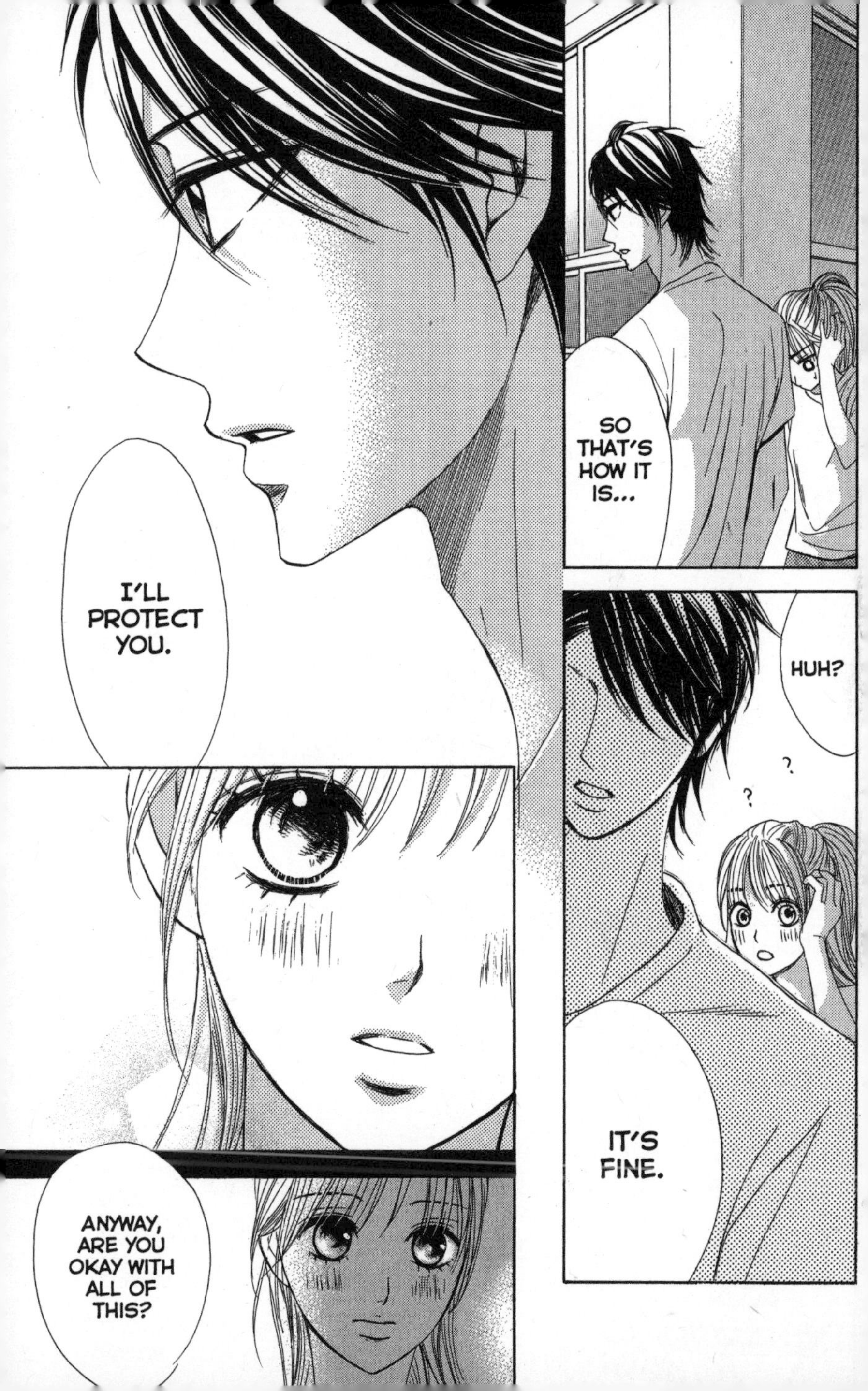
SO THAT'S HOW IT IS...
HUH?
IT'S FINE.
I'LL PROTECT YOU.
ANYWAY, ARE YOU OKAY WITH ALL OF THIS?

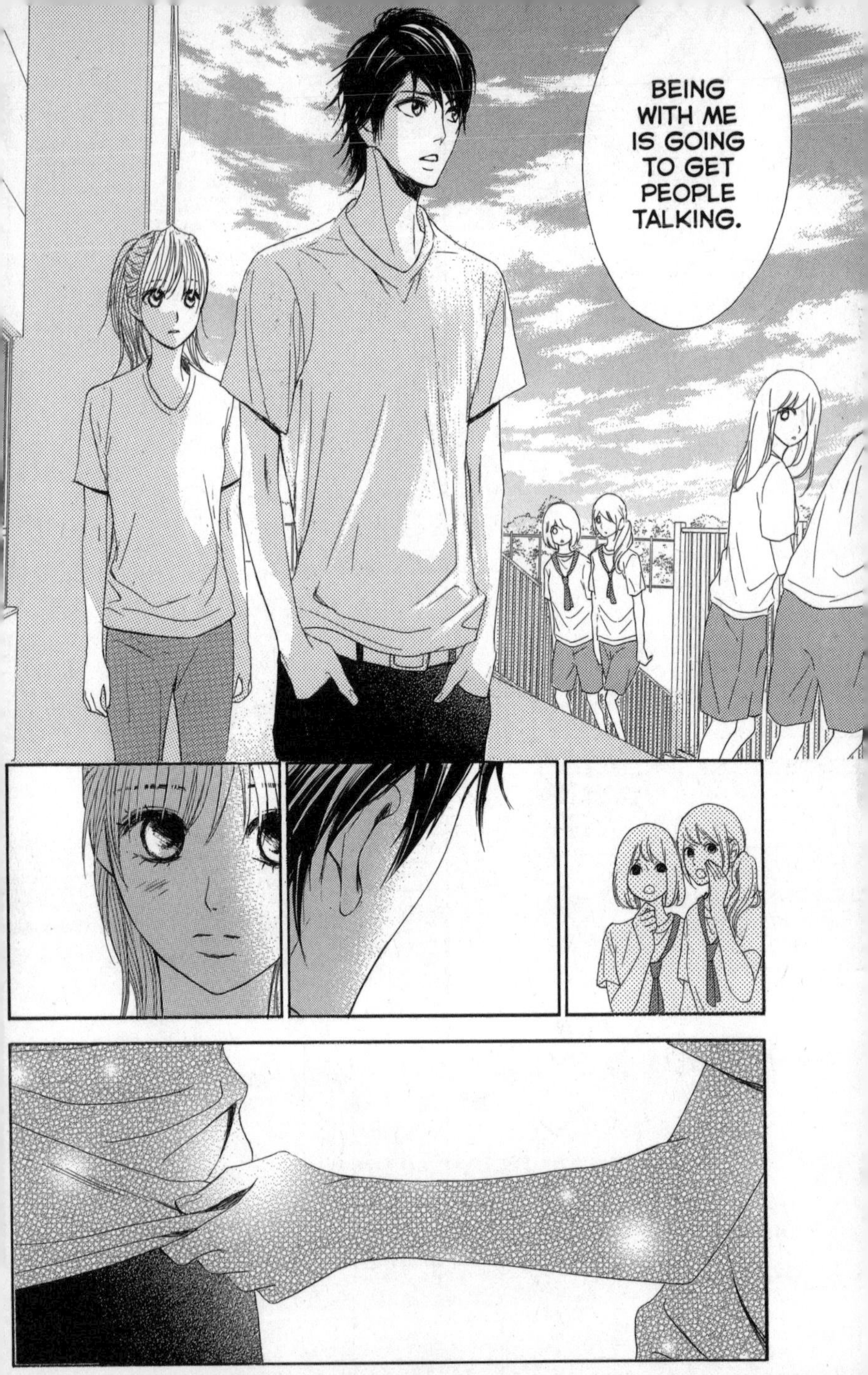
BEING WITH ME IS GOING TO GET PEOPLE TALKING.

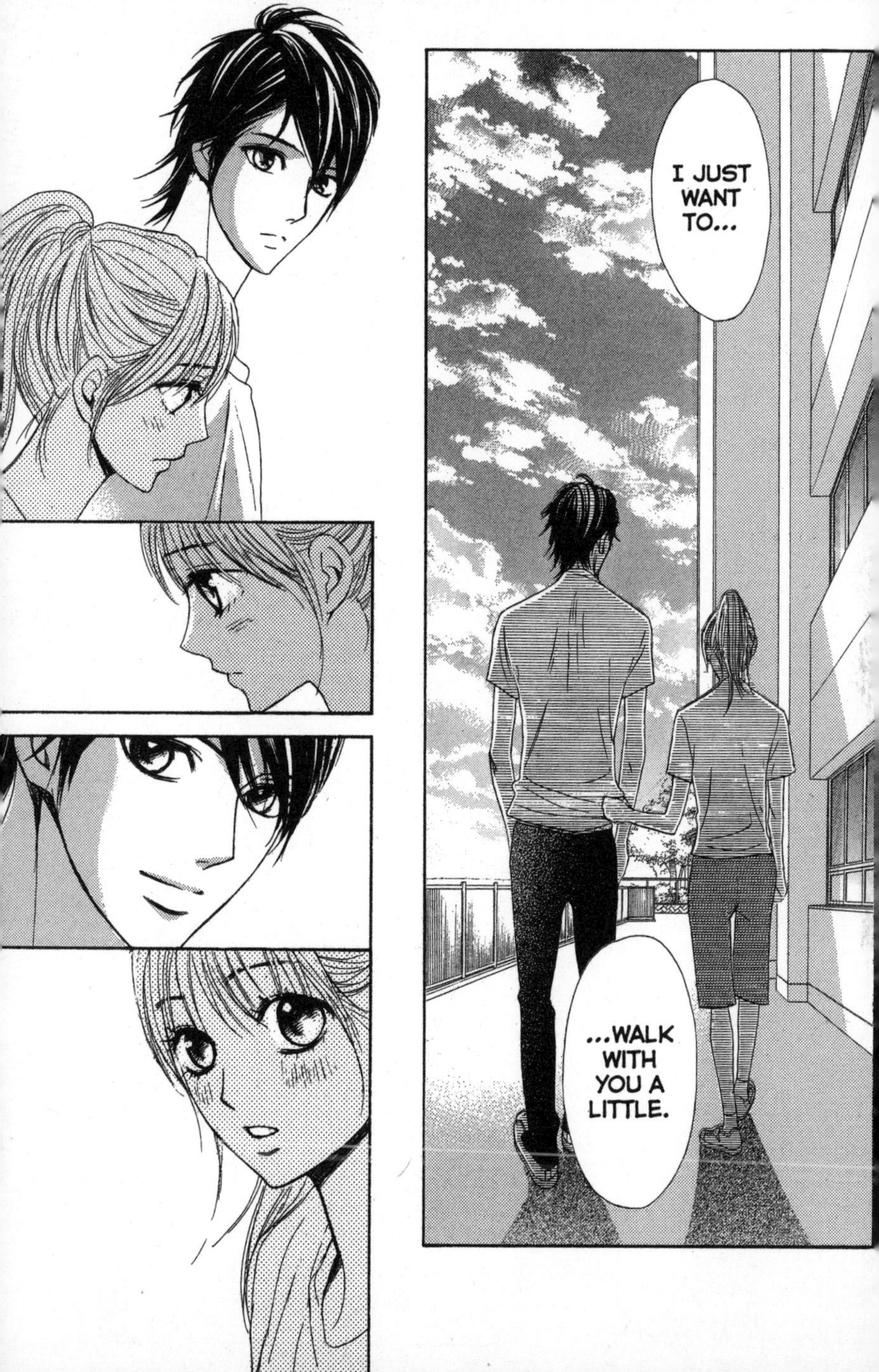
I JUST WANT TO...
...WALK WITH YOU A LITTLE.

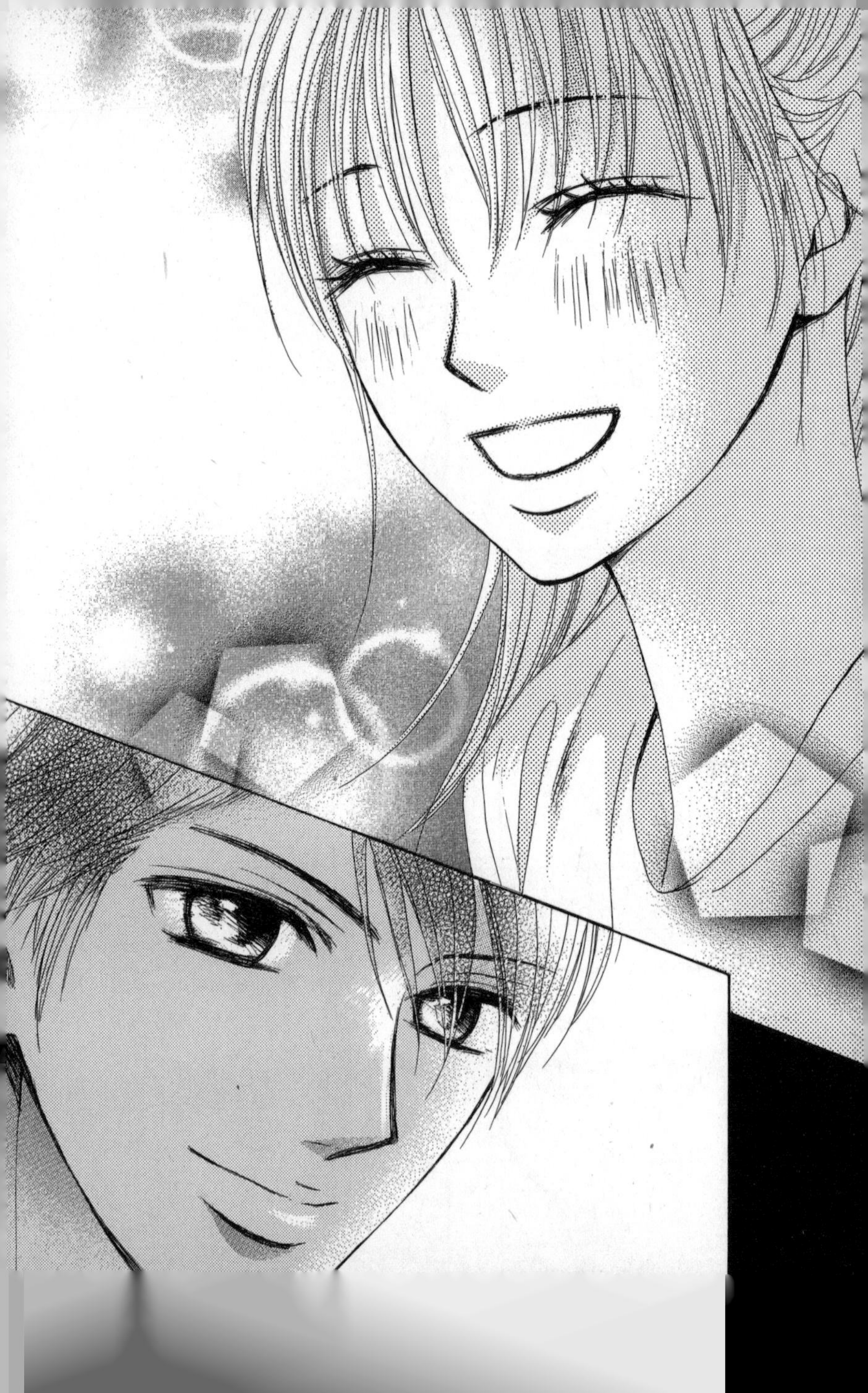

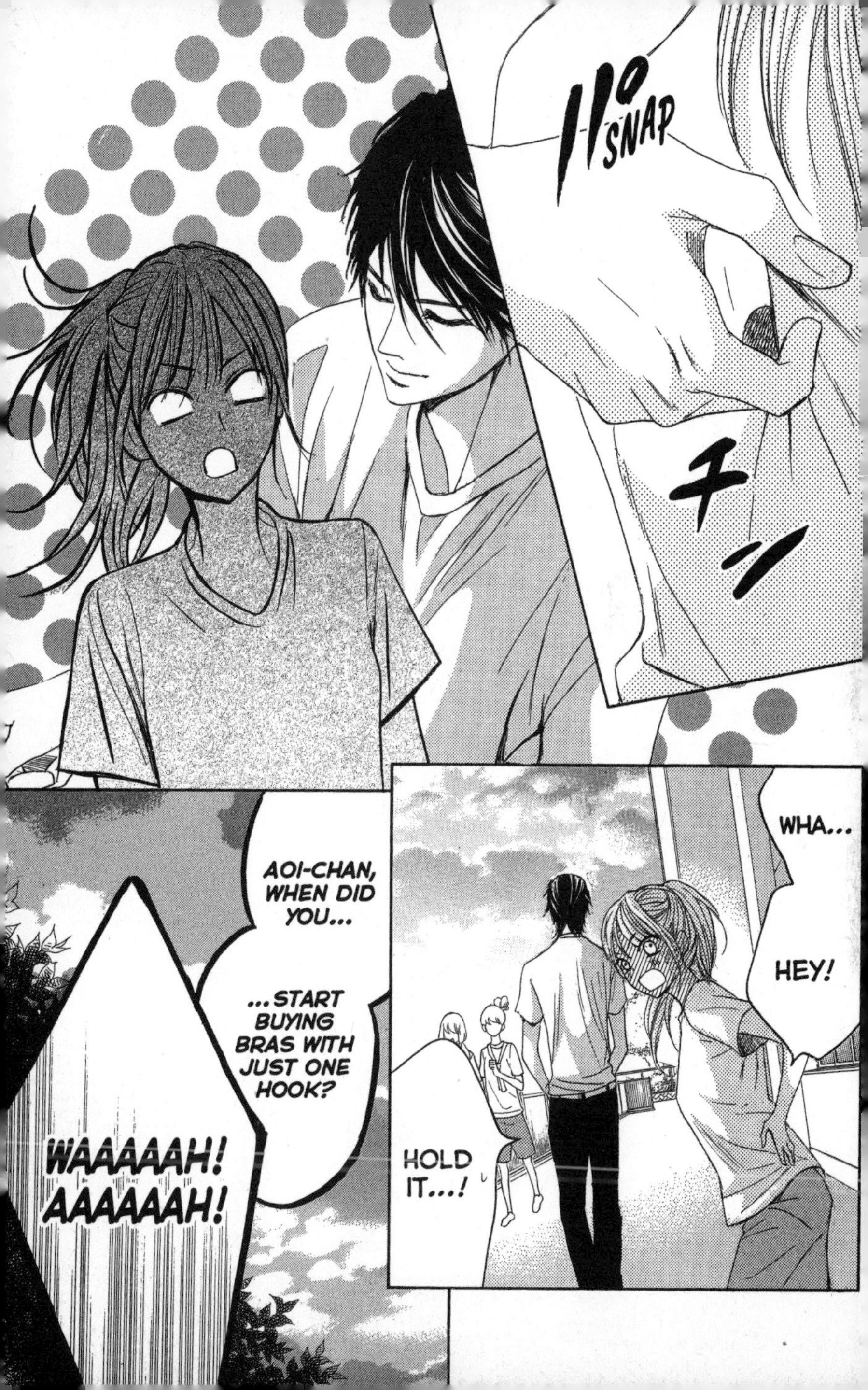
SNAP
チン
WHA...
HEY!
HOLD IT...!
AOI-CHAN, WHEN DID YOU...
...START BUYING BRAS WITH JUST ONE HOOK?
WAAAAAH! AAAAAAH!

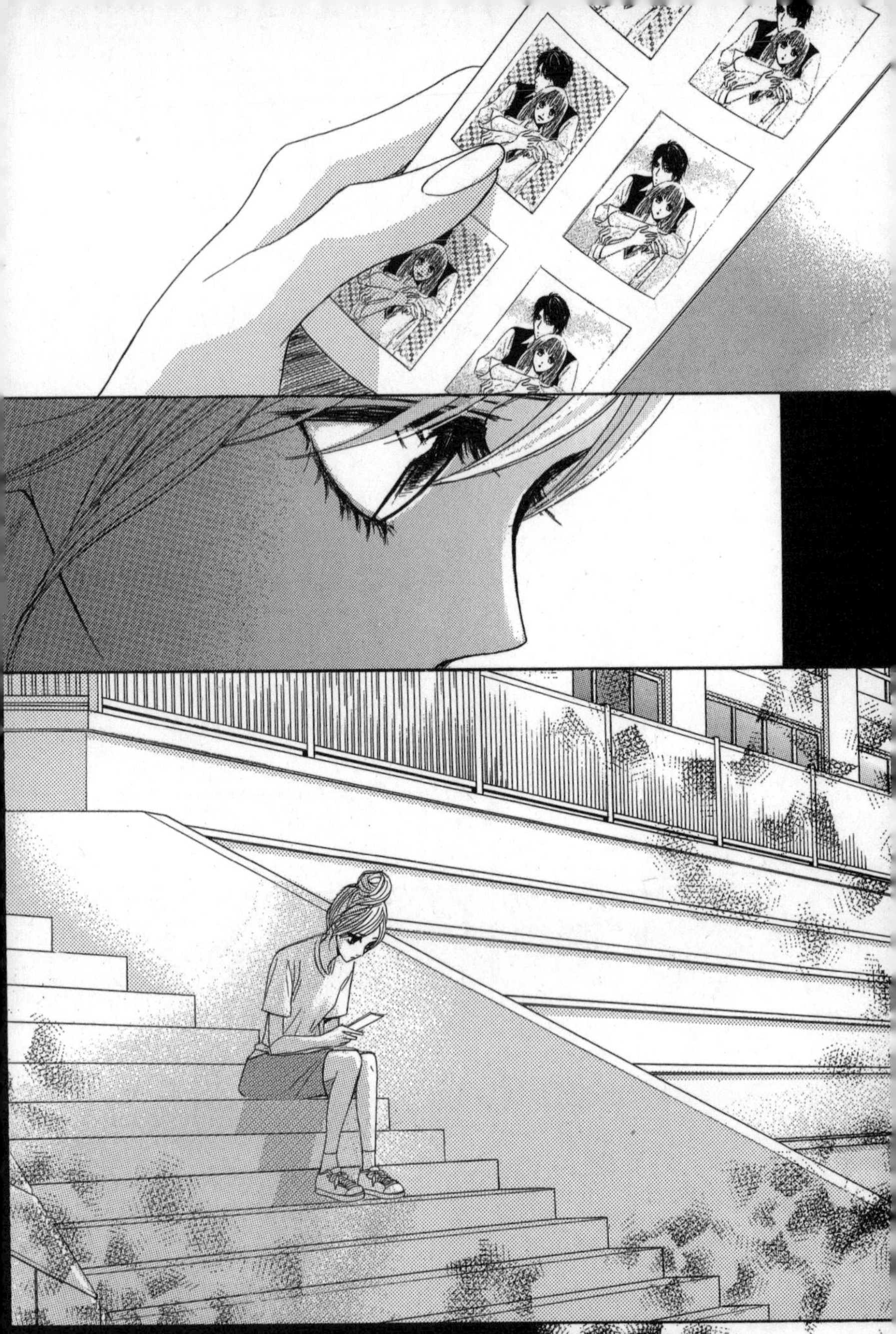

To Be Continued in L♥DK 12

L♥DK

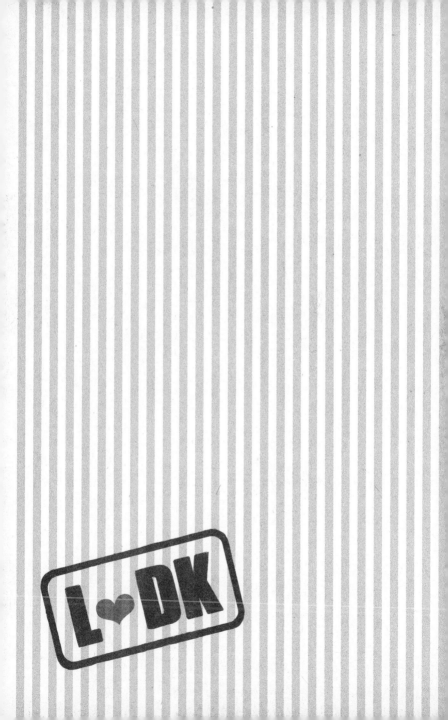

Shusei Kugayama

- Height / Weight: 182cm / 67cm
- Blood Type: AB
- Birthday: January 14, Capricorn
- Favorite animal: Dog (French bulldog, etc.)
- Favorite color: Black, indigo blue
- Favorite class: History
- Skills: Basketball, English conversation (hates grammar)
- Likes: Sleeping (especially falling back asleep), Good-wear T-shirts, sugar
- Dislikes: The heat (also can't stand the cold)
- Catchphrase: "Whatever."

Aoi Nishimori

- Height / Weight: 156cm / not telling
- Blood Type: O
- Birthday: July 16, Cancer
- Favorite animals: Rabbits, hamsters
- Favorite colors: Red, white, pastel colors
- Favorite class: Gym, home ec.
- Skills: Cooking (especially Japanese cuisine)
- Likes: Incense, karaoke (singing in the shower), soaking in the tub, white things
- Dislikes: Ghost stories, loud noises
- Catchphrases: "Hey!" (especially in reply to Shusei's pranks)

GREETINGS.

Hello, everyone! This is Ayu Watanabe. Thank you for picking up *L♡DK* volume 11. I'm sitting here at my desk with kombu and candy in one hand.

Drawing manga is really a deep process, and no matter how many years I've been doing it, I'm always reminded of the more difficult components of it that I'll just never get used to. When the set-up and development of characters get more typical, you have to figure out how to make the action work and more powerfully portray the characters. So these days I spend a lot of time thinking about how to get better at that (it's really more like zoning out about it). It's something I want to apply myself to.

ꕥ On another note, lately I've been visiting the blast-from-the-past "*Nounai** Maker" (©Usoko Maker-sama). It's an online game where, when you input a person's name, it'll show what that person's thinking. When I input the names of my manga's characters, I got some very interesting results.

**Nounai* means "inside the brain."

- Shusei Kugayama's Brain

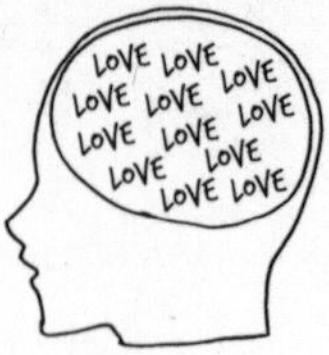
LOVE LOVE
LOVE LOVE LOVE
LOVE LOVE LOVE
LOVE LOVE
LOVE LOVE

Wow!! It's love across the board!! How starved for love is this guy? Or perhaps he's thinking he wants to have love in his life.

Then, Aoi Nishimori was...

- Aoi Nishimori's Brain

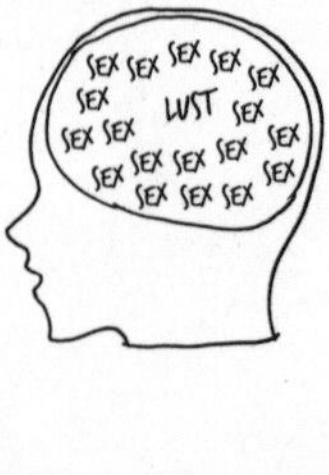
SEX SEX SEX SEX
SEX SEX
SEX LUST SEX
SEX SEX SEX
SEX SEX SEX SEX SEX
SEX SEX SEX SEX

?!! Her brain is apparently full of carnal desires!! What a mental state for our heroine to be in...

Since I found that interesting, I also tried it out with the newer "*Meigen** Maker." First was Shusei:

*Meigen means "famous quote."

> "THE MOMENT WE KISSED, A NEW COSMOS WAS BORN."
>
> SHUSEI KUGAYAMA

W-what the?! How literary!! I was moved to see that Shusei and I are on the same page.

Now let's see Nishimori.

> "THE WORD 'SELF-CONTROL' DOESN'T EXIST IN MY DICTIONARY."
>
> AOI NISHIMORI

?!!!! This girl's in trouble. She's a stalwart pervert. And I have to say I'm not surprised.

I'd like to see the results of these tests actually come to fruition. (Heh, heh!)

🙞 There are plenty more twists and turns in store for these two, and I hope you'll stick around to watch their lovey dovey living situation evolve. It makes life easier when you avoid confrontation, but facing mountains and overcoming them is what makes you grow up, and I think that's important, too... Hmmm. I guess that means I'm still a kid.
Well, see you in the next silly and lovey-dovey volume!!

special thanks

K.Hamano
N.Imai
Y.Negishi
S.Mitsuhashi
M.Nagata
Mosuko

my family
my friends

M.Morita
Y.Ikumi
M.Horiuchi

AND YOU

Ayu Watanabe

Nov.2012

Translation Notes

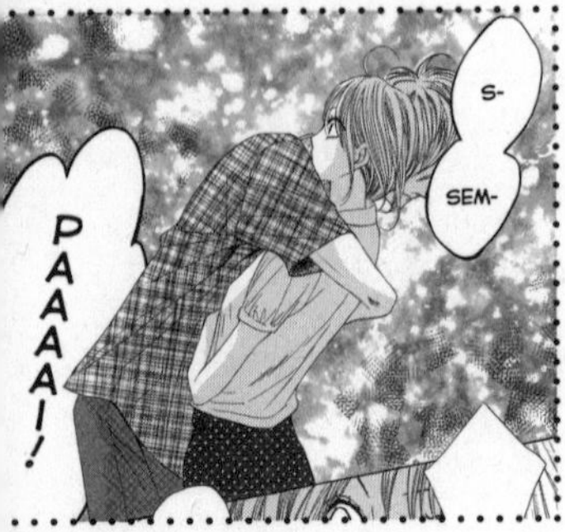
S-
SEM-
PAAAAI!

Sempai, page 26

Sempai is an honorific that is used when one addresses someone who is senior within a group. It is commonly used in a school setting where underclassmen refer to their upperclassmen as "sempai."

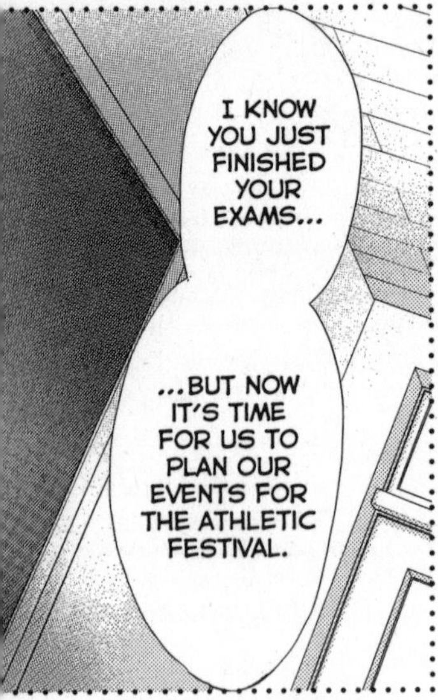
I KNOW YOU JUST FINISHED YOUR EXAMS...
...BUT NOW IT'S TIME FOR US TO PLAN OUR EVENTS FOR THE ATHLETIC FESTIVAL.

Athletic festival, page 81

The Japanese term is *taikusa*, also called *undōkai*. These sporting events are sometimes compared to what is known in the US as "field day." The festivals are an integral part of Japanese school culture. Students form teams and compete in a variety of athletic and gymnastic (*taiku* is Japanese for phys. ed.) skills. The tradition is rooted not only in athletic competition but is also a festive cultural celebration that fosters teamwork and builds a sense of camaraderie.

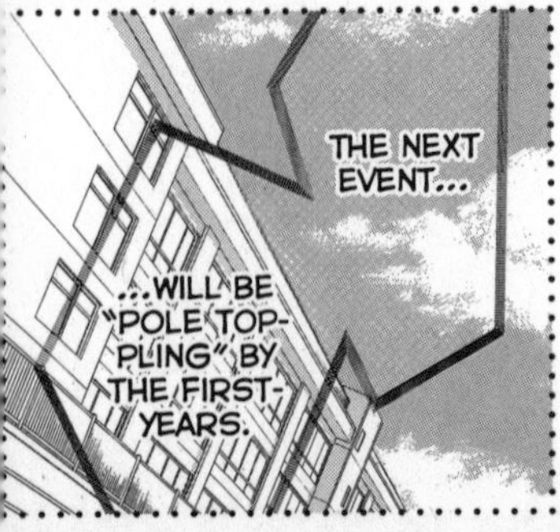
THE NEXT EVENT...
...WILL BE "POLE TOP-PLING" BY THE FIRST-YEARS.

Pole toppling, page 113

Athletic festivals in Japan feature common, distinct events. Some are known universally, such as tug of war. Others, such this one called *bōtaoshi* in Japanese, are less familiar outside of Japan. This scrum-like team competition is sometimes compared to "Capture the flag."

**Everyday Essentials, Item 11
Robotic Vacuum**

While I'm deep in my storyboarding stage, this little guy keeps whirring away doing its job and is a very reliable presence in my life. Occasionally, I'll lose track of it as it'll go missing somewhere, but I find even that endearing. Today we're also working side by side again.

BAYA

LDK volume 11 is a work of fiction. Names, characters, places, and incidents are the products of the author's imagination or are used fictitiously. Any resemblance to actual events, locales, or persons, living or dead, is entirely coincidental.

A Kodansha Comics Trade Paperback Original.

LDK volume 11 copyright © 2012 Ayu Watanabe
English translation copyright © 2018 Ayu Watanabe

All rights reserved.

Published in the United States by Kodansha Comics, an imprint of Kodansha USA Publishing, LLC, New York.

Publication rights for this English edition arranged through Kodansha Ltd., Tokyo.

First published in Japan in 2012 by Kodansha Ltd., Tokyo, as *L♡DK*, volume 11.

ISBN 978-1-63236-164-6

Printed in the United States of America.

www.kodanshacomics.com

9 8 7 6 5 4 3 2 1

Translation: Christine Dashiell
Lettering: Sara Linsley
Editing: Tomoko Nagano
Kodansha Comics Edition Cover Design: Phil Balsman

JUL -- 2018